I0592243

Samuel Royce

Deterioration and the Elevation of Man through Race Education

Vol. I

Samuel Royce

Deterioration and the Elevation of Man through Race Education
Vol. I

ISBN/EAN: 9783337209551

Printed in Europe, USA, Canada, Australia, Japan

Cover: Foto ©Suzi / pixelio.de

More available books at **www.hansebooks.com**

DETERIORATION

AND

THE ELEVATION OF MAN

THROUGH

RACE EDUCATION.

BY

SAMUEL ROYCE.

THE SACREDNESS OF HUMAN LIFE INCREASES WITH CIVILIZATION.

IN TWO VOLUMES.

VOL. I.

THIRD EDITION, REVISED AND ENLARGED.

BOSTON:

LEE & SHEPARD, PUBLISHERS.

1880.

1877, BY

SAMUEL ROYCE.

DEDICATED TO

MRS. ELIZABETH THOMPSON,

THE PATRIOT AND PHILANTHROPIST,

WHO DEVOTES HER ENERGIES TO THE ELEVATION

OF THE MASSES THROUGH INDUSTRIAL EDUCATION, AND LABORS

FOR THE IMPROVEMENT OF THE CHARACTER OF

THE MEN AND WOMEN OF AMERICA

THROUGH THE KINDERGARTEN,

BY THE AUTHOR.

PREFACE;

LETTER OF INTRODUCTION.

My Child :—Amid the severe pressure of daily labors and cares I have tended you. Under deprivation and humiliation I had but a cheerful countenance for you. Many a long winter's night I have watched over you, nursed and taught you until the sun rose, and my weary head without repose entered upon the struggle of the day. It is time you go forth and stammer your lesson to the world. Your dress is simple, for service and not for parade, but your armor shall make you strong in battle.

There is no loss of force. The life and spirit of my sweet little Julia, which floated away from her while I attended to you and your wants, will be with you ; and however much you may be abused, never mind, if only thereby other children will be treated more tenderly, and will be kept alive and be made happy.

The perishing masses are the import of thy message ; nothing can save them but an Education aiming in all its parts at the preservation of the individual and the race. Nothing but the solidarity of mankind, or, in more homely phrase, the feeling of mutual responsibility, can give stability to society tottering to its very base. Want almost general can only be allayed by industry as universal. Home, the school of great and small, health of body and mind, city and country, institutions, and whatever influences the well-being of individuals and States; the jail, the hospital, the battlefield, the shop and the banking-house, the past as well as the present, whatever touches man, is part of thy message—be brief, but hide nothing.

Proclaim *the true spirit and principle of Education;* when you will have done that, the people will know the rest, as Education embraces the whole of life, and ten thousand times ten thousand rules would leave the subject as incomplete as ever.

When your message, burdened with facts and figures, fatigues the listener, retire not unwillingly to the shelf, satisfied that the solidity of thy arguments will secure to your message another hearing.

And now, child of my riper age, of many labors and anxious hours, I trust you and your message to justice that never fails in the end.

May success attend you, not for my sake, nor for your sake, but for the sake of the Education of the Race, and the saving of the masses that perish to-day.

THE AUTHOR.

PREFACE TO THIRD EDITION.

NEW YORK CITY, *November*, 1879.

TWICE thou hast gone forth on thy mission. If thy work was arduous, still it was not wholly without success. For since thy message has been delivered, some of the most baneful prejudices have lost some of their hold upon the educational world ; industrial Education has received more proper attention, and the dwellings of the people and their sanitary condition have been seriously looked into. A third time thou art sent forth to plead for the perishing masses ; stand by them and suffer with them, if there be need, but falter not, knowing that thine is the victory.

THE AUTHOR.

CONTENTS TO VOLUME I.

PART I.
RACE DETERIORATION.

Symptoms and Causes of Deterioration 13
Rate of Mortality 18
Rate of Insanity 22
Rate of Crime 29
Blindness and Deaf-muteism 38
Unfitness for Military Service 39
Factory Population 41
Consumption 42
Scrofula 45
Changes of Mortality Rates 47
General Deterioration. 48
Pauperism 49
Remedies 58
Education and Race Preservation 62
Degenerated Tribes 65
Degeneracy in Tenement-houses 66
The Evolution of Education 67

PART II.
HEREDITY AND RACE EDUCATION.

Heredity 69
Race Education Defined . . . . , . . 76
Race and Scholastic Education 80
Race and Scholastic Education Compared . . . 82
Systems of Education 90
Race and Individual Education 100
Race Education Further Expounded 105
Race Education and Division of Labor 111
Woman's Work 112
The School and the Home 115

The Development of Education 117
Our Civilization and Deterioration 119
Education and Individualism 121
Race Education and Hygiene 124

PART III.
KINDERGÄRTEN AND INDUSTRIAL EDUCATION.
Kindergarten 133
Education and Social Science 146
Industrial Education 152
The Progress of Industrial Education . . . 161
Industrial Education in the United States . . 170

PART IV.
THE PROGRESS OF CIVILIZATION.
Trades and Tools our Civilizers 185
First Improvements 188
Modern Conveniences and Foods 196
Progress in Cotton and Iron Manufactures . . 201
Progress of Manufactures in the United States . 203
Industry and general Civilization . . . 205
Industry, Science, and Education 206
Industry, its Work and Cycles 208
War and Army Mortality 222
Mortality in Public Institutions 226
Industry as a Deteriorator 229
Suicide 231
Social Murder 235
Supreme Law of Humanity 238
Slaughter-pen Civilization 241
Humanity Suffering 242
The Sanctity of Human Life 248

PART V.
THE PROGRESS OF EDUCATION.
The Progress of General Education 251
Cost of Education and Crime 261
Does our Common Education Prevent Crime . . 263

Does our Common Education Prevent Pauperism . . 263
Intellectual Pleasures 264
Education and the State 265
Education and our Financial Crisis 266
Eras of Civilization 269
The School the Miniature of the World . . . 269
The Period of Crime and of Education . . . 270
Our Wordy Education 271
Education and Industrial Labor 272
Race Education described 291
The Education of the old Greeks 292
The Education of Massachusetts 294
The Demands of Race Education 295
Race Education and a Rational Idealism . . . 298
The Claims of Classical and Scientific Education . 303
The Proper Employment of Time 332
Men and Women, and their Spheres. . . . 334
Industry, Health, Comfort, and Happiness . . 335
The Science of Things 335
The Cultivation of Altruism 337

PART VI.

THE PEOPLE AND THEIR HOMES.

Home the Climate of Man 348
Home in City and Country 349
Home and Property 352
Manufacturing in Rural Districts 352
Commerce and Starvation in England . . . 354
The City the Workman's Ruin. 355
Condition of Operatives in French towns . . . 358
Condition of Operatives in English towns. . . 365
Tenement houses in New York City. . . . 369
Tenements in Boston and other towns . . . 379
Tenement house Mortality in New York City . . 384
Industrial Building Societies 386
Degradation of Laborers in Cities 392
Epidemics from Crowding 399
Sins and Evils of Crowding 401

Infant Mortality and Crowding. 402
Crime and Crowding 404
Misleading Averages 404
Mortality in City and Country 405
Cities with More Deaths than Births . . . 407
Surplus of Births in City and Country . . . 407
Cholera and Density of Population 408
Births and Deaths in London 408
Infant Mortality in New York City and in the Country . 409
Table of Births, Deaths, Fertility, &c. . . . 410
Vitality in City and Country 411
Growth of Cities 412
Legislative Restrictions against Crowding . . 415
Vitality in its Moral Bearings 418

PART VII.

THE SCOURGES OF HUMANITY.

Drunkenness Deteriorating the Race . . . 424
Drunkenness and Expectation of Life . . . 429
Drunkenness and Rates of Insanity. . . . 430
Causes and Prevention of Drunkenness . . . 431
The Virus of the Social Evil 437
Spread and History of this Poison 438
Cause and Prevention of this Evil 444
Standing Armies Deteriorating Nations . . . 448
Prisons 448
Trade Diseases and their Prevention . . . 448
Employment of Children in Factories . . . 458
Our Resources and our Greed 460
Crime and Education 461
Crime, Pauperism, and Insanity Increasing . . 462
Ratio of Increase and Birth Decreasing . . . 468
Blindness, Mental Disorders, and the School . . 471
Crime and Industry 472
Moral Basis of Education 475
Manufacturing in the Country 476
Crowding and Crime 477

EDUCATION:

A SOCIAL STUDY.

VOLUME I.

The nature, function and importance of public education under the powers, possibilities, dangers and responsibilities of modern civilization are as yet not half understood. Six dull hours daily passed upon school benches are but a parody upon Education, which should be as real and multifarious as life is; aye, it must be life itself lived under the eye of the State and its ministers, who are to fashion our outer as well as our inner life, the one by rightly starting our practical activities, and the other by effectually regulating our passions, and thus remove the double source of human woe, outer want and inner misery, a consummation to be brought about by the co-operation of men who have before their eye the love and fear of God as well as the good of their fellow beings.

NEW YORK CITY, *November,* 1879.

INTRODUCTION.

DETERIORATION is the foundation of our work, which we bring forward, that we may convince men of the necessity of aiming at race amelioration. Certainly, the gradual descent from the meridian of life to natural death is but an inevitable process of individual deterioration, and when, again, whole species and genera of plants and animals become extinct, as the geological strata attest, that is general deterioration. The whole of life, therefore, is a constant struggle of the individual and the race against a world of hostile forces ever tending to deteriorate them.

A healthy rural population crowding into unwholesome city quarters, and transmitting to an enfeebled progeny a constitution deteriorated by the conflux of adverse circumstances is not unworthy the attention of men.

The removal of the preventable causes of deterioration becomes the more urgent in this country, where a comparatively new soil and a foreign climate conspire against the exogenous white race, as has been noticed from Buffon down to our day, and is patent to every observer from the lesser development of the muscular system, the narrow chest, the pale face, the delicate constitution, the premature dental decay, the greater frequency of consumption, especially among the female sex, and the small fertility even of foreign born women after their acclimatization.

Society and the means of preventing ever present morbid tendencies from settling into abnormal and anti-social formations must be the chief study of the future teacher in our normal colleges.

We recognize the importance of the study of man, but, alas! look for it in musty chronicles instead of in the living present spread out before us like a feast. We might just as well seek the key to the enigma of life among rattling bones.

What a world of thought the structure of a prosperous society presents to us! and what lessons are to be compared in importance to those the morbid conditions of society offer us.

The application of physical, mental and social hygiene to the physical, mental and social degeneracy as manifested by an excessive rate of mortality, insanity, pauperism and crime is the great work of the teacher.

This truth is sure of finding acceptance at last, as we are beginning to be oppressed with taxes for the erection of hospitals, mad-houses, jails, poor houses, asylums for the blind, the deaf, the dumb, the idiotic, etc., etc., all the fruit of sin or our indifference for man, his happiness, or misery.

The very word *Education* in our day suggests the school, studies, hieroglyphics, and what not. The writer of this work sets out with an inquiry into the condition of the people, and from a vast

DETERIORATION

AND

THE ELEVATION OF MAN.

THROUGH

RACE EDUCATION.

PART I.

RACE DETERIORATION.

WRITERS and thinkers, according to their standpoint or method of investigation, base their systems of Education upon religious or philosophical principles, as God-likeness, duty, humanity, usefulness, happiness, etc.

Most children are not educated at all. They are simply taught the three R's. Many are brought up to get along in the world, no matter how the world gets along; and a small minority is taught in schools devoted to the promotion of learning, but regardless to the advancement of humanity, while denominational schools care more for the propagation of their peculiar tenets than for anything else; and only the fewest children are educated upon anthropological principles.

Upon a careful study of the social condition of

the people, we venture to advance the principle that the general tendency of human deterioration must be counteracted by Race Education aiming directly at race amelioration.

Statistics prove that a deterioration of the physical, mental and moral tone of mankind, induced by the present state of civilization, is undermining the race.

Many Utopian theories have been advanced against the various ills of society, but a race ameliorating Education alone can stop humanity in its downward career.

Pauperism, with all the misery and barbarity inseparable from it ; drunkenness, crime and insanity, a growing morbidity, leading through heredity to race deterioration, and a fearful infant as well as adult rate of mortality, such are the tendencies that surround us on all sides, and must be combated by Race Education.

Maintaining, as we do, that the one great aim of Education must be to counteract the cause of human deterioration, the first step in our inquiry must be to prove the actual existence of such fatal agencies. Deterioration is contingent on our present state of civilization, as labor, especially in factories, is productive of metal, mineral, vegetable or animal dust and deleterious gases, all favoring phthisis. Not infrequently rank poison, such as copper, lead, arsenic, phosphorus, etc., have to be handled and are absorbed by the system. Many manufacturing processes require degrees of heat or moisture varying from what the human body can well bear; and often the posture of the laborer, attending one or another technical operation, interferes with the free action of one or more organs. Mines, barracks, damp and dark tenements, filthy lanes, crowded towns and factories, penitentiaries, want, commercial crises, epidemics, poverty, misery, degradation, drunkenness, tobacco, opium, and other influences too numerous for mentioning, contribute to this deterioration.

It would open too wide a field for discussion were we to enter upon these and kindred causes of human deterioration, the existence of which alone concerns us here, and which we shall prove by the rising rate of mortality as well as of insanity and by the nature of crime.

The profound Morel says: " My conviction is that in the majority of cases the insane are of a deteriorated constitution, suffering from a long line of hereditary degeneracy." Everywhere, the same writer continues, insanity increases, so does general paralysis, and a general collapse diminishes the chances of curability. Hysteria and hypochondria, often accompanied with a suicidal mania or tendency, are becoming alarmingly common among the working people and even in the country. The increase of misdemeanors, crime against property, juvenile criminality, and a physically degenerated community that has not men enough fit for the service, are incontrovertible facts, alarming European governments and engaging their most earnest attention. A brigade raised among the weavers in England measured mostly less than five feet. At Spitalfields, the men are not good enough for cannon fodder. "The constitution of these degenerated men," says Dr. Mitchell, "does rapidly descend to the size of the Lilliputians; the old men among them surpass in strength the young ones."

At Birmingham the men cannot be said to be all sick, but neither are they all well. Among 613 men, only 238 were approved for the service. The spinners and weavers are stunted and rickety. So they are in France and everywhere else. Upon investigation, scrofula, diseases of the digestive organs and inflammatory affections of the eyes are most common. Abortions and distortions of the spinal column are almost universal among the working people. Often the children manifest an early arrest of their faculties; they learn but little, and even of this they soon lose every recollection. Often three to four years are not sufficient for these degenerates to learn a little reading and writing. Their language, their morals, their conduct are all low, loose, and shameless. All about them is degenerate. Their pale physiognomies are mute, hard, showing nothing but resolution to persevere in evil. These types shock us; and well they may, for they are personifications of the degeneracy of our race, caused by evils which are more fraught with danger for modern society than the invasion of the barbarians was for ancient Rome. This degeneracy might be stopped if society would consent to be anything else but a machine, grinding humanity, even at the risk of conjuring up a revolution, to which the present state of affairs must lead sooner or later.

Having described the symptoms of human deterioration among the English working people, Morel proceeds to trace the same symptoms in France, where he finds the masses to have lost the power and inclination for fixing their attention upon subjects of a higher order. Such is the imbecility of the young or their intellectual faculties that the priest has to defer their confirmation. In Rouen, as in most manufacturing cities of France, the population is born and develops under conditions favorable for the formation of phthisis, cancer, inflammation of the kidneys and of the digestive organs, hysteria, chlorosis, and general, progressive paralysis. The factory children are puny, their intelligence torpid; and most characteristic is the

degeneracy which slowly, but surely, undermines the
health of body, mind, and morals of the population,
visibly nearing a fatal transformation into a fixed
order of diseased specimens deviating from the normal type of humanity, in whom the average intellectual life is low; and the double characteristic of
their moral and physical shortcomings is reflected
in the form of the body as well as in the disposition
of the mind.   In the absence of regenerating measures these diseased specimens are bound to form
progressive types of degeneration.

Having established the progressive hereditary deterioration of the normal type of humanity among
the masses, and the necessity as well as the possibility of a complete regeneration by the removal
of fatal causes, from the labors of Morel, we pro-
ceed to the still higher authority of a million statistical facts, and we shall set out with those of
mortality rates as best studied, and the sure indi-
cators of the vitality and the ameliorating or deteriorating tendencies of the world.

RATE OF MORTALITY.

To those who consider mortality rates a sentimental question, we would recall the words of
Europe's greatest statistician: "The people themselves are by far the most important capital of the
State; and the industrial capital stored up in the

living generation surpasses the sum of all other species of capital. Every injury to the physical condition of the people is a loss of the noblest capital of intelligence and physical strength of the nation, and is an absolute destruction of capital."

Dr. Engel, to whom we have just referred, has established the average age at death in Prussia to have been as follows:

1821–1830	28.39 years.
1831–1840	28.34 "
1841–1850	27.23 "
1851–1860	26.40 "

In Bavaria lived, after the first year, of

1,000 born, 1841–1848 . .	701 children.
" " 1848–1855 . .	697 "
" " 1855–1862 . .	681 "
" " 1862–1869 . .	673 "

In Basel, Switzerland, survived the first year of

1,000 born, 1821–1840 . .	879 children.
" " 1841–1850 . .	830 "
" " 1860–1865 . .	802 "
" " 1866–1870 . .	783 "

Marc d'Espine shows the expectation of life for Geneva to have been as follows:

1814–1836	47.29 years.
1838–1845	43.62 "

In Wurtemberg lived, after the first year, of

1,000 born, 1846–1856 . .	697 children.
" " 1858–1866 . .	646 "
" " 1866–1868 . .	640 "

In Muhlhausen lived, after the first year, of

> 1,000 born, 1830–1842 . . 745 children.
> "   "   1860–1868 . . 670   "

In France lived, after the first year, of

> 1,000 born, 1840–1851 . . 834 children.
> "   "   1851–1860 . . 826   "

Neison shows in England an increased mortality, notwithstanding all sanitary improvements. It has been as follows :

1838–1844.	1845–1854.
For males, 2.27 per ct. pop.	For males, 2.364 per ct. pop.
" females, 2.104 per ct. pop.	" females, 2.209 per ct. pop.

This shows an increase of mortality of 4.141 per cent. in males, and 4.8 per cent. in the female portion of the population.

W. R. Gray, in a paper published in the *Statistical Journal* of 1842, says that the rate of mortality has increased in England since 1820 10 per cent. and probably 12.50 per cent.

Mr. S. Shattuck, in a paper on the vital statistics of Boston, says: " The average value of life is greater now than during the last century, but not as great as it was twenty years ago. It was at its maximum from 1811–1820, and since that time it has somewhat decreased." He also says: " It is a melancholy fact, and one which should arrest the attention of all, that 43 per cent., or nearly one-half, of all deaths which have taken place within the last nine years, are of persons under nine years of age; and the proportional mortality at this age has been increasing."

The average mortality of children under five years in 1866–1870 amounted in the city of New York to 50.6 per cent., and but 4.4 per cent. of all who died during the same years reached seventy years. Of 492,262 deaths in the United States in 1870, 7,986, or 1.6 per cent., were of old age, while 69,896 died of consumption alone. Fully a hundred thousand children die annually in this country beyond what is natural, and with them twice as many hearts are broken. But hearts do not count in this matter-of-fact world. The loss of labor during gestation, lactation and the sickness of the child, medical attendance and funeral expenses foot up at least to one hundred dollars in each case, and in the aggregate to ten millions per annum, to a class generally in such precarious circumstances as to be crushed by this additional burden; and the fifty thousand adults, who die annually purely from degenerating causes, can we estimate them individually to be worth less than a thousand dollars? Or is the loss of the State in the citizen, or of the wealth of the country in the producer, and of the wife and the children in the husband and father, less than this paltry sum? This, then, is

another loss of fifty millions per annum. But a
hundred and fifty thousand avoidable deaths mean
two millions of avoidable cases of sickness and
their cost ; and, worse still, so much sickness means
so much deterioration of the race, and multitudes
of men, women and children decrepit in body and
soul, fit inmates of all sorts of asylums and candi-
dates for early graves—the last of which is not the
worst for them.

But one glance more at the most degenerate.
Among the most destitute at Manchester, of 21,000
children 20,700 die before they reach five years.
In Lille, in France, 94 per cent. of the same sort
of children die before this age. In very deteriorating trades, of 1,000 born, but 15 reach the age
of fifty. Without entering upon details and causes
beyond the proper limit of our inquiry, we have
established the fact of a rising death rate, which
proves a degeneracy Education must protect us
against, and this Race Education or Hereditary
Culture only, and not school pedantry, can accomplish.

RATE OF INSANITY.

The daily increasing rate of insanity is another
symptom of human deterioration.

Maudsley says : " In the hard struggle for existence, men of inherited weakness, or some other
debility. break down in madness. Overcrowding

deteriorates health, favors scrofula, phthisis, and faulty nutrition, all of which open the way to insanity; and whatever deteriorates mental or bodily health may lead to insanity in the next generation."

Galton says: "Social agencies are unsuspectedly working toward the degeneration of humanity, and it is a duty we owe humanity to study this power and to combat it to the advantage of the future inhabitants of the earth."

Griesinger, a great authority in Germany on insanity, decidedly believes in its increasing rate. He says: "Misery and privation are its chief causes. Bad nourishment, hunger, cold, fatigue and over-exertion, which of necessity accompany misery, are important physical causes of insanity, and, hence, of race deterioration. Typhus, intermittent fever, cholera, pneumonia, acute rheumatism, tubercular, constitutional diseases, and anæmic states—all scourges of the poor—induce insanity. The monotonous and hopeless condition of many factory hands, depriving them of all interest in a higher life, is favorable to dementia."

Such are the opinions of the leading minds of Europe on the spreading causes of insanity.

We shall now prove the terrible fact of an actual race deterioration by statistics, which, though sufficient to convince the earnest inquirer, do not begin to display all the facts of the case.

Making every allowance, the following table of
the number of lunatics and idiots in England and
Wales and of their annual admissions, shows that
the increase of want, worry, over-work, crowding,
drunkenness, etc., have their effects on the mental
condition of the people :

Years.	Insane and Idiots.	Admissions.	Years.	Insane and Idiots.	Admissions.
1859	36,762	9,310	1868	51,000	11,213
1860	38,058	9,512	1869	53,177	11,194
1861	39,647	9,329	1870	54,713	11,620
1862	41,129	9,078	1871	56,755	12,573
1863	43,118	8,914	1872	58,640	12,176
1864	44,795	9,473	1873	60,296	12,773
1865	45,950	10,424	1874	62,027	13,229
1866	47,648	10,051	1875	63,793	14,317
1867	49,086	10,631	1876	64,916	14,386

The statements of Dr. Simon, the medical officer of the British Government, Maudsley, and Dr.
Robertson, lead all to the same conclusion.

In Ireland, were in

1844	....	10,855 insane.
1863	....	16,256 "

In France insanity has most fearfully increased
during the last ten years, though there were already
in 1866, 90,684 insane and idiots, including those
in private institutions. The following table is taken
from the Report of the Inspector-General of the
Insane, and takes only notice of the poor insane in
public asylums :

January 1, 1835, in the asylums . . 10,529 insane.
"   1840,   "   .   "   . . 13,243   "
"   1845,   "   "   . . 17,089   "
"   1850,   "   "   . . 20,061   "
"   1855,   "   "   . . 24,869   "
"   1860,   "   "   . . 28,761   "
"   1869,   "   "   . . 38,545   "

Belgium had in its asylums in

1852 . . . . 4,054 insane.
1856 4,278   "
1860 4,832   "
1864 5,441   "

In the Netherlands there were in the asylums in

January 1, 1844 . . . . . .   837 insane.
"   1850 1,187   "
"   1856 1,828   "
"   1862 2,317   "
"   1868 3,179   "

Norwegia had in

1835 . . . . 1 insane in 334 population.
1845 . . . .   "   309   "
1855 . . . .   "   239   "

In the Rhenish provinces of Prussia the ratio of the insane to the population was in

1828 . . . 1 insane in 1,027 population.
1856 . . .   "   666   "

In Nassau the ratio of the insane to the population was in

1840 . . . . . 1 insane in 607 population.
1858 . . . .   "   318   "

In Wurtemberg insanity has increased since 1832 76.3 per cent., while the population has increased 13.5 per cent.

Baden shows in

1848	100 insane.
1851	158 "
1854	187 "
1857	231 "
1860	255 "
1862	306 "

The official reports of Berlin show an increase of cases of mental aberration or melancholia in

1864	275 cases.
1865	337 "
1866	377 "

Massachusetts had in 1870 in a population of 1,457,351, 3,194 insane. Dr. Jarvis shows in the Fifth Annual Health Report an annual increase of fresh cases. In

1867 . . .	1 for every	1,546	population.
1868 . . .	"	1,486	"
1869 . . .	"	1,533	"
1870 . . .	"	1,350	"
1871 . . .	"	1,389	"
1872 . . .	"	1,357	"

The intensity of this disease of degeneracy has equally increased, so that at Bicêtre, among 100 insane were afflicted with general paralysis, the very worst form and the most incurable, in

1828–1829	9	cases.
1832–1833	16	"
1836–1837	19	"
1840–1841	25	"
1844–1845	27	"
1848–1849	34	"

A glance at the following figures will show the disproportionate increase of the insane in the United States. In 54 asylums were in

1839 . .	1,329	insane, with	961	annual new cases.
1849 . .	7,029	"	"	2,961	" "
1859 . .	13,696	"	"	5,342	" "
1869 . .	22,549	"	"	8,769	" "

The State of New York had in its various institutions in

1870	4,761	insane.
1871	5,073	"
1873	6,003	"
1874	6,279	"

What a commentary these increasing ratios of insanity form to Galton, when he says: "Our race is overweighed and likely to be drudged into degeneracy by demands that exceed its powers. With the deterioration of the condition of the masses, their organizations and functions, there will be plenty of idiots, but very few great men; and, hence, under the miserable conditions in which the masses of the people live, the general standard of mind is but little above the grade of trained idiocy."

The eager pursuit of wealth, says an eminent writer, as well as the dread of poverty, have their ill effects. Men are excited, anxious, absorbed in the state of the market, petty gains, meanness and dishonesty, until their moral nature and character are sapped, and their nature deteriorated. Overwork, depression, exhaustion, want of culture, poverty, drunkenness, licentiousness, are all favorable to the development of insanity; and the number of the insane is rising. The same author relates a number of cases of financial operators, whose speculative, selfish minds show their morbidity in the diseased minds of their children, who are either morally defunct or wholly insane.

The increase of insanity has been for a century steady, large and universal in the ratio of the spread of our present civilization.

Is this lesson not plain enough, when the universally educated Scandinavians have 3.4 insane in 1,000 population; the cultivated Germans, 3 in 1,000; the less educated Romanic nations, 1 in 1,000; and the most barbarous Sclavonic races, 0.6 in 1,000; and, again, when the ratio of the insane to the population is larger in cities than in the country, and the professionally educated, who compose 5.04 per cent. of the population, yield 13.8 of all the insane? If, then, our civilization and Education are especially productive of human deterioration and insanity, is it not reasonable to ask that Education should studiously avoid and oppose whatever degenerates mankind?

CRIME.

Crime may have decreased numerically but it has deepened in quality, and has become a low, permanent type of humanity. The crime of former times was rude force cropping out under other influences as stern virtue, and needed but the restraint of force. The crime of to-day is disease and insanity, and cries for help. Sporadic crime is individual, habitual crime is social; for society engenders it by deteriorating humanity, though it denies the paternity and evades the responsibility. An English judge says, insanity and criminality are convertible terms. Plato and Aristotle held crime and insanity akin, and so do Pinel, Esquirol and Prichard in our own day. Morel says, we have hidden in us the germs of the fatal disposition of which we are the victims.

But our position that the criminal class is evidence of a deep-seated social deterioration, calls for more than a mere incidental verification. We shall, therefore, sustain it by the observations of Bruce Thompson, than whom none has brought greater experience and thoroughness to the treatment of this question. "Intimate and daily experience," says he, "have led me to the conviction, that in by far the greater proportion of offences, crime is hereditary, which tendency is in most cases associated with bodily defect, such as spinal deformities, stammering or other imperfect organizations of speech, club-foot, cleft palate, hare-lip, deafness, congenital blindness, paralysis, epilepsy and scrofula."

"The criminal class," says this great officer and observer, "has a stupid, sullen look, the complexion is bad, the heads and outlines are harsh, clumsy, and angular; the women are positively ugly in form, feature and action. The frequency of tubercular diseases among habitual criminals is proof of a low type and a deteriorated system. Most of them die before the meridian of life is reached, and hardly any see old age. The post-mortem examinations show a series of morbid appearances very remarkable; almost every vital organ of the body being more or less diseased; few dying of one disease, but generally worn out by a complete degeneration of all the vital organs. Everything indicates a deteriorated hereditary organization."

The low state of intellect among criminals shows them degenerate. One-third of the juvenile criminals are imbeciles. According to the reports of the English common prisons, one in every twenty-five of the males is weak-minded, insane, or epileptic. Of six thousand prisoners in Scotland, 12 per

cent. are mentally weak, imbeciles, suicides, epileptics, besides the fully insane. According to the
official report of the Millbank Prison, of 943 convicts, 218 were weak-minded, 34 insane, besides
many epileptics. One in 27 was insane, and the
great majority had some inherited physical infirmity or defect of intellect. Out of 6,273 prison
population in Scotland, fully 1 per cent. were epileptic, and, of course, enfeebled in mind and irritable in temper. Morel shows that crime and insanity lapse into each other congenitally.

Bruce Thompson further shows by the number-
less recommittals returned to prison, not three, four
or five, but thirty, forty and fifty times, by the
utter remorselessness, grossest habitual lying, and
total want of all self-respect, that professional criminals are hopeless imbeciles and hardly amenable to
moral treatment. What else is this but a degraded
organization?

The criminal classes are especially liable to brain
diseases and insanity, and many of the great criminals died in lunatic asylums; and madness among
criminals in prison is extremely frequent. In Scotland, of 2,690 criminals, 57 are insane, or 1 in 47 of
the criminal population, while of the whole population, 1 in 432 is the common proportion.

In England, during 1860–1868, 1,244 criminals
were detained as insane. In 1857–1867, of 664

homicides, 108 were declared by the courts of
England as insane. Among the habitual female
criminals, 1 in 30 is the proportion of the insane
to the sane.

Frederic Hill says: "Crime often proceeds from
father to son in a long line of succession." Prof.
Laycock says: "The line of hereditary transmission
of mental and moral qualities is as inexorable in
these moral imbeciles as in other men, and adds to
the imbecile, vicious and degraded part of the
population."

Dr. William Guy, upon a thorough research of
the judicial record of the Millbank Prison during a
period of thirty years, shows that of 5,598 criminals
convicted of rape, arson, horse and cattle stealing,
burglary, homicidal attacks or violence, and fraudu-
lent offences, 232 were insane, weak-minded, and
epileptic; 657 were scrofulous or lung and heart
diseased; 1,434 were deformed or defective, and
3,399 were sound.

The same great authority says: "We have at
this moment at the Millbank Prison 200 convicts,
who would be much more in their place at an insane asylum."

The late Governor of the Chatham Convict Prison
declared: "I have known as many as 50 per cent.
and more of the inmates of an Irish convict prison
mentally affected."

E. Gordon, the late Lord Advocate of Scotland, testifies to the great weakness of intellect among those placed at the bar of justice.

Dr. Wilson, in a paper read before the British Association, in 1869, reported that from the examination of 460 heads of criminals, and from observations he had made, he had no doubt that cranial deficiency, associated with a real physical deterioration, is the cause of crime, and that 40 per cent. of all convicts are invalids more or less, and that the percentage is largely increased in the class of professional thieves.

Dr. Campbell found in 50 prisoners, after death, the weight of the brain 2 lbs. and 14¼ oz., while the average weight of the brain in other men is over 3 lbs. The average height of 6,022 male prisoners, who passed through the Worcester Prison, was found two inches less than the average height of Englishmen, and their weight was lighter in proportion.

The physical aspects of convicts have become almost proverbial. Bullet heads, low brows, projecting ears, weasel eyes, and other bodily indications of deficiency, are but too general among them. In some of the most ferocious criminals there have repeatedly been discovered after death morbid conditions of the brain or other organs, as tumors, cancers, ulcers, or irritating secretions,

which fully accounted for mental or moral defi-
ciencies and for murders committed.

Dr. Wines cites many cases of congenitally weak
minds, idiots and insane, which came under his
notice among our own criminals.

Miss Dix has in two years traced twenty-six
persons convicted for crime in the Eastern Penitentiary of Pennsylvania, who were insane. Every
month, she says, men are convicted and sentenced
as if they were responsible, when, in fact, they
were not.

Among 233 convicts, whose personal relations
have been carefully studied under the auspices
of our eminent sanitarian and prison reformer, Dr.
Harris, 54 were found belonging to families in
which insanity, epilepsy and other disorders of
the nervous system are reported. Eighty-three
per cent. belonged to a criminal, pauper or inebriate stock, and were, therefore, hereditary or congenitally affected ; and, hence, nearly 76 per cent. of
their number proved habitual criminals. Dr. Harris states, also, that the general observation in the
counties of our State goes to prove that crime,
pauperism and insanity revert into each other congenitally, so that disease or insanity in the parent
produces crime or pauperism in the offspring, or
vice versa, crime or pauperism in the parent produces disease or insanity in the offspring.

The progress of culture and civilization has certainly lessened the crime of unrestrained passion and rudeness; but has the criminal class, until quite of late, been reached?

In England and Wales were committed in

1805	4,605 individuals.
1815	7,818 "
1825	14,437 "
1835	20,731 "
1845	24,033 "

According to Potter, crime has increased in England and Wales since the beginning of this century to 1850, to five times; in Ireland, from 1805 to 1849, to twelve times; and in Scotland, since 1815 to 1849, to seven times. While the population has increased 79 per cent., crime has risen 482 per cent.

In France were committed for common offenses in

1826–1830	178,021 individuals.
1831–1835	203,207 "
1841–1845	195,542 "
1846–1850	221,414 "

Incendiarism has in 1826–1865 increased in France over 200 per cent.

In London, the proportion of incendiarism to buildings was:

1845	1 in 2,990,
1850	1 in 2,673,
1855	1 in 2,585,

1861	1 in 2,370,
1862	1 in 2,180,
1863	1 in 2,064,
1864	1 in 1,980,
1865	1 in 1,900.

In Holland, according to Guringar, crime has in the last years increased 72 per cent., and the prisoners 34 per cent. Norwegia had in 1815, 480 criminals, and in 1845, 1,782!

And what progress have we made in the United States in lessening the number of the great and habitual criminals who crowd our State prisons? In 1850 the entire population was 19,553,668, and the inmates of our State prisons numbered 5,646. In 1860 the population was 26,922,537, and the criminals in the State prisons numbered 19,086; and at the last census, in 1870, the population of the United States amounted to 33,589,377, and the number of criminals was 32,901.

We see here at a glance, that crime has increased beyond all proportion to population. Neither will it answer to lay it to the foreign element, the criminal rate of which has remained the same, or even lessened, while the native criminals have increased during 1860–1870, from 10,143 to 24,173.

We have proven that the criminal class is a deviation from the normal type of humanity, and is, therefore, an evidence of actual race deterioration. Statistics have shown us that no decided decrease

of crime has attended our late general progress of
civilization ; and, in fact, the recommittals, especially of juvenile criminals, the frequency of female
criminality, suicides, infanticides, prostitution and
illegitimate births, show all a deep-seated human
deterioration. Of course, illegitimate births mean
a rich harvest for the grave, the jail, and prostitution, the latter of which avenges itself on society
by insidious venereal deterioration, which inflicts
upon its unborn victims blindness, idiocy, phthisis,
scrofula and a most degenerate system in general.
But we must forbear entering here upon this form
of human deterioration though not to mention it
would be a gross oversight.

The causes of human deterioration are vast and
many, but the right sort of Education may conquer
them all.

When the hero of Wagram, Austerlitz and Jena
stood at the gates of Berlin, Fichte addressed to
the German nation, in the midst of the thunder
and storm which burst forth from the brazen throats
of a thousand cannons, the potent word, *Education*,
and the relative position of the French and Germans to-day proves the wisdom of the patriot and
philosopher. Like an ancient, renowned legislator,
he thought Education was the sole function of the
Government ; for, where the people are rightly educated, war, prisons, courts, asylums of all sorts,

poor-houses, hospitals and other institutions of the same kind cease to have an existence.

BLINDNESS AND DEAF-MUTISM.

Blindness and deaf-mutism are common, fearful, expensive and preventable. Europe has 500,-000 blind, Asia 2,000,000 and the United States 25,000. What a growing misery and public expense. Blindness, congenital in one in ten cases, and then the offspring of a deteriorated parentage, results in the main from causes accompanying misery. Scarlet fever, measles, smallpox, typhoid and other fevers, all preventable diseases, raging among the poor, give rise to this terrible visitation and great public burden; and so does scrofula. Ophthalmia is another disease of poverty leading often to blindness. The strain upon the eyes of tailors, dress makers, needle makers, watch makers, blacksmiths and other operatives causes much blindness; but lace making is the most fearful trade as far as blinding poor operatives is concerned.

Deaf-mutes, Europe counts 250,000, and the United States 20,000. That congenital deaf-mutism is a deterioration of the system is obvious from the fact that whilst in Europe 1 in 1400 is a deaf-mute, there are poor regions there in which 1 in 44, and even 1 in 20 of the entire population is a deaf-mute!

Of 644 deaf-mutes in Massachusetts, 350 are congenital and traceable to a deteriorated stock, whilst 304 are post-natal, of whom 112 are the result of scarlet fever, and the rest are the victims of other fevers, diseases and accidents peculiar to the tenements and condition of the poor.

The blind, deaf-mute, as well as the idiot, are but chargeable to removable causes and conditions of our half civilization. Inherent weakness is the cause of many a form of degeneracy. Under different conditions the local or general congenital weakness leads to blindness, deaf-mutism, idiocy, or other morbid formation, still-birth, deformity, general weakness, or death in early infancy.

UNFITNESS FOR MILITARY SERVICE.

Michel Lévy, the highest sanitary authority in France, cites the following facts as evidence of a general race deterioration : From 1816 to 1840, of 7,321,609 recruits, 1,416,527. or nearly one-fifth, have been rejected for being below the requisite stature or on account of infirmities. In comparing the exempted prior to 1816 with those of 1840, the latter are twice as numerous, though the standard has been lowered from 1 metre 57 centimetres, to 1 metre 56 centimetres. There were rejected in

1852	. .	3.34	per cent.	for deficient growth.
		15.55	"	" infirmities.
1853	. .	4.75	"	" deficient growth.
		21.03	"	" for infirmities.

The steady deterioration of the people necessi-
tated a continual lowering of the military standard,
as the following table will show :

It was, 1701 . . . . 1.624 metres,
  "   1803 . . . . 1.598   "
  "   1818 . . . . 1.576   "
  "   1860 . . . . 1.560   "

and to-day of every 325,000 young men who survive their twenty-fifth year, 108,333 are rejected on
account of low stature or infirmities.

According to the statement of Dr. Mayer, the
average of nine years shows 176 out of 1,000 con-
scripts under the standard measure, and 399 unfit
on account of bodily ailments. Berlin could not furnish its quota in men fit for service by 156 in 1856.

If, on an average, 352 in 1,000 men of the most
favorable age are rejected by the recruiting officer,
what must be the condition of the people at large ?

Among 8,794,674 examined recruits of European
countries between 1837 and 1856, 1,576,815, or 17.9
per cent., were found below the standard measure,
and 3,097,016 sickly, crippled, feeble and otherwise
unfit for military service. What a condition ! About
53.1 per cent. of men, at their best age, sickly or
stunted in their growth.

The official report of the canton of Zurich shows,
for the agricultural districts, 29 in 1,000 young men
disabled ; for the industrial, 35.

FACTORY POPULATION.

The deterioration of the factory population in England is seen from the fact that, on an average, the measure of 1,000 factory boys aged 18 years, was 55.28 inches, of non-factory boys, 55.56 inches —a difference of .28 inches in favor of non-factory boys. The same official report shows 2,000 factory boys, aged 9–17 years, weighing 3 pounds less each than as many non-factory boys.

Upon examination

51 farmers' boys, old 10 y., 9 m., measured in height 51 inches.
51 mining boys, of the same age, measured 47.3 inches.

An official examination of the health of 350 factory, and as many non-factory boys, showed of

	Factory.	Non-factory.
Bad health	73	21
Middle health	134	88
Good health	143	241

These examinations have been varied without any material change in the result.

The following official list of the diseases of the factory and agricultural population of the canton Zurich, in Switzerland, is suggestive. In each 1,000 population were found :

	Factory.	Agriculturists.
Eye diseases	13	7
Injuries from accidents . .	14	7
Rheumatic diseases . . .	13	9

	Factory.	Agriculturists
Lung diseases	37	10
Abdominal diseases . . .	9	3
Scrofula and infirmity . .	11	5
Ulcers	8	3

The deteriorating influence of the trades is only so fearful because they are divorced from science and Education, which alone can find the means of rendering them innoxious, and dispose the men engaged in them to be more on their guard.

Workers in white lead, arsenic and phosphorous compounds, who deteriorate most fearfully in most factories, suffer hardly any where the employers are highly intelligent and conscientiously disposed, and·the government keeps a strict watch over the hygienic management of factories.

Nothing calls louder for the association of science and Education with the trades, than the present outrageous poisoning of humanity throughout more or less all the factories of the land.

CONSUMPTION.

As consumption shows more degeneracy and deteriorates humanity more fearfully than any—and we might almost say than all other diseases put together—we will just refer to its deteriorating influence in the trades divorced from science and Education upon the men engaged in them. In Berlin, the observation was made, that the whole population being taken, of 1,000 deaths of men over 20 years, 344 are caused by tubercular consumption, while among mechanics, 497 die from this fearfully deteriorating disease.

This observation is confirmed by the experience of Dr. Hannover, at Copenhagen, who found that upon 60 deaths from consumption among the people at large come 96 among the mechanics and laborers.

According to the observations of Benoiston de Chateauneuf, among 43,010 hospital cases 18 to 48.4 of every 1,000 died from consumption, according to the nature of the different trades and the deteriorating influences, as dampness, dangerous fumes, dust, etc., accompanying them.

Lombard found that, while among men who live in perfectly healthy surroundings, 50 to 89 in a thousand die from consumption; men working in the close air of factories, as they are managed to-day, die in 138 cases in 1,000; those working in dust of any sort, die in 137 to 152; and those exposed to the evaporations of ethereal acids, varnishes, etc., die in 369 cases in 1,000 from consumption.

In the always reliable statistics of Geneva, we find among men living under the best possible conditions the death rate from consumption in

1,000 deaths	50
Among the tailors	601
Machinists	497
Book binders, calico printers, painters, gilders, stone masons, type founders, and millers	482
Jewelers, watchmakers and day laborers.	460
Silk workers	333

Fifty in a thousand we may, then, call the natural proportion of death from consumption to the deaths from all other causes. How loudly, then, do these high ratios of death from consumption call for bringing to bear science and Education upon these race-deteriorating trades, in many of which men grow gray before they live half their years. The dry-grinders die in the majority of cases before they reach thirty-six years; so do the manufacturers of watches and others exposed to fine, hard dust, like cutters of crystals, stone cutters, etc.

It is impossible to pass unnoticed this great cause of human deterioration; but to state in full the disease, deformity, death, and even hereditary corruption of body and mind entailed by each of two hundred trades deprived of the safeguards and thoughtful precaution of science, the school and Education, upon the producers of the wealth of the country, would fill many volumes.

SCROFULA.

The tendency of the masses toward degeneracy is obvious from the character and spread of scrofula—significantly called by some the people's malady—a constitutional, hereditary and deteriorating disease common among the poor. Mr. Phillips, the greatest authority in this field of inquiry, says that in the cottages of the poor we find the child with a scrofulous constitution, often pallid, puffy, insensible, listless; and, if it be not altogether deprived of force and energy, what remains is soon wasted by taxing it beyond its force.

In an extraordinary experience extending to the examination of 133,721 children, 24.5 per cent. presented a number of scrofulous symptoms; in 3.5 per cent. the disease was so marked as to be obvious to the eye. Among 95,586 recruits, 800, or 1 in 119, were rejected on account of scrofulous marks. At the examination of 660 persons, between 10 and 18 years, at the house of correction, 95 showed symptoms of scrofula.

Mr. Phillips sums up his wonderful experience as follows:

1½ per cent. of the children of the poor show apparent scars; 3 per cent. show at a glance enlarged glands; 24½ per cent. show these enlarged glands under close examination; 8 per cent. of the

adult poor show the same scrofulous symptoms;
3 per cent. of the population are under treatment
for scrofula.

In some districts Mr. Phillips found only 11 per
cent. of the children of the poor scrofulous, and in
other districts 72 per cent. were thus affected.

Barier found, upon examination of 166 strong
children, 21 tuberculous, or 1 in 8; 114 moderate
children, 27 tuberculous, or 1 in 4; 99 feeble children, 49 tuberculous, or 1 in 2.

How closely want and misery in the parents and
children are allied with scrofula, is obvious from
the fact, that we find affected with this disease:
4 to 5 per cent. of all the sick in hospitals; 40 to
50 per cent. of foundlings; 50 to 60 per cent. of
children received into orphan asylums.

When we consider that insufficient or improper
food, dark, damp and unventilated apartments, insufficient clothing, etc., engender scrofula, it becomes plain that, with the increase of poverty,
scrofula must increase; and, as this disease is of
a tubercular nature and akin to consumption—
into which it reverts hereditary—the impoverished
masses must of necessity degenerate.

Scrofula, says a noted American author, that
once was a rarity among us, has of late become
quite common.

CHANGES OF MORTALITY RATES.

Many causes contributed to improve the chances of life from the sixteenth to the beginning of the nineteenth century, as the growth of science, the spread of intelligence, the general prosperity springing up with the small trades, which brought with it improved dwellings, food, clothing, etc., the disappearance of periodical famines, the cessation of former ravages from smallpox through Jenner's great discovery; and, finally, another cause of the apparent great reduction in the old mortality rates, is to be found in the prudentially reduced modern birth rate, caused by later marriages, as the mortality is always greatest among infants.

But with the large industries, the former master has become again poor and dependent; large cities sprang up with all the unwholesome elements of thick populations, crowded tenements with their vices, drunkenness, worst of all, alcoholism, illegitimate births, the trade diseases of modern factories, and all contributed to swell of late the list of mortality. The ravages of our largely increased factory towns make up for the former victims from the smallpox, and our periodical business stagnations are as calamitous to the working people as former famines were.

There is none but will agree that there are elements in our civilization tending toward the deterioration of mankind which must be combated; our position, therefore, cannot but be tenable that our Education must strive to preserve the race, which it can only by being physiological, scientific and ˙ industrial—making us healthy, intelligent and prosperous.

GENERAL DETERIORATION.

A picture of France of but a few years ago may serve us as an illustration of our civilization, which strives for perfection in art and literature, for accumulation of wealth and everything else, save the one thing needful—the amelioration of mankind. France, with a population of 35,783,170, had

Blind	37,662,
One-eyed	75,063,
Deaf-mutes	29,512,
Insane	44,970,
Goiter and hunchbacks	42,383,
Deformed spinal column . . .	44,619,
Loss of one or both arms . . .	9,077,
" " " legs . . .	11,301,
Club foot	22,547,
Total	317,134.

This picture of misery is far from being complete. The charity murder of tens of thousands of foundlings, the massacre of factory hands and miners, a fearful infant mortality, paupers, criminals, prostitutes, infanticides and suicides, should all be added as evidence that our pretentious age understands but little of the art how to prevent the deterioration of mankind.

What a picture the whole of Europe presents of what we call in this age civilization, with its 300,000 deaf-mutes, 500,000 blind, as many insane and idiotic, and as large a criminal class!!

PAUPERISM.

Pauperism, like insanity, does not exist in the natural state of man. Under the sweet influences of the skies, he is in the woods as quick and nimble as the bird or deer he pursues. Only in the atmosphere, thick with moral and physical poison of crowded cities, he degenerates into a pauper, robbed of all that elasticity and high potency by which man masters every resistance and subjects everything to his will. Pauperism being the parent as well as the offspring of human deterioration, forms such an entanglement of causes and effects as to render it difficult to hunt it down. Our poorhouses reveal at a glance the genesis of pauperism, for there we find the congenitally blind, deaf and mute, the insane, the idiotic, the epileptic, the deformed, the inebriate as well as the pauper; and they are not only inmates of the same building,

3

but are members of the same family, united by all
the ties of consanguinity. This idiot is that pauper's nephew; this deaf-mute is his own child;
that inebriate is his brother; and that mount in
view covers the bones of an old inmate, who found
his last resting place in the pauper's field forty-five
years ago—his uncle; what are we to conclude from
all this but that the pauper is the child of a degenerate blood and family?

We do not mean to deny that poverty, with its
harassing care, misery, squalor, crowded tenements
and poor fare, with everything adverse to human
health and development, is the generating cause
of a deterioration that, deepening still more, settles
in that apathetic state of the pauper, which is the
beginning of a line of deformities ending in complete extinction.

If a pauper meant a man without money, we
should not care about him. If it meant a man
without pleasure, we would not care. If it meant
a man of sorrow and much trouble, we might, perhaps, not care. But it means more than this, it
means a man robbed of his very manhood; and
even more than this, he is corruption and the deformity of everything that is manly; he is a dis-
seminating mass of crime, insanity and disease;
an infernal brood springing up from him and poisoning all around him; an avenging Nemesis get-

ting even with society that mocked a brother in his deep fall and degradation.

Pauperism is, as a rule, attended by anæmic states of the blood, which make continuous exertion impossible, and dispose the poor to scrofula, subject them to a most frightful rate of infant mortality as also to a very high figure of adult death rate ; and, during epidemics—as the black death, the cholera or typhus—the degenerate poor are the first and often the only sufferers, as the power of resistance is in these deteriorated men reduced to almost nothing.

In 1862, among the 963,200 destitute or paupers of England and Wales, were 30,905 insane, which makes 1 in 31.8. If we consider that these insane are adults of from 20 to 45 years of age, which form but one-fifth of the whole population, we will find that one of six adults among the destitute and congenitally poor is insane. And in this frightful amount of mental disease 10,311 idiots belonging to the same destitute poor of England and Wales are not included. And this fearful rate of insanity was gradually rising from 1852 to 1869, until the ratio of the insane to the sane amounted, among the paupers of England and Wales, to 1 in 25, and in the metropolitan district to nearly 1 in 20.

In the United States it is not much better. In 1854 the legislature of Massachusetts appointed a commission on insanity. They reported: "We find the pauper class furnishes in the ratio of its number sixty-four times as many insane as the other classes."

Dr. Wm. Guy says, frequent as insanity is among criminals, it is still more so among paupers.

Epilepsy, that fearful malady, affecting and enfeebling the mind more than any other, is getting most common among the poor. Dr. Nattuck, physician to the Bradford infirmary, has searched the register of patients for more than thirty years—from 1825–1859—and found the proportion of this malady to other diseases as follows:

1825–1835	15 in 1,000,
1835–1845	18 in 1,000,
1845–1855	24 in 1,000,
1855–1859	34 in 1,000.

Balbi observed the same increase of epilepsy among the poor of Vienna and Milan.

These facts, together with the observation of the hereditary nature of pauperism—which congenitally reverts into insanity, disease or crime—leave no doubt but that pauperism is one of the worst forms of race deterioration, and that the paralysis of the human will and its energies is but the result of a fearful dissolution in progress. But, as we have already mentioned, human deterioration is also to a large extent the result of pauperism.

Dr. Prichard, the famous author of the " Physical History of Man," says : " The conflict in England in the seventeenth century drove many of the natives to the mountains of Sligo and Mayo. Here they have been almost ever since exposed to the worst effects of hunger and ignorance—the two great brutalizers of the human race — gradually producing in their case open, projecting mouths, with prominent teeth and exposed gums ; their advancing cheek bones and depressed noses bear barbarism in their very front. Five feet, two inches, on an average, pot-bellied, bow-legged, abortively featured, these spectres of a people that were once well-grown, able-bodied and comely, stalk abroad diminutive and deformed, while they are specimens of human beauty and vigor in other parts of the country where they have never been subjected to the same causes of physical degeneration. Such are the deteriorating effects of misery !"

Is the pauper condition of the world not a reproach to the nations, and will it not soon involve their very existence? To say, simply, pauperism forms in Germany, France and England respectively, 3, 4 and 5 per cent. of the population, or that in these countries 30,000, 40,000 and 50,000 of each million population are paupers, gives no conception of the existing evil. We appreciate more truly the situation when we consider that at

the slightest rise of breadstuffs or financial disturb-
ance, this army of paupers swells to double and
triple its usual proportion. So was in 1847 every
tenth man in England and every eighth man in
London a pauper. In 1852 every thirteenth man
in Paris, every seventh man in Marseilles, and even
double as many in Lille, in France, were paupers.
In 1855, every twelfth man in Italy, every sixth
in Belgium, and nearly twice as many in Flanders
were paupers.

In 1847, 183,447 individuals were assisted by the
public authorities of Paris, and this number has
gradually risen to 237,393 in 1866. But how many
hearts agonized in secret, and would not appeal to
a public board of charities?

The following statement of Jules Simon gives us
a full insight into the extent of public misery. He
takes 1,700 francs to be the lowest possible sum a
working-man can subsist upon a year with a family
of two children. He further states that actually
of 500,000 work-people of Paris earn per annum

35,000	1,600	francs each.
60,000	1,400	"
44,000	1,150	"
160,000	450	"

The remaining make even less. But, then, how do
workmen fare with five, six and seven children on
such scanty incomes? And the condition of this

half million may fairly be taken as the average state of the masses.

But we are permitted to approach still nearer the problem of the actual condition of the people. In 1874 the tax roll in Prussia proved that 58.5 per cent. of the population earned individually less than $100 per annum, and 34.1 per cent. less than $150. Here, then, we have more than nine out of every ten in the proud Empire of Bismarck struggling with poverty; and, in fact, less than 1 per cent. has an income of $1,500, while the great wealth of the country is held by less than one-tenth of 1 per cent. of the nation.

The tax roll of England betrays the same sad condition of the people there. In 1865, of a population of 24,127,013, only 332,431 were taxed on incomes, while the rest of the nation struggled with poverty, their incomes falling below three hundred dollars per annum.

In Belgium, in 1856, of 908,000 families, lived

Upon alms	226,000 families,
In utter misery	220,000 "
In poverty	273,000 "
In comfort	89,630 "

Of 100 Belgians, 49 live in utter destitution; 42 live very poorly; 9 live in comfort. That corruption and mortality are in proportion hardly needs being told; 44 per cent. of the children are illegiti-

mate, and 1 in every 150 population is a prostitute.

The fact is, we have volumes upon volumes written by the conservative Le Play, Ducpetiaux, De
Gerando and the like authorities, full of figures
like Napier's tables of logarithms, about the wages
of every trade for the last hundred years; the price
of bread, meal, cheese, meat, beans, onions, soap,
rent, articles of furniture, clothing, and what not,
the weight in grains of carbonaceous and nitro-
genous food indispensable for the support of a
man, woman or child at the different seasons of
the year. Governments are turning pale at the
ominous results of these accounts, all tending to
establish in a variety of ways how the people are
wasting away.

The Blue Books of the English government, in a
lengthy and learned Report, officially advise the
people of her British Majesty not to indulge in
daily evacuations of the bowels, which are promo-
tive of too vigorous a digestion. Two or three
a week will do for people in straitened circumstances. . . . .

Do not the very heavens blush at such misery
and insults? Poor humanity that calls for such
official dissertations, and such royal philanthropy.

Calamitous as 40,000 to 50,000 paupers in the
million are, the most desponding fact is the hope-

less struggle of the whole million, save fifty or a hundred thousand who are well off. With the pauper—the degraded and ruined pauper—pity comes too late, he does not care for it, nor can he be bettered; those who have not yet given up the struggle against the stream, and are still to be saved, should most excite our sympathy.

What a mill that does such grinding, turning out to the million fifty thousand paupers of whom a couple of thousands go down in lunacy, and all end in total human brutalization, filling the world with bastards, prostitutes and sneaks, of whom England and Wales alone count 127,839.

The following table proves the deteriorating power of pauperism. Caspar showed that there are left of 1,000 born:

	Among the favored.	Among the poor.
10 years after birth . . .	943	598
25 " " . . .	852	553
45 " " . . .	624	396
55 " " . . .	464	283
65 " " . . .	318	172
85 " " . . .	29	9
90 " " . . .	15	4

Wherever, says a very able writer on medical statistics, pauperism with its want and misery prevails, there the mother is more likely to die in labor; there still-births will be more frequent; there the deaths during infancy will be more numerous; there epidemics will rage with more violence; there

3*

the recoveries from sickness will be fewer, and death will usually happen at an earlier period of life. All Education is thrown away on men in this condition, for *you cannot engraft virtue on physical misery.*

The advocates of the old *régime* claim for slavery that pauperism did not exist under it. But are we not to bear the sight of a brother with a square meal and a decent bed and shelter to rest him from the fatigue of an honest day's work without we own him like a sheep, a horse or a cow?

The rates of mortality of poor-houses are often higher than those of prisons, insane asylums and even than those of hospitals. Is this not proof enough that pauperism is one of the worst phases of race deterioration? That the county houses, in which the poor are collected, hardly harbor a man, woman or child with a sound limb, organ or brain, establishes only our proposition, that pauperism is evidence of a deteriorating humanity.

REMEDIES.

This tide of human corruption, wrong and infamy has ceased to be a subject for the consideration of curious students; the despairing millions are putting their hands to it; the very names of their societies and organizations and public organs all over the world, fill volumes. To prevent a war more bloody and desolating than the world has yet seen, what is proposed? Communism, public charity or co-operation.

Communism, destructive of liberty and individuality, is complete despotism. Besides, by destroying individual motives and responsibility, it decreases productiveness and increases poverty, want and misery.

Public charities were nowhere organized on so great a scale as in England, which raised a poor tax equal to the entire revenue of a kingdom, and they failed; for they are but an ill-concealed communism, and share in the same improvidence. But even co-operative societies would bring but little help, as with the present remorseless competition, societies would wage the same ruinous war against one another as now individuals do.

The world of the future is not to be a monster soup kitchen. The conception is poor, paltry and impossible. We want a more varied and higher productive power and moral energy. The world is becoming a school house, training the race for more efficient and more perfect work. Forty years ago the total value of the school property of the State of Massachusetts was half a million; to-day it is seventeen and a half millions. The school property of the State of New York amounts to thirty millions. This shows the direction we are marching in.

Pauperism is want of energy, power, health and strength. We must, therefore, introduce into our system of Education the element of physical work to train the rising generation to labor and exertion. Better we combine work with Education, than build poor-houses and penitentiaries, and introduce work at that late stage.

When labor and intelligent reflection accompany each other in childhood and youth they will remain united through life, and the social problem will be solved. The productiveness of labor will increase then in more than one way; the laborer will lessen his expensive and injurious indulgences, while he will increase his substantial comforts and nobler pleasures, which add to his power and efficiency.

Nothing but Race Education, training all classes —capitalists as well as laborers—for accomplishing together the great work of saving, elevating and preserving the race, can deliver us from the violent revolution that threateningly overhangs the social sky.

Our present school system breaks a boy from any inclination he may have had for physical labor; it fills the country with seekers for clerkships and office hunters of all sorts; and the laboring people feel that the children who are to take up their work are not benefited by such schools. Through union with labor the school becomes the institution of the people, and renders Education common and universal, as the lovers of the race ever wished to see it, and solves every problem, as an active and intelligent people will ever be able to cope with the difficulties of their situation. Or does any one pretend that pauperism offers no problem for solution this side of the Atlantic?

Let us, then, just glance at the Empire State, and notice the progress of pauperism, which includes every other private as well as public vice and misfortune, and we will find its rate rising from year to year.

	County Poor-house Population.	*City Poor-house Population.*	*Total.*
1871 . .	18,933	39,286	58,219,
1873 . .	20,193	41,737	61,930,
1874 . .	26,094	43,719	69,813.

But the army of the poor that had to be relieved by the board of charities was much larger than the one supplied inside the poor-house, and amounted in 1874 to 122,391, which, added to the first, gives 192,204 individuals provided for by the public charities.

But to form a correct idea of the deterioration, that is partly the cause and partly the effect of pauperism, let us look at the 18,933 paupers inside the poor-houses of the State of New York in 1871, and the causes which brought them there:

Drunkenness	4,846,
Debauchery	616,
Idleness	873,
Vagrancy	1,023,
Lunacy	1,652,
Idiocy	416,
Blindness	204,
Deaf-mutism	70,
Sickness	1,327,
Lameness	730,
Decrepitude	427,
Old age	942,
Indigency	1,735,
Orphanage	249,
Bastardy	311,
Not ascertained	3,058.

What a system of Education, life and philosophy the fruitage of which is such a pandemonium compounded of hundreds of poor-houses, each teeming with prostitutes, bastards, drunkards, insane, idiots, epileptics, orphans, lame, sick, blind, deaf-mutes; and yet this queer medley of vice, misery and corruption is but a sharply drawn picture of the outside world.

EDUCATION AND RACE PRESERVATION.

We must organize schools which will make poor-houses, penitentiaries, insane asylums and the like institutions unnecessary. A school which cannot do this has no right to exist, and it will most assuredly fail to bring about such a consummation, if it does not strive for it directly, studiously and intelligently. Or has Education no higher aim than geography and grammar, and does it take no interest in the weal or woe of man, and in the calamities and misfortunes of life which develop from habits contracted in early childhood?

Race Education must lay a new and deep foundation in the heart, head and hands of the people. It must discard shams and illusions, restrain our selfishness, and set us to work for one another. It must stop our crime-creating society in its work of scattering broadcast the seeds of death and disease, of raising one crop after another of half a million of defectives and of undermining the health of all, as none can be all well in an atmosphere which breeds such a distemper. Necessity will force us at last to give heed to these lessons.

The capital absorbed in the State of New York in insane, blind and deaf-mute asylums, in poor-houses, houses for orphans and hospitals, amounts to $50,000,000, and the yearly outlay on these institutions is fully $10,000,000. Correctional institutions, criminal courts and penitentiaries, police force, etc., are not included in this sum. And as we cannot long continue the present barbarous fashion of lumping together all sorts of defectives in these sinks of wretchedness and misery we call poor-houses, and will have soon to put the blind, the deaf-mutes, the insane the idiot, the re-

spectable but indigent old, and, finally, the children, into institutions their condition calls for, we
shall have to double the sum presently expended
upon them. To save the State from these burdens we must save humanity, and the prevention
of human degeneracy must become the great aim
of public Education.

Education is the natural function of parental aid
extended to the undeveloped young for its preservation ; and while among animals it stops at the
individual, among men it takes in the race, the preservation of which is the only natural and sensible
function of Education.

Our educators study to reduce the statistical figures of illiteracy, but look upon those of insanity,
the blind, the deaf-mutes and the idiots as God-
appointed social quantities. The high figures of
these miseries are so constant, because our barbarity is ever the same, and we make no attempt at
lessening them.

Noble men have plead for the bettering of the
condition of the insane, the idiot, the blind and the
deaf-mute ; but what is wanted is an earnest effort
for the prevention of these miseries, which are all
the offspring of a constitution weakened by wretched
living and other unhygienic conditions, under which
mostly the poor degenerate.

In pleading for the tens of thousands of insane,

idiotic, blind, deaf and dumb we plead for a hundred
times as many outside the asylums; for nature tol-
erates no quick transitions, and we differ all but in
degree from one another; and for every one who is
all insane, idiotic or criminal, hundreds are partially
so, and that just in proportion to their coming
under the control of the same wide-spread causes.

To prevent human deterioration means to
strengthen and purify the whole nation, and to
defer its extinction a thousand years. And is such
an aim unworthy of our schools?

DEGENERATED TRIBES.

Degeneracy, surrounding us on all sides, appears
to us as the normal condition of mankind, which is
not apt to lead to the disintegration of the race
and the nation. But a little reflection and observation may convince us that the process of deterioration, though working by imperceptible degrees,
brings about in the end fearful results.

The earth is full of kindred tribes, of which some
are mean in body and spirit, brutal, lazy and stupid,
by reason of the barren territory they occupy, and
which starves and dwarfs them, while tribes of the
same descent, but more favorably placed, are well-
formed, active and intelligent.

Europeans, who, by their enterprise and valor,
have made noticeable maritime conquests, have

through unfavorable surroundings fallen behind the very savages their ancestors have subdued.

A most appalling illustration of the low type of humanity into which whole communities may degenerate from want of pure air, water, light and food, is afforded by the disgustingly deformed and idiotic cretins, found in great numbers at the base of great mountains and in deep valleys, with the air stagnant, in certain localities of Germany, Switzerland, France, Italy, Denmark, Norway, the Highlands of Scotland, Turkey, Russia, China, Sumatra, South America, etc.

DEGENERACY IN TENEMENT HOUSES.

But the crowded tenements of our large cities contain all the elements of the climatic influences which produce cretins, and we need not roam the world over to find illustrations of permanent types of a degraded sort of humanity. The pauper and criminal class show all the characteristics of a specific low type of humanity, and not only threaten our future, but are a burden to the present generation.

How unsound must be our general condition and how unsafe our future, with half our dead dying from unnatural causes, with three millions of avoidable cases of sickness per annum, half a million of habitual drunkards, criminals and paupers—not to mention an army of defectives of every description.

The duty of Education to counteract this degencracy, and the system it must pursue to reach this important end, will form the contents of the following chapters.

THE EVOLUTION OF EDUCATION.

The catechism formed once the entire outfit of the school. Education meant then *to believe*. The reaction followed, and Education meant next *to know*. This, too, was found hollow, and Education was next taken for teaching us how and what *to be*, which again ended in moral formalism and in a refined sentimental self-seeking. We expound Education as the art of preserving the race by training us what *to do*. *To believe, to know, to be, to do*, and, finally, the synthesis of all the four form the complete evolution of Education springing up in the order of the human faculties, perception, reason, emotion and the will.

The three distinct ages of childhood, boyhood or girlhood, and youth or maidenhood, indicate three phases of Education. In the first, our being is to be developed in the infant training school; in the second, the opening mind is to be furnished with knowledge in the common school, and in the third we are to be set to work in the school of

industry preparatory to life we are about to enter.
Our being, knowing and doing are to be determined
at these three different ages. Our present Education plainly teaches by its practice, never mind
what you are or what you do, if you only are knowing; and, hence, cunning rather than character and
useful activity is fostered by our schools.

How long, oh! how long does the watchman of
the night cry, When shall the blind see, the deaf
hear, the dumb speak, the simple understand, the
lame walk forth, the sick take up their bed, prisoners go free, and the people's dead rise?

How long, how long? does the voice of reason
and experience respond to the voice of the watchman in the night, until the art of raising men will
come to honor, and mothers will learn how to educate children, and children will be trained for virtue
and activity in the infant sanctuaries of the nation,
and young men will be prepared in temples devoted to art and manual skill for usefulness; until
the body and its physical powers will be inured to
active work. Not until then will men be healthy
and honest, will the blind see, the deaf hear, the
dumb speak, the simple understand, the prisoners
go free, and the people's dead rise.

PART II.

HEREDITY AND RACE EDUCATION.

HISTORY joins her testimony to that of statistics, and the decay of Egypt, Assyria, Greece, Carthage, Rome, the Byzantine Empire and the Saracens gives evidence of the deteriorating tendency inherent in human society.

Only an Education wisely directing its efforts toward counteracting this deterioration can delay the death of a nation.

Despotisms, aristocracies, democracies; in short, distinctive forms of government have distinctive vicious tendencies, so have the different pursuits—as agriculture, manufacturing, commerce, or the different stages of civilization; and each of these varying conditions requires a distinctive system of Education for counteracting its peculiar degenerative tendencies.

As the masses live under conditions tending almost universally toward their deterioration, Education must directly aim to counteract this deterioration through measures leading to hereditary improvement. The principle of heredity or the transmissibility of structural peculiarities from parent to offspring has already been recognized by Hippocrates, and has been fully established by Darwin and other naturalists. The principle of heredity has been fully discussed in regard to genius by Galton; in regard to psychological morbidity by Lucas, Despine and Mireau; in regard to crime by Bruce Thompson; in regard to insanity by Morel, Maudsley and others, and in a more general way by Herbert Spencer, Ribot and others.

Nobody doubts but that the general nature of the parent is transmitted to the child. That less important peculiarities are transmissible is not so plain, nevertheless established. Many families have been known in which four, five and six generations had more or less than five fingers on each hand. Baldness, defective teeth, deafness, cataract, have been known to be congenital, and the gout, consumption and insanity are universally so; other affections are more or less so, and nervousness in parents generally appears in the children.

Singular habits are often formed through peculiar surroundings, and give rise to peculiar structural formations. Domestic birds that have no use for flying lose the power of the wing. Cave fishes, like moles, lose the organ of sight almost entirely. Domestic animals, which are not exposed to hostile attacks from other animals and do not raise their external ear in the act of spying the feared danger, lose the power of doing so just as man has lost it ; and, hence, the importance of fostering mental habits, as attention, reflection, self-observation, will, etc., as these habits condition corresponding structural peculiarities in the brain, become transmissible, and, after ages, permanent features of the race.

That even newly acquired habits are transmissible has been established beyond contradiction. It is maintained, with much reason, that merely the predisposition to disease and malformation, insanity, dipsomania, crime, consumption, etc., is transmitted and only developed under conditions favoring the formation of these peculiarities. This explains why often the peculiarity which appeared in the parent does not appear in all the children, and often shows itself only after two, three and four generations, when surrounding conditions conspire with the innate tendency they make actual.

Let the educator bear in mind that human deterioration can only be prevented by calling to his aid influences adverse to the development of undesirable hereditary tendencies, and that the improvement of mankind can only be secured by conditions favorable to the development of desirable hereditary tendencies.

It is not often that the one or the other set of

qualities is so unalterably fixed in the mind of the child as to leave nothing to be done by Education.

We are the work of two factors—of innate tendencies, which are the work of nature, and of surroundings and habits, which are the work of man and of Education.

Heredity and human agency have each their limits, which it is well to bear in mind in order to avoid opposite, but equally dangerous mistakes. We cannot do all, but neither is our agency reduced to nothing. Only by realizing the power of heredity as well as the power of external conditions, are we sure to press both into the service of mankind and thereby prevent human deterioration.

We hold with Dr. Carter that the habit of exercising the judgment increases the power of this intellectual operation by stimulating the growth of its nervous organ, and that, as a general rule, a *man's brain grows to the kind of activity most habitual to it*—whether sensational or intellectual—and a tendency to the character thus impressed upon it is transmitted in some measure to his offspring. Or, as Darwin and Herbert Spencer show, external influences may considerably change functions which in their turn modify the organ which becomes permanent and fixed in the race through heredity.

Our mental powers have attained their present

perfection through the cumulative or hereditary effect of a thousand generations, and are as capable of hereditary improvement in the future as they have been in the past.

It is high time the hereditary tendency of mental characteristics be intelligently applied in the Education of the race. The presumption is that, as the organ is hereditary, the function must be so, too. Thinking improves the brain under certain conditions, and with the improved brain the thinking is transmitted. Dr. Gall has maintained as much sixty years ago, and Auguste Comte recognizes the fact. Thomas Buckle was still in doubt, but observation has established the hereditary nature of our moral and intellectual faculties. Both Senecas were noted for their extraordinary memories. So were Annaeus, father and son; and in modern times the Porson family. The hereditary nature of the imagination is illustrated by the poetic eminence of the Greek poets Sophocles, his son and grandson; Aristophanes, the famous comic poet, and his three sons; Ariosto, of the "Orlando Furioso," his brother, Gabriel, and his nephew, Horace; Tasso, the renowned author of "Jerusalem Delivered," and Bernardo Tasso, his father, the greatest poet of his time, though eclipsed by his great son; music has descended through two centuries in the family of the Bachs.

4

The family history of scientific men shows the intellect just as subject to the law of heredity as the imagination; an observation holding true from Aristotle down to Darwin, and of which we will cite a few instances. Jacques Bernouilli, a distinguished mathematician and scientist, had two sons, four grandsons and two great-grandsons equally renowned in one or another branch of science. Cassini, a celebrated astronomer, had a son, grandson, great-grandson and a great-great-grandson, all distinguished astronomers and naturalists. Euler, the celebrated mathematician, had a father and three sons, all great mathematicians. Gregory, the distinguished mathematician, counted fifteen members of scientific ability in his family. Sir William Herschel, the renowned astronomer, his son, John Herschel, his daughter and two grandsons, are among hundreds of illustrations of the principle of heredity.'

The will-power, prominent in statesmen and soldiers, follows the same law, as is manifest from the names of the Adams, Colberts, Foxes, Guises, Medicis, Pitts, Peels, Richelieus, Walpoles, Charlemagne, Collignys, Gustavus Adolphus, Maurice of Nassau, and many other equally distinguished families.

It is not pleasant to dwell upon the shady side of human nature, or we could cite as many illustrations of the hereditary nature of drunkenness, theft, suicide, homicide and other crimes and vices. We shall illustrate this tendency by the sketch of one or two unfortunate families.

Jean Chrétien shows the following descendants by three sons:

Two grandsons condemned for life to hard labor for robbery and murder; one grandson condemned to death; one great-grandson transported for robbery; one great-grandson died in prison guilty of many robberies; one great-grandson died falling from a roof he was scaling in the attempt of robbery; one great-grandson died guilty of many robberies; two great-granddaughters died in prison, where they were sent for theft; one great-great-grandson condemned to death for murder and robbery.

Bruce Thompson tells of 904 convicts at Perth, 404 of whom were recommitted. In a house of detention were 109 convicts belonging to 50 families, and 8 members of one family.

A most striking illustration of hereditary degeneracy offers the Thirtieth Annual Report of the Prison Association of the State of New York.

The Juke family, located in the State of New York, is descended from five sisters who were born 1720–1740, and counts among its members 140 criminals and offenders, 60 habitual thieves and 50 common prostitutes. Seven murders have been committed by this family, and one and forty years have been spent by it inside the prison.

The reporter of this case asks: "Do our courts, our laws, our almshouses and our jails deal with the question presented?" To us it seems, when once the problem reaches the court, the almshouse or the jail, it is already too late, and matters but little how they deal with it. The far more important query is, does our system of Education deal with this question? Shall we, by example, surroundings and judicious training, produce generations of Fénélons, Franklins and Aragos, or let heredity uncontrolled breed families and generations of the Chrétien and Juke style, and bankrupt humanity?

RACE EDUCATION DEFINED.

But Education to be hereditary must be something different than a mere cramming process. True Education is the constitutional improvement of the whole man. Man, and not scholarship, is the aim of Education. The constitutional improvement of man is effected by the training of the body, the senses and the functions of the brain to the highest degree of power and active use.

This training must take place in the formative period of earliest infancy, in order to improve the very organization, that it may work rightly and automatically through life.

Education must be functional and affect the organization of man, if it is to be hereditary.

Education, when hereditary, is not lost with the individual, but is what it ought to be—Race Education.

Education, when so constituted as to become hereditary in its effects, forms a truly National Education.

An Education that affects the constitution of man through habitual training in the formative period of earliest infancy, forms man's character; and if the training is of the right sort, it makes him a good man; and a like training of the whole people forms a noble national character.

The practical training of the eye, the ear, the hand, the intellect and the will in the formative period of earliest infancy makes an effective, industrious individual, and a like general training renders a nation industrious, inventive and prosperous. Our bookish Education keeps us from observing and using our senses with accuracy—a power of universal usefulness, and yet so rare.

The present bringing up called by a misnomer Education, neglecting the child in the formative, and, therefore, most susceptible and assimilative period of its earliest infancy, fails to form its character or to develop its powers; it fills the world with conceptions lacking execution, aspirations unsatisfied, promises unfulfilled, beautiful theories and poor practice, and, hence, the conflict between the ideal and the real, which constitutes the contradiction and the misery of the times.

Education must put the child to work; for by work man is perfected. And what he does not achieve, he never comprehends; and, hence, the barrenness of the word-learning of the schools. It profits but little the individual, and none at all the race or nation.

Habit and heredity, judiciously controlled, ameliorate man; left to themselves they deteriorate him.

We have to this day neglected to aim at the cumulative effect of Education through the principle of heredity, and have failed to secure as great an abundance of good and wise men, inventors, statesmen and sages as we might, while the vicious have even by the power of this principle spread themselves through generations until they threaten to curse the nation with a brood of criminals, paupers and imbeciles.

There is something of the infinite in moral obligation; and our duty toward the present, to be rightly performed, must take in the remotest future. The solidarity of mankind extends through all time as through all space, or as far as man's existence spreads. Only when based upon the principle of heredity we shall educate man for the future of the race, will the individual be blessed in his present relations; while an Education that ignores the future of the race sacrifices likewise the true interests of the individual and of the present, which are inseparably linked to the whole of humanity.

Only when national infant schools will watch over, cultivate and direct the growth of the bodies and souls of the dear little ones of the nation; and the future mothers of the race, instead of being unsexed in factories, will be trained in these national schools for their truly noble work in the nursery, will our homes be co-workers with our schools; and people and teachers will form one great educational association, joining heart, head and hand in the great national work of rearing up the rising generation.

Only when the principle of heredity will be made the foundation of a system—which will be the Education of the race and the nation as well as of the individual—will men of enlarged capacities of head and heart consecrate themselves to the work of Education, which under their hands will no more be a thoughtless routine, but science, life and practice. There was a heathen age, when it was the ambition of the great and the wise to guide and teach the young, who grew up to men worthy of their teachers, who were sages ; that time must and will come again, and then humanity will be blessed.

Nothing but a thorough, consistent and well-directed Race Education will free the masses from the blight of pauperism, madness and crime, and remove from us the disorganizing selfishness and incapacity for good that sadden us on every side.

Education at public expense, directed by the nation, must be national, securing the perpetuity of the commonwealth and the well-being of the masses, and that can only be achieved by hereditary Race Education, which is improving the quality and increasing the energy of every God-given power of the body and soul of man.

RACE AND SCHOLASTIC EDUCATION.

Race Education is the only solution of the great social problem arising from hereditary defectiveness and the consequent increase of pauperism, misery, crime and insanity.

While our routine Education is scholastic, exercising the memory at the expense of every other faculty and to the injury of the force of body and soul, Race Education, or Hereditary Culture, is hygiene applied to the physical, mental and moral nature of man.

Race Education, by training the present generation, determines the condition of the next one; it watches over the first hours and days of man, when the foundations of his character are laid; it watches with unwearying solicitude over the waive in its charge, as a mother does over her babe.

Race Education makes physical culture the basis of its future operations; and, hence, gymnastics form an important part of its system.

Race Education, by its own hygienic tendency, inures the people to an habitual observance of the sanitary laws of body and mind, and secures thereby the health and strength of the nation.

Race Education, or Hereditary Culture, makes the practice of art and industry integral parts of its system; first, because activity is health, and, secondly, because activity transforms the physical world into things of beauty and use, which, in their turn, become means of a more perfect life; while the scholastic system has its eye fixed upon an artificial literary standard, unconcerned about life, health and power, and is entirely theoretical and notional.

Race Education, or Hereditary Culture, as it differs from scholastic Education in aim and method, so it differs from it in the objects of knowledge, or the subjects it gives prominence to in its course of instruction. It cultivates the study of hygiene, of

4*

nature, art, industry, economics and government, whatever concerns life and action, and looks to the future of man ; while scholastic Education concerns itself about words, opinions, archæological lore, and looks to the past.

Race Education, or Hereditary Culture, considers function, organization, power, work and character, or a complete human existence, as the end, and knowledge as but one of the means for securing this end.

RACE AND SCHOLASTIC EDUCATION COMPARED.

Race Education, or Hereditary Culture, aiming at mental quality is averse to stuffing by lectures or text books. The mind must be exercised on the object of thought in the only natural and old Socratic way by dialogue, which alone develops the power of thought, and by showing the student how to find knowledge in and by himself, makes it part of himself and a possession forever.

It was not books, but the discourse, says Thornton, that developed the Grecian mind for the appreciation of Eschylus and orators of the metal of Demosthenes.

Race Education, caring above all for man, chooses subjects and methods of instruction suited to the age and the development of the faculties of judgment, reason, sensibility, invention or imagination.

The scholastic system, caring more for scholarship than for man, adopts methods calculated for the promotion of learning, unconcerned about the effect upon man, as it cares more about a complete body of rules of Latin composition or Greek particles, than about the body and soul of humanity.

Race Education, aiming at a harmoniously developed and happy humanity, recognizes the claims of the young to the happy days of childhood, which it will not sacrifice for the sake of producing intellectual prodigies.

Race Education, or Hereditary Culture, directing its efforts against human deterioration, guards against premature mental strains in infancy; it takes measures against the mental equilibrium disturbing predominance of one faculty over another; it aims at soundness and efficiency all over, which secure the present success and happiness of the individual as well as the health and strength of the race in the future; while our scholastic Education, which has only in view the individual and its accomplishments, cultivates the memory and imagination at the cost of the highest reasoning and moral faculties, and makes men selfish, proud and unjust; and, hence, the strife, ambition, disappointment, increase of insanity, suicide, premature death and social decay, so glaring in our day.

Our chiefly literary Education stimulates mostly emotion and fancy, which are the life of the passions, and it secures the application of the student by working upon his pride, and thus nurses the flame which consumes us ; for pride or morbid selfishness is half insanity, and passions uncontrolled are insanity complete ; and pride and passion, as they disorganize the human economy, so they disorganize the social ; and, hence, our charge against the doubly fatal tendency of our scholastic Education upon the individual as well as upon society.

However loyal schoolmen may be in theory to the principles of development in Education, do they recognize them in practice ? Do they give due weight to the training of the physical forces, the senses, and, especially, to the moral faculties and the powers of observation, invention and practical execution or industrial skill ?

Do they supremely aim at forming sound minds in sound bodies, which help themselves by efficient hands, restrained from working injury to others by fortified morals and habits of honesty ?

As all evils tend to race deterioration, and not infrequently spring from it, Education, the great social preserver, has to be moulded in every particular, in aim, means, method, scope and surroundings, in keeping with the one great aim of race amelioration or Hereditary Culture, to which every part of Education must tend as the radius points to the centre.

Our scholastic tattooing, with all its ornaments and accomplishments, is shallow patchwork, while Race Education recognizes no improvement unless it enters the blood and marrow of body and soul, and becomes, by its organic nature, hereditary.

Unless our partly ineffectual and partly selfish culture is given up to Race Education, Pariahs will spring up among us stunned in body, low in perception and defective in moral sensibility, who will drag the nation into the vortex of their own corruption; for the virtue and intelligence of a select few are too narrow a basis for a great nation to stand upon, and the few are absorbed by the many.

Upon the foundation we indicate here, physiologists, psychologists, statesmen and educators must raise a system, in which every step taken shall advance the race as well as the individual in very deed and forever.

The formation of desirable hereditary habits does not only call for infant schools, but also for long-continued training. To render the association of occupation and virtue more permanent, we must make it continuous to the age of sixteen or eighteen years; this alone can deepen the better disposition, render it organic and hereditary, and thus improve the race as well as the individual.

Theoretical knowledge has assumed vast proportions, and its power and efficiency are marvelous, where physical resistance is to be overcome by mechanical elements. More indefinite is the power of science in modifying organizations, which, growing from within and averse to direct external interference, yield only if put in surroundings, where they may—as if it were at will—seize upon the means which are to our purpose and assimilate them as desired. We know we have to adapt the medium a fauna or flora lives in to the qualities we wish them to develop; and yet, when we deal with the cultivation of man, we fancy that we can talk him into virtue, wisdom and efficiency, without adapting the conditions and surroundings to the desired end; as if, like savages given to sorcery, we believed in the enchanting power of magic words and formulas. We forget that our actions very much depend upon our affective and passional nature, which almost wholly depends on the organic functions, in their turn determined by the nutritive condition of the entire state of the body and mind. Dejection, fear, grief, despair, uncertainty, anger, sorrow and the like affections, disturb the organic functions, which in their turn disturb the brain. And yet we consider the brain and its functions as if they were independent of all these affections.

But, if the outer world has to yield the elements for a healthy nutrition, the individual must, by an ever-active habit, contract such affections and mental tendencies as are most desirable for his own development and that of the race.

Only when we behold in our Education the Education of the race are we likely to see in our contact with men and nature and in our inner and outer experience, grand educational influences, the end of which is our own development as well as the culture and development of the race.

Men cannot be talked into living for the race; they must be trained and be brought up for the race, and they will live for the race.

Race Education, bringing up the individual for the race, develops the altruistic feelings, by which we feel the weal or woe of others as if it were our own, until conscience acts as an unerring and spontaneous force, and the religion of doing good becomes as hereditary among men as brute instinct among animals.

Does our position that the individual belongs to the race want a proof? Is there a power or faculty in him that has not descended to him from the race, and ought he not to make a faithful return for the trust with which he has been honored?

Humanity has hitherto progressed from mere brutal strength to intellectual force, and must advance to moral power. Violence has but shifted the scene from muscle to brain. The three powers in man seem to have divided the rule of the ages among themselves. The first age of the world belonged to the brutal force in man. The second age belonged to reason. The empire of both these powers is equally remorseless. The third age of the world belongs to love, which rules only to serve.

God comes to us in humanity, and, above all, in helpless children, and calls upon us in their divine capabilities, which wait for our maturing them.

Education must not be a trade, but a worship; and the school must become a temple, in which the teacher officiating at the altar of humanity, makes a sacrifice of himself that the race may live a better and happier life.

Science pushes us to these conclusions. For every function has for its end self-preservation; and the function of Education must have for its purpose the preservation of the race, and, hence, the individual must be brought up not for ambition, wealth or power, but for the race. If we lived in isolation like animals, their brutal, individual Education might do for us as for them, but as we are by our families and states linked with the whole of humanity, the condition of the race determines our own preservation.

Not only the moral law with its sanctions of a sweet inner reward or remorse, but also the inexorable law of physiology, with its long catalogue of most hideous diseases, enjoins upon us Race Education, or Hereditary Culture.

The importance of physical Education has been insisted upon by all great writers on Education, so the training of the senses, the development of the mental faculties, the formation of character and the strengthening of the will, so have the means of doing this great work been tried and studied; but, though the highest induction contains nothing but what lies in the scattered facts, it throws a flood of light upon them, and so will the principle of Race Education, or Hereditary Culture, give definiteness and union to the principles and practice of Education, which it will guide and direct by keeping in view the highest aim, by inculcating the subordination of the individual to the race, of which it is but a part and for which it must live and be educated.

The necessity of basing Education upon the principle of race amelioration was first suggested to us by the overwhelming evidence of an actual deterioration of race, forced upon us by a pathological study of labor. The study of heredity convinced us, in the next place, of the transmissibility of improved mental states, and, therefore, of the practicability of race amelioration through improved methods of Education.

Our doctrine is supported on every page of Carpenter's remarkable work on Mental Physiology, which must suggest our doctrine that *the hereditary defectiveness of the masses must be corrected by Education and Hereditary Culture ; that an Education that does not affect its subjects organically and permanently—even as far as the race is concerned, and for future generations—is not deserving the name of Education.*

This is our principle of Education, and all the means and appliances of study and training of mind and body must tend toward it as the planets do to the sun.

The great social problem of the condition of the masses, the latest development in biology, and the progress in the separate parts of Education, all point to the doctrine of Race Education, or Hereditary Culture, as the principle of gravitation of a strictly scientific system of Education upon which the whole science—in all its parts—is to be reconstructed.

SYSTEMS OF EDUCATION.

Others before us have laid stress upon Education ; have singled out the various parts of Education ; have, perhaps, seen in part the importance of our principle, as Spurzheim and others of the same school ; none, however, have recognized in it the principle that contains all others and much more beside, and that alone is comprehensive enough to rear upon a complete system of Education.

Penn's first word to his colony was, " Educate," and Washington's last bequest in his farewell address to the people he so well loved, was again, " Educate."

Education, says Rénan, is with modern society a question of life and death. It contains, as Laboulaye says, the solution of the problem that troubles the age we live in. But what is commonly called Education, makes of us, as Göethe expressed it, bags filled with words, figures and facts. What we want is men of vigor, action and character. "It is the early training that makes the master," sings Germany's great national poet. Strength, will, power, mental activity, work and a harmoniously developed humanity must be aimed at in Education—such are the utterances of our great thinkers.

Our higher reason is but the accumulated capital of the progress of the ages, says science. Thankfully we receive at the hands of the heroes of human progress the requisite material for our structure of Race Education, and trace step by step our principle in their labors.

Already the Lacedemonians gave supreme attention to the physical condition of the parents.

The Old Testament almost on every one of its pages, lays stress upon the early training of the young.

The genealogical history of individuals and families proves the truth of the heredity of mental traits. Physiology teaches that systematic thinking enlarges the brain, and craniology establishes this principle by the exact measurements of the skulls of races and ages belonging to different stages of civilization. We acknowledge our indebtedness for these and other labors.

Happiness, truth, goodness, activity, reasonableness, virtue, God-likeness, etc., are unquestionably important elements, but they lack direction, definiteness, compass and scientific basis; they contain no principle that secures what they aim at, and each and every one of them considers only the individual, who, if he is to live for humanity, must be educated for it.

There is not a principle suggested by our system but has the support of the earliest thinkers of the race.

The divine Plato largely discourses how manners are implanted in early infancy, and virtue gathers strength from habit. He insisted upon bringing together children from three to six years of age for the purpose of being trained at their self-originated games. He already considered compulsory Education the safeguard of the State. Careful training in gymnastics, music and science he insists upon as the means for the attainment of strength and beauty of mind and body, so highly prized among the Greeks.

Aristotle, who furnished the world with its intellectual food for over two thousand years, like his great master, urges State Education to begin in early childhood, the very playthings of which should have a bearing upon the life and work of the man, whose ethical culture must be secured by early habits of right feeling and correct action, under teachers of political knowledge, whose aim must be not to form merely useful, but perfect men, by the means of art, science and discipline, the tools of Education.

Plutarch, in his inimitable essay on Education, tells us of Lycurgus showing the Lacedemonians in a public meeting the effect of early training on two dogs of the same dam, the one running to the platter, and the other starting after the hare ; the one made voracious, and the other an excellent hunter.

Early exercise, says the same author, gives

strength ; good habits lead to virtue, and wisdom leads to happiness and a good old age.

Training of body and soul from earliest infancy, the solid things of science, the living example of parents and teachers, and upon the like topics, Plutarch gave us in these essays his thoughts with a freshness, which makes them delightful reading to-day.

Montaigne said : " Bookish learning is a poor stock to go upon." Again, he said : " Our understandings are no more formed by learning by rote what other men said than we learn riding, handling an axe or playing a tune, by discourses without practice."

Lord Bacon said : " Our speeches take after our learning, our thoughts after our inclinations, and our deeds after our habits, which are fixed by the force of early custom."

Milton indignantly descants against the waste of time in our schools with a miserable little Latin and Greek, and pleads for a virtuous and noble Education, consisting in studies, exercises, diet and music, likest to those ancient and famous schools of Pythagoras, Plato, Isocrates, Aristotle and others, and of whom were bred such a number of renowned philosophers, orators, historians, poets and statesmen.

John Locke held that a sound mind in a sound

body — as already Juvenal aptly expressed it — is the chiefest happiness, and, hence, the chiefest care of Education. Education makes the man, and the commonest and weakest impressions in childhood have most important and permanent consequences for us. Morals and good habits come first, the knowledge of things next, and languages last. The treatment should be mild, natural and suited to the temperament, inclination and character of the child, which the educator has to study carefully.

Leibnitz, who, by the universality of his genius, has thrown out many ideas ahead of his age, advanced the teaching of the arts and trades in public schools as a matter of highest utility to the State.

Montesquieu said, Education has for its foundation the same principles as the State—fear under despotism, pride under a monarchy, and virtue under a republic. And since virtue is formed by early habit, a republic must train children to simplicity and self-restraint. Attachment to the laws of the country demands a preference of the public good to narrow self-interest. Everybody participates in a free country in the government of the State, and must love to preserve it. Nothing but virtue and intelligence can save a republic from ending in despotism, corruption and anarchy.

As the great Cominius, the John the Baptist of universal Education, was the apostle of the study

of method, to the spread of which all over Europe
his agitated life has been devoted, so was Rousseau
a hundred years later the apostle of the study of
the child and its nature. According to him, the
full activity of our senses and faculties and the
skill of acquiring knowledge are the ends of Education and are to be attained by actual observation, but not by mere words thrust upon children,
to whom they have no meaning and whom they
can but stupefy. Like Locke, Rousseau insists
upon the propriety of every child learning a trade,
which not only bestows independence, but cultivates reflection far more than books do at that age.

Basedow, who first reduced to practice whatever
was tangible in Rousseau's " Emile," insisted equally upon his pupils to engage at least two hours daily
in the mechanical exercise of some useful trade.

None lived in deeper sympathy with the race,
shared its miseries, loved it more truly, or worked
more earnestly for elevating and saving it through
life-long labor in the schoolroom, than Pestalozzi,
and none has effectually more reformed our system
of Education than he. He has clearly worked out
the principles of developmental Education, object
teaching and the whole modern system of primary
Education; and he, above all, is the prophet of the
school house and the schoolmaster of Europe.

Man's love of liberty, says Kant, is so strong that

if he is not early subjected to discipline, he inclines, especially under a free government, to lawlessness, which is barbarity. To habituate the child to submission to reason is the first aim of Education, which must lead the race to its highest destiny, the development of its faculties. The great philosopher of Königsberg insisted that the child is not to be educated for the world as it is, that it may get along in it, but that it must be brought up for humanity and a better future; and that a bringing us up for the good of the world cannot injure us in our own life. Education is discipline or correction, culture or instruction, and exercise of the faculties of prudence and wisdom, and at last the formation of the moral disposition or of character. The child must learn to use its freedom and its powers, act upon principles and develop its character by order and steadiness. Work is the chief element in human life; the school should, therefore, train children to work, and as this requires strength and energy, physical exercise must form the prelude to Education, and is a chief part of it. So far the founder of the critical school of philosophy of Germany.

Mackintosh wisely says, Education is a proper disposal of all the circumstances which influence character, and of the means of producing those habitual dispositions which insure well-doing.

5

According to Froebel, indolence, love of pleasure, want of sense and energy, lead to vice and crime. He insists, therefore, upon work, as activity takes delight in its own creation, and develops intelligence and energy of will. Rousseau, Pestalozzi, and others before them, have seen that work develops virtue. None but Froebel has realized all the applications this principle is capable of developing in man. The Kindergarten is the door by which we re-enter the garden of Eden. As work was the first means in educating the race, when the soil was cursed with sterility that man might be blessed through work, so in the Education of the individual, work is the first means of blessing him; and the restless activity of the child is the foundation of the indefatigable enterprise of the man. Industry, which is the characteristic feature of the age, must be made the school of humanity. Life, energy and power, like wisdom, are not to be plucked from trees; they come only as responses to an earnest will, as the prayer which ends in work as its amen.

And in earliest infancy this training must begin. Spelling, grammar and arithmetic may be learned at ten or twenty years, or later. The man, the character, says Juvenal, is made at seven; what he is then, he will always be—in spite of a thousand teachers you may give him after that period has passed.

Maudsley says, the true aim and character of Education are unhappily not yet understood. Man should understand himself and nature, of which he is a part; and with which himself, his thoughts and actions should be in harmony; that through knowledge of and obedience to the laws of nature he may represent the highest physical, mental and moral evolution. Our present Education must be revolutionized; for to-day, riches, position, power and the applause of men are the chief aims, and not culture, development and character; and, hence, anxieties, disappointments and jealousies break down the soul in madness, which nothing can cure more radically than a sound Education.

John Draper maintains, Education should represent the existing state of knowledge and not the pretended wisdom of past ages. He treats with deserved contempt the pretended training obtained through the study of Latin and Greek. The American political system is founded on the principle of public intellectual culture, and the organization of the intellect is to be the great work of this continent. The only method of ameliorating the condition of men is by acting on their intelligence. Our aspirations have been hitherto physical; they must and are now becoming spiritual and intellectual. Our personal ambitions must retire, that we may share in the development and accomplishment of a far higher result.

There is not a principle of Education but we may glean it from some ancient or modern writer; but Race Education, or Hereditary Culture, is a formula that embraces all the hitherto separated tendencies, each of which is but part of Education. It embraces the physical, mental, moral and industrial elements; it suggests the method, means and end, and sets before us humanity as the highest aim; it is above all practical, and looks to the solid welfare of the individual, nation and race, and indicates the necessity of a National Education, as none but the nation can educate the individual for the race and nation.

RACE AND INDIVIDUAL EDUCATION.

Man, standing on the border of the brute world, cares only for himself. He mounts the first step of civilization and lives for his family; the second, and he lives for the State. He is to-day called upon to mount the third and live for the race. Or, is it asking too much, after ages of spiritual culture and political Education, that man should feel his unity with, and his place in the race, from which separated he has no more life nor purpose than the eye, hand or foot has apart from the body?

Is it not unscientific and leading to mischief, if the school treat man as a complete and unitary being that has its end outside of the race?

Should we not live, and, therefore, be brought up for the race? Or, are we to be brought up for ourselves, and be told afterward that we must live for the race? Does not this doing one thing and saying another, sow in us the seeds of hypocrisy and contradiction? Does not our every act bless or curse the race, ameliorate or deteriorate it? Why, then, should the preservation and amelioration of the race, which enters our every act, not be made especially the aim of Education?

If a decent regard for the rights of conscience keeps out of schools disputable points, what is there to hinder us from introducing into them the purest ethics of science?

The training of man for his place in a world of law, order and justice, that the race may be preserved and live, grow and develop in harmony with the conditions of being and universal progress and development, is the work of Race Education, or Hereditary Culture.

Everything serves a purpose outside its own existence; it is the law of nature in which everything is means as well as ends. Man, a conscious being, feels the void of a life that serves no higher purpose and ends with its own being. Race Education

points out to us humanity or the whole as the end
of the individual, who is but part of the whole, and
is only possible in and through it.

The individual who, in passion or ignorance,
silences this inner voice of nature, which pushes
man to be means as well as end in a world of mu-
tuality, will soon perish in his isolation.

Every great reformer of Education was a great
lover of the race. So was every extraordinary
teacher. The worst method in the hands of a
teacher full of love to his race, is preferable to the
best method in the hands of a teacher whose soul
is dead.

The highest scientific induction places the spirit
of saving, elevating and preserving the race, which
has led all the great reformers of Education into the
discovery of improved methods, and has strengthened and upheld their hands in the performance of
their arduous work, as a constructive principle, at
the very head and front of Education, and builds
upon it a system in keeping with the great end to
be attained.

Of course, routine pays no attention to the aim
or principle of the teacher, whom it considers a
tool working well with the method, books and
charts furnished by the man of genius who has a
soul for him.

We deny the proposition. Man is not made of

wood or leather, and cannot be manufactured ma-
chine-like. A man must have a higher life in his
soul, or he cannot kindle it in others. In every department even this is the mischief, that
forms and methods so useful supersede the life
and spirit which generated them ; and, natural
enough, lose their efficiency with the spirit that
departed.

The highest generalization alone can teach us
the proper means and methods, and put into them
life and efficiency.

Civilization will not long tolerate the barbarism of
our present poor and mad-houses or killing jails.
The care of our defectives is becoming very expensive ; the lessening of public burdens, therefore, by
lessening public miseries, is the rightful domain of
public Education, the sphere of which is the public weal and not fashionable accomplishments, leading to fashionable vices and corruption, and ending in human degeneracy—the very thing public
Education is to prevent.

If we are to succeed in stopping race deterioration or lessening defectiveness, we must aim
directly at it and work hard for it ; sailing at
large on the wide ocean of Education will not
do it.

Theorists may dream ; still the indications are the
world is not to be improved by being turned into

a vast monster kitchen, but by being made into a grand school house, where the present generation will train the next one, that every man may live in harmony with the laws of his own individual being, of society and of the entire universe ; that all discord may disappear ; vice, misery and crime may only live in name as sad memories of the past, and men may no more imbrue their hands in each other's blood, nor may be driven annually by the half a million to madness or unnatural self-destruction. The common consciousness of the nation and the world at large is, that its future salvation is Education. Of course, we ascribe such potency, no more than Herbert Spencer does, to mere ciphering, or spelling, or geography, or algebra.

Make the individual the end of Education, and his partial culture will be taken for his full development ; make individual development the means and the race the end—as nothing else is—heredity becomes then our great ally and human degeneracy our great adversary, of which the one can only be secured by early infant training and discipline throughout the whole of Education, and the other can only be combated through industrial training, the only sure preventive of pauperism, the main source of misery which opens the flood gates of human degeneracy.

RACE EDUCATION FURTHER EXPOUNDED.

Physical, intellectual, moral, scientific and industrial Education have each attracted more or less attention. We deal with Education as a social science and with the chief end of Education. Men of mere routine care not about ends, but the sight of the end of the journey keeps us on the right track. The end once clearly perceived, and the means and method for obtaining it are clear. The putting of the problem right is half the solution ; and, hence, our solicitude for ascertaining the great end of Education and for finding the formula, which embraces the whole of Education.

Race Education implies that Education has its tangible foundation in the physical nature of, and its moral purpose in devotion to, the race. And we must lay stress upon the moral element, which is crowded out of Education by the multiplicity of modern studies.

Virtue, says Locke, is to be aimed at in Education, and not forward pertness or any little arts of shifting. The teacher should know that Latin and language are the least part of Education, and that virtue and a well-tempered soul are to be preferred to any sort of learning.

Lord Kames says: "Our teachers direct their instruction to the head with very little attention

5*

to the heart. And yet, surely, a man is intended to be more an active than a contemplative being; and right action is infinitely more important than rare scholarship." Bacon and Milton, like all great leaders of the race, speak in the same strain.

But this right disposition can only be formed in the mind while it is in its very making, by our stamping devotion to mankind upon every exercise of the school, be it gymnastics, music or industry, and that we can only effect by engaging in every exercise for the purpose of enlarging the capacities, efficiency and happiness of the race.

The whole of Education must be a consecration of the individual to the race, in which it is to be merged, and life from the cradle to the grave has to be a sacrifice of the present to the future, and of the individual to the race. Still, this sacrifice is only one in appearance, as we can do nothing for the race, which does not further our own individual growth and true happiness.

Race Education, or Hereditary Culture, renders the adaptation of the Education of every individual to his own peculiar organization only the more imperative, as no permanent improvement is possible which is not based on physiological conformation; and, hence, the development of the race and the individual is best secured when the one is treated as the end, and the other as the means.

The gala or state morality, or moral mask and prudery, of a lesson or two a week in a moral text book, would not be worth pleading for. The whole of Education and every act of it must be permeated by a spiritual element, which is at the same time the last and most sober word of science, without cant or weakness, and in which science and religion are wedded to each other—and that word is Race Education.

In the multiplicity of means and methods for doing this, that and something else in the mechanical routine of our crowded school houses, the physical basis, and the moral purpose of all true Education can only be kept in view by the magic word of Ra'ce Education.

A teacher cannot develop hereditary culture or build up a desirable national character, if he has not risen even to the bare conception of Race Education. He, who aims may hit; he, who does not even aim is sure to miss.

Only national infant schools moulding the character and organization of a people by habit and training, and nothing else can build up a desirable hereditary national character. Every peculiarity of the skin, muscles, bones and nerves is hereditary, and so is that of the brain, especially when the whole of the nation is trained and educated in the same direction, and the surroundings are made subservient to the same common end. It is almost beyond the power of the individual to dispose the forces of nature and of society in a manner as will develop his character in the right direction. This requires the almost infinite means and power only at the disposal of a nation, which, to say the least, largely shares in our individual responsibility, which it controls mightily in its right or wrong development. And, hence, the duty of our public Education to use all the powers at the command of the state for the elevation of the character and efficiency of all.

Race Education, or Progressive Hereditary Culture, has a double function to perform—the correction of physical, mental and moral morbid tendencies and the developing and strengthening of the normal activities of man in the most susceptible and pliable period of infancy and youth.

Enlightened thinkers insist that a criminal should not be treated as a blank, but as a collection of hereditary tendencies; and, certainly, the school and the teacher should not be behind the prison and its keepers in scientific method and treatment. Let the school correct some of our hereditary tendencies and cultivate others, and there will soon be no call for prisons and the like institutions. Better the teacher study the hereditary tendencies of the child than that the same study be forced upon us in the end for the purpose of correcting pauperism, insanity and crime.

The constitutional deterioration of the masses induced by want, misery and neglect, begins its destructive work in the mind with the highest functions, the moral sensibilities, or the conscience, spreading to the will, the seat of the character or energy, until it reaches at last the power of thought; and, hence, the increase of crime, pauperism and insanity.

The physical powers may seem unabated, but the decay is apparent in the higher functions and the moral sensibilities are defective, rendering men hardly accountable. With the progress of deterioration the function of the will is attacked, and the man is no more to be blamed for his lethargy, than the idiot for his obtuseness.

The corruption of our time and its general confusion, as our lack of organizing capacity, are all symptoms of deterioration not likely to be met by Latin grammar.

We over-estimate in our scheme of Education the ideas of other men which, coming to us without thought or observation, are but half understood words, adding nothing to our real strength. Knowledge, like wealth, looks tempting; but only when obtained by long and hard labor do they develop the power of employing them wisely. Our thirst for knowledge is as morbid as our greed for gain. Wealth and knowledge are both but means of which humanity is the end; knowledge, however, instead of developing humanity by being assimilated into character or incorporated into institutions, is left by us unapplied. We hurry from idea to idea, like images in a phantasmagoria; one gives way to the other; all solves itself into relativity; and, hence, the apathy and anarchy of the age in which truth and goodness have ceased to serve as standards of life and action.

Ideas are so far ahead of the actual condition of mankind that the application of the one to the other is almost out of question; the one advancing at high speed, the other lagging lazily behind at a great distance, until hardly anything but violent revolution can bridge over the chasm between the actual and the ideal; a contrast too painful long to be borne and which must have its adjustment.

Race Education strives for a strong, healthy and normal humanity; scholastic Education sends its literary firework up into the clouds, unconcerned about the benighted masses of mankind below.

Religious men feel the defect of the position of men, who cultivate science and literature unconcerned about man. We have applied science to almost everything and have made it pay, save to humanity itself, which has become almost worthless. It was otherwise with the Greeks. True, they knew but little of machinery, but their men were God-like. The realism of science may become as dangerous to humanity, and even more so, than the dogmatism of past ages, which it replaces by the worship of wealth it develops.

Spain, doting upon the gold mines of the New World, neglected the richer treasures of her own soil and got poor. We get rich by trade and commerce, and neglect the cultivation of humanity, more rich in treasures than even the bosom of mother earth under our feet. Poor and paltry, indeed, are our richest possessions compared with the material wealth of the future, and this is but as the dust of the balance to the power and the resources of the mind, which creates it all.

Science in its most perfect form leads to the highest evolution of humanity, and is more truly religious than anything else, because it is most humane.

We believe with the great positivist, that the re-organization of Education must precede the re-organization of society; as all legislation is but a dead letter as long as public opinion is unimproved.

RACE EDUCATION AND DIVISION OF LABOR.

Race Education leads to a proper division of labor, the chief part of a proper organization of society.

For National Infant schools, a chief feature in Race Education, train young women for their future work and duties as mothers and educators of the race. The children are kept first in the infant, next in the elementary, and, at last, in industrial schools; and grown men alone are to work in factories. Here, then, is a most simple and natural division of labor initiated, resting upon the difference of sex and age, decidedly restricting the present murderous competition of labor. All the vast interests and the very existence of humanity call imperatively for this step in the re-organization of society, a step supported by public opinion and meeting with but little resistance, everybody feeling the need and naturalness of this measure.

We shall not lose by this division of labor, for we produce values in proportion to our efficiency; and, if we are better educated, the production of material values will be enhanced, besides that the more perfect and normal man is the chiefest wealth of the state.

WOMAN'S WORK.

Woman holds her commission from God; her natural sphere is the nursery and the Infant Training school, where she continues her work of gestation, which is not completed until she has formed the character of her offspring.

The factory is not woman's place, as Gladstone says: " He who will free woman from labor in the factory will be a benefactor of the family;" still, as we cannot afford to lose the labor of half the race, woman must work for the race by working upon the race, fashioning and developing its character; and that she only can do when Kindergartens cover the land in which she is prepared for her work.

Why were the Romans during the better ages of the republic the model citizens of the world? Because they had model mothers for their educators. Fill the land with Kindergartens, training women for their future duties as mothers; and, as we shall have then more than Roman mothers, we shall also have citizens who are more than Romans.

Woman in the barbarous state of society is the slave; in the semi-barbarous she is the toy and the tyrant, and in the perfect state of society she is the educator.

When women will be educators of the race they will be its saviors; to-day, show, pride and vanity make them its destroyers, leading on men by their extravagance to corruption in private as well as public business, until confidence in men and institutions is to-day fairly gone, and the downfall of the nation almost inevitable.

To let a woman speak about her own sex, we will quote the well-known and competent Emilie Davies, who said before the National Association for the Improvement of Social Science: " Is it

not true that to amuse themselves and other people is the great object in the life of women ; and
is it possible that their sedulous devotion to this
one object can fail to react upon the men with
whom they associate ? Who gives the tone to
what we may call lax and luxurious homes ? Who
teaches the boys that hard work is foolish self-tor-
ture, that an easy life is more to be desired than
the fine gold of intellectual attainment ? Not their
fathers. What is the ideal presented to young girls?
Is it anything higher than to be amiable, inoffen-
sive, always ready to give pleasure and to be
pleased ? Could anything be more stupefying
than such a conception of the purposes of existence ? As long as women live only for trifles, men
will only live for making money."

Only when women will be brought up to be the
educators of the race will men live for great purposes, and every family will be a centre from which
saving influences will go forth to bless the race.

Women have infinitely more tact for developing
character than men, though they may have less fit-
ness for teaching Aristotle's metaphysics, which,
however, are best not taught at all.

Pessimists may stamp every thought of an upward tendency as an idle dream, but we cannot believe men, women, the government and our whole
civilization hopelessly corrupt.

Race Education, or Hereditary Culture, aiming at the prevention of race deterioration, insists upon fitting woman for her domestic duties, upon the proper performance of which many lives depend. She has under her supervision the home, the food, the clothing, the exercise, the rest, sleep and the entire habits of the family. She nurses them in sickness, and by her economy or lavishness brings comfort competency, and general improvement, or poverty, with all its want, misery and deterioration.

For the children, the home and the school are the place, and not the factory.

For men and their powers the factory and the workshops of art, science and industry furnish opportunities, according to their aptitudes.

Reactionists may force upon the world revolution; thinkers work for normal development; and the soul must be dead that does not feel that there is a divinity in reason that shapes the progress of the race.

THE SCHOOL AND THE HOME.

Race Education interests itself in the homes of the people, without the co-operation of which its own success is utterly impossible.

The school can at best do but half its work with children housed like swine.

The cry of the educators of the land must, therefore, be: "Homes for the people and schools for the children."

Race Education, in which training predominates, exercises more the will, the central faculty of the mind; and by moulding the heart and character of man leads through correct feeling to sound thinking.

Race Education antagonizes in the pliant state of the young organism all vicious hereditary tendencies, physical or otherwise, and corrects the passions which unbalance the mind.

Race Education improves the race by fostering individual skill and aptitudes, which increase the effectiveness of the race as well as of the individual.

Race Education does not consider man as a separate being, divorced from the past, present and future of the race. Man exists only in, through and for the race, and can only be understood and prepared for his destiny in harmony with the race.

Race Education, aiming at the improvement of the race, seeks to elevate the masses; while scholastic Education, aiming at literary excellency, the prerogative of but few, sacrifices to this small minority the many.

Education, fitting man for all his functions in society, must take council with social science. The teachers of Greece and Rome were social and moral philosophers, hence their great influence upon their disciples and upon the lives of the men of their times.

The characteristic morbid tendencies of the minds and morals of individuals and communities, the vices and miseries peculiar to the age, their spread, cure and prevention deeply interest the educator.

THE DEVELOPMENT OF EDUCATION.

The Education of modern Europe began with the catechism, or belief, progressed to the study of the languages of Greece and Rome, and is thought to have reached its goal in our day in aiming at knowledge, which, we maintain, must give way to Race Education. Belief, language, knowledge and humanity form the complete cycle or evolution of Education. We begin with instinctive hope and assurance, the prophecy of future realization ; and, hence, belief, or the catechism. As language is the first step and mark of growing intelligence in the child, so it is with the race. Language, the instrument of thought, must be brought to some degree of perfection before men can think with precision and advance to scientific knowledge. Language, having the full impress of reason, is the best means for developing the mind ; and, being the storehouse of the intellectual acquisitions of the race, acquaints us with the labors of those who preceded us before we advance to original research. But even knowledge is not the last word, for ideas must become things, leading to the improvement of man and the elevation of the race.

We are far from undervaluing knowledge; still nothing less than the preservation and improvement of the race can be the aim of Education.

We object to the display made of a showy sort of learning in our higher institutions, while the people are refused in their elementary schools the solid instruction of science that would assist them in the use of the tools they are to handle in their future practical pursuits in life.

Our histories, with their royal pedigrees, political intrigues and battles, must give way to the study of the rise and development of cities and states; and physics, chemistry, physiology, botany and the other sciences must be taught in the common school chiefly in their applications to life and industry. Our common schools better teach a little less geography and a little more of Youmans' Physiology and Hygiene, a little less grammar and a little more of Youmans' Household Science. The subject matter of our Education is not life, but literature, the heroes of which we worship, while we neglect the only true hero of the world—toiling humanity.

Race Education, or Hereditary Culture, implies progress, a power by which we are striving for an excellency not yet attained, and which assists us more in our endeavor to work up to the high destiny of man than any other idea or principle.

Race Education, improving the masses, lifts all to a higher plane of common sense, where all see at a glance what the interminable discussions of former ages could not make clear even to the wise surrounded by general darkness.

OUR CIVILIZATION AND DETERIORATION.

The whole of our civilization is a series of life-deteriorating processes. The producing classes degenerate in mines and factories; adulterations and artificial wants do their work on the consumer; luxury deteriorates the one, and want and misery degenerate the other. The records of the nobles of Venice, of the old aristocracy of France and England, prove the almost general disappearance of families living in great affluence after a few centuries; while our factory and poor laborers in great cities, left to themselves, die out in three to four generations.

There is not a relation in life but tends toward race deterioration; and, like past nations and civilizations, we dig our own grave if we fail to oppose to this degenerating tendency an Education, which

is a persistent system of race amelioration, inspired
by the spirit of altruism, the saving genius of the
race, and the only possible correction of an age
selfish to the core.

Race Education cultivates in the teacher, who
brings up the child for the race, devotion to humanity, which from him spreads and imbues all.
The system in vogue appeals to the scholar's pride
—a passion that stirred up the first rebellion in
heaven ; a passion fierce and anti-social underlying
one-half of all mischief and oppression in the world.

Are men never to be brought up to work for one
another? Is the kingdom of heaven never to become a fact and a truth? Are justice, peace and
good - will among men but a dream and not a
prophecy as well?

Individual Education means selfishness, which,
winding its way from the school room to the cabinet, creeps down thence to the lowest shop, and
involves the nation in ruin.

Not without mighty reasons, and the testimony
of the universal facts of history as well as the judgment of the best of mankind, has Rousseau de-
nounced civilization as the mother of the chiefest
of our woes, which denunciation falls still justly
upon the culture of to-day, that often is but another name for refined selfishness, considering itself
the highest end instead of serving and improving

the race. Within reasonable limits this terrible in-
dictment of all past civilization is more than a mere
morbid fancy of the over-sensitive . Jean Jacques.
The clear-sighted Lessing, than whom none loved
truth more ardently, moaned over the displacement
of the practical wisdom of Socrates by the dreams
of Plato and the syllogisms of Aristotle—for both
these men were but toying, the one with philosophy and the other with science—while none of
them cared for humanity, at least not in the great
style of the master, who discarded the high-sound-
ing philosophy of the schools and set about teaching men how to live.

Other sages spoke words of love, equally drowned
by the jargon of the schools, which ever preferred
what pedants call scholarly accomplishments to
humanity, which they left to perish.

Words cost less than deeds, and learning is
cheaper than goodness; and, hence, scholarship is
more popular than humanity.

This evil, therefore, is not of yesterday, nor is
its denunciation new; but, as the lesson is not
heeded, men must not complain if it is dinned in
their ear over and again.

EDUCATION AND INDIVIDUALISM.

Neither the promotion of the individual nor the
establishment of any truth or principle, but solely

6

the preservation and improvement of the race are the aim of the new Education.

Or do we aim too high, when we are asking for the masses of the people a sound body and a well-balanced mind, the first requisite of Race Education?

Nothing but the bringing up of every child for the race can bring those better times, the belief of which is implanted in every human breast.

Race Education, with heredity, its foundation principle, impresses parents and all with the sense of the responsibility arising from the knowledge that by any imprudence, which deteriorates the race, we may give the world maniacs, criminals, paupers and idiots, filling individuals and communities with sadness and decay, and even lead to a degeneracy which may seal the doom of our country.

Individual happiness as the aim of Education, and, therefore, of life, is mean on the very face of it; and yet the aim of individual perfection leads invariably to the same selfish end and defeats its own better purpose.

Considering the culture of the select few of our own class as the sole aim of humanity, we reduce mankind to beasts of burden in order to subserve our own selfish purposes, call it culture or what you may, and thus we find that neither the divine

musings of Plato nor the science of Aristotle discovered to the one or the other the inhumanity of
slavery, which they deemed the necessary condition of their own culture.

Race Education, setting up the claims of the race
above those of the individual, makes universal benevolence, the sum total of all morality, the foundation of our Education and of our conduct in life.

In our endeavor to be unsectarian we become
inhuman to piracy. But humanity will not always
be cheated out of the great principles springing
from the eternal relations of the individual to
the whole of humanity and the Cosmos, advanced
by every founder of religion and adhered to by a
sound philosophy. Every man who sacrifices the interests of humanity to his own narrow advantage, or
who is proud, oppressive and inhuman, has not risen
to the high plane of humanity, and is a brute. Education must be organized on the highest principles
of humanity, or society will break up into fragments. A half a million of men have fallen as if
it was yesterday, before the violated majesty of the
higher law, and if it cannot be done otherwise, millions more will fall—but the higher law of the subordination of the individual to society will be vin-
dicated. Men sneer at patriotism, honesty and
honor, and confess money their deity. Wealth
takes off the ugly looks of vice, and poverty de-

prives virtue of its charm. Ostentation makes riches a necessity at any price, and all at war with one another chase for gold. A nation may live for ages under traditional slavery, but a state, in which all deliberately violate the known laws of nature, cannot long continue to exist ; and that this is our condition is the open secret of the nation to be read on every countenance. And are we to be told by pedants that this condition of affairs matters nothing to the school ?—perish the state, literary culture is the thing !

Since, then, nothing but subordination to the higher law, or the subordination of the individual to humanity, and general regard to the good of mankind can preserve a state or government, Educators must rear their whole structure upon this foundation, and, hence, the necessity of Race Education, or Hereditary Culture, which subordinates in every particular the individual to the race.

Under the system of Race Education self-culture is not a debt we owe merely to ourselves, and which we may slight—if we so please—it becomes rather a duty we owe to others, and which to neglect is a crime against the race.

RACE EDUCATION AND HYGIENE.

Race Education does not trust to the power of mere words; it looks to material conditions, from which ever ideas and principles spring, as effects do from their causes; for folly or wisdom, and vice or virtue, are but the inner aspect of the outer condition of man; and air, bread, clothing and shelter are full of moral significance.

Do we expect to pluck figs from thistles? Why, then, should we look for sound principles in an unsound body? We treat the mind and take no account of the body—the common vice of the quack, who treats the symptoms and leaves the deeper seat of the disease untouched.

Race Education studies its subjects in their homes and in connection with their hereditary family relations.

Plants, to be understood, must be seen in the soil in which they grow; and children can only be understood in the home in which they are rooted with their vices and their virtues.

The scholastic system injures body and soul by the cramming process; the æsthetic system cultivates unduly the imagination and the passions; the moral system, relying upon precepts, neglects the material conditions of what it aims at; the practical system makes time-serving men, and even the harmonious development of the faculties of the individual is defective in principle, as man must be brought up chiefly in harmony with the race and the future of humanity

Race Education lays its foundation in the body, watching the physiological formation, in which are the beginnings of the higher development.

Emotion, will and perception originate in sensations, and these depend upon the state of nutrition; and we might just as well try to transplant the flora of the tropics to the rigid zone as try to inculcate noble conceptions into children, whose nerves, suffering from want of proper nutrition, give rise to vicious sensations.

The school often debilitates children by mental overstrain, physical inactivity, too long hours of study, want of pure air and ozone, seats and postures interfering with the natural functions of one or the other of the organs, overheated rooms, depression arising from fear or dislike of the teacher or the school restraint, envy of the more gifted and preferred students, self-distrust, want of cheerfulness or lack of harmonizing physical and moral surroundings.

With so many drawbacks to health, strength, working capacity and good-will, what wonder that the funneling system of the schools interfering in so many ways with individuality and energy, furnished so small a quota of the great men of the world.

Sir Isaac Newton ranked very low in school until the age of twelve. Sheridan was pronounced an incorrigible dunce. Goldsmith was dull in his youth, and Shakespeare, Gibbon, Davy and Dryden have given at school not the slightest evidence of their future success. The character given to the great Swedish chemist, Berzelius, in his school certificate, is "Indifferent in behavior and of doubtful hope." Walter Scott passed for "the thickest skull in the school." Milton and Swift were justly celebrated for stupidity in childhood.

That our schools look more to geography, grammar and spelling than to life, health and strength of the rising generation may be seen from the last report of the Commissioner of Education, in which Dr. Thomas F. Hunter, of Buffalo, is quoted to have said in his inaugural address before the Medical Society of the State of New York: "In the primary department little children have hardly room to breathe and stretch out their little arms. The United States hospitals allow from 800 to 1,200 cubic feet of air to the individual. The British India jails give the prisoners 648 cubic feet of air. Some of our schools give our (growing?) children 56 cubic feet! No wonder that scarlet fever, diphtheria, typhoid fever and blood poisoning of every sort are more or less prevalent. A large proportion of these dread disorders are generated and propagated in our public schools. But acute diseases are not the only results of this criminal

crowding. Tuberculosis, scrofulous and brain affections, developed at various periods, are generated
in our schools. Better for society and better for
themselves would it be that these infants were not
educated at all than at such risk."

And such schools may be found in every large
city of the land !

The average number of cubic feet to the scholar
in the schools of Philadelphia is 143. The proportion of carbonic acid to the air is 500 per cent.
larger in these crowded rooms than in the normal
atmosphere, and cannot but vitiate the blood.
Every individual, says Dr. Bell, requires 2,000 feet
of fresh air every hour, and if only 300 feet are
allowed to the scholar, the air must be changed
every twenty minutes, and with less provisions con-
tamination is sure to follow; the sensibilities are
blunted, the intellect is obtused; stupidity, idiocy
and physical deformity are promoted. The depressed condition of the children in our schools
predisposes them to epidemics, from which they suffer also more intensely than others.

An examination of the public schools of Brooklyn, in 1874, showed 50, 49, 30, 29 and even as little as 24 cubic feet of air to the scholar. Such is
the condition of the schools in Brooklyn. It is, as
we have seen, not much better in Philadelphia,
and very much the same all over the country.

Dr. Howard shows that our present system of Education, treating alike all scholars, is injurious to many, weakens body and mind, and is one of the causes of the increase of insanity.

Is it not time, then, that our schools be put under the sanitary supervision of competent physicians, as advocated by the Social Science Association?

Theory and practice have both established the hygienic effect of gymnastics, never more indispensable in childhood or mature age than under our present division of labor, which affords hardly to anybody the harmonious exercise of all the parts and organs of his body. Still our schools are criminally indifferent about this reform, alike necessary to the health and development of the human system.

The one-sided mental culture of our seminaries leads to mental degeneracy. The criminal pride and foolish vanity of the world, the excess of imagination and passion, and other disturbing elements cultivated by our literary schools, prepare the way for insanity, to which students thus deteriorated fall an easy prey in after-life.

But it is not necessary to enter upon a hygienic analysis of our present scholastic system. Dr. Ray, a most eminent observer, sketches in a few lines the future mothers of our physically enfeebled race, as sickly young women, daughters of healthy moth-

6*

ers who went to school hale and hearty, and returned with an enfeebled constitution, the face pale
and the spine not infrequently curved, to give existence to children as weak as themselves.

The examination of a noted physician proved
the fact that there was not one girl out of forty
who have spent two years at a boarding-school that
was not more or less crooked.

Horace Mann said : " Degeneracy must not only
be considered as one of the greatest calamities that
can befall a people, but it must be entered on the
catalogue of its greatest sins." Again, the same
eminent educator says : " As the inevitable consequence of unhealthful habits, debility or sickness
ensues, old age is anticipated, feeble parents are
succeeded by feebler children, the lineage dwindles
and tapers from less to less, the cradle and swad-
dling clothes are frequently converted into the
coffin and shroud, occasional contributions are sent
off to deformity, to idiocy and insanity, until sooner
or later, after incredible sufferings and abused and
outraged nature finding all her commands broken,
her admonitions unheeded, her punishments con-
temned, applies to the offending family her sov-
ereign remedy of extinction." The same veteran
says : " On the broad and firm foundation of health
alone can the loftiest and most enduring structure
of the intellect be reared."

Nervous diseases are daily becoming more frequent, and our mad houses, though of the size of towns and daily increasing in number, are overflowing with their unhappy tenants.

We, therefore, insist upon Race Education, or Hereditary Culture, which clearly implies a humanity, sound in body, vigorous in mind, skilful in performing, inventive in conception and well-balanced all over.

Our definition of Education excludes both extremes, the past ineffectual formalism as well as the anti-ideal or unethical realism, which would fain press Education into the service of a selfish industrialism.

Health is the first condition of success and happiness, and, hence, hygiene and gymnastics are the first steps in Education. Gymnastics direct the organic activity of the body from the great nervous centres to the muscular system, and lessen thereby an excess of sensibility, which, among other baneful influences, counts also that of a premature and morbid sexual development, ending in that terrible vice which destroys the youths of the land by the tens of thousands. Our one-sided Education, failing to combine physical with mental exercise, is greatly responsible for this race-deteriorating pest.

Too many lessons lead to evening studies, an

excited brain, an unsound sleep, dreams and self-pollution. Muscular exercise and fatigue induce a sound sleep and a clear head for morning study.

Germany is following in the traces of ancient Greece, and gymnastics form a part of its common schools, of which it is fast reaping the benefit.

Prof. Tyndall, like others, strongly condemns our one-sided culture. "Few persons," he says, "are aware how great a promoter of study labor is. Those whose occupations are of the intellectual kind, frequently become brain-weary, and this sort of weariness is very exhausting. The brain needs rest, gets it most effectually in muscular toil, and returns to study with a keen appetite." Tyndall recommends alternation of farm and shop work with study, and concludes, "*This habit of work should be formed early in life, if we would have it a source of pleasure.* Work is the greatest educator and blessing that we have or are likely to have." And this initiation in the mechanical arts, horticulture or agriculture, while affording relaxation from mental exercise, would prepare us for the active duties of life, and add greatly to our material wealth.

PART III.

KINDERGÄRTEN AND INDUSTRIAL EDUCATION.

FOR hundreds of years universities absorbed all the care of governments; to-day the vaster importance of common schools is conceded. But we venture to say, the foundation must be laid deeper and lower still—in infant schools, where the senses are developed, moral and industrious habits are formed, the taste is improved, and the finer feelings, which give fibre to the will, are cultivated.

But while the highest interests of humanity demand the formation of national infant schools, the immediate material interests of the industrial classes call for them as an opportunity for early art training, the development of the faculty of form, combination and invention, as they can only compete with machinery in art and ornamental industry.

The daily increasing temptations of all classes convince all of the urgency of moral training, the want of which has not a little to do with our almost universal loss of trust and confidence, and the consequent crisis we are passing through.

Through the inactivity of our intellectual faculties in early infancy we become more apt to imitate and form habits good or bad, and, hence, the importance of training-schools at that age.

Our sensations and their gradations, even those of touch, smell and taste, and especially those of sight—which suggest form and magnitude and lead to the perception of order and beauty—and those of hearing—which imply a succession of time and harmony—are all elements of thought and lead to the formation and development of the mind. This cultivation of the mind begins, then, with the exercise of the senses, and especially of the eye, best cultivated by Kindergarten training adapted for the purpose and by the art of drawing continued in after years.

From the very birth of man, sensations deepen into perceptions, perceptions by repetition form memory, memory develops into imagination; the absent object is imagined and calls forth desire, which grows into passion; impressions force a comparison and give rise to judgment, which again develops into reason; and, hence, the importance of coming in contact with living nature and her grand living realities, the source of all healthy sensation and perception, the fountain-head of all higher mental life, and the necessity of feeding the minds of children through their senses and not to blur their minds through words — the imperfect shadows of things. It is from the freshness of the sensations and perceptions, derived from the constant intercourse with living nature, that the self-made man obtains his vigor and success in life.

When character and individuality and the cultivation of virtues, like order, steadiness, neatness, industry, wisdom and love, and, in general, a better and happier humanity will be aimed at in Education, Kindergarten, in which the development of these traits is the only business of the teacher and his young pupils, will be assigned the first place in the rearing of the race. As long, however, as the cramming down of the fragments of half-digested knowledge is taken for the proper work of the school, the race will be uneducated and suffer severely and variously, in spite of our boasted institutions of learning, and in proportion to the undeveloped nature of its positive elements of physical, mental and moral strength.

The words of Lord Brougham are always worth considering, and he dwells upon it as a weighty matter in connection with national infant schools, that a child can and does learn more before the age of six years than it does or can learn after that age during his whole life, however long it may prove to be. Children, he says, with curiosity, frankness and candor, become soon unwilling to learn, turn stubborn and sullen, and even full of base fear and falsehood, from want of early Education and infantile tuition.

If colleges and universities turn out men full of fine speeches and sermons, only Kindergarten schools can turn out men and women of fine moral dispositions and such sterling mental parts as will make them citizens of solid worth.

Kindergarten sounds very poetic, though its origin is deeply realistic. Froebel's heart sunk within him at the misery of the masses, whose children are pining away within the dingy walls of dark and damp tenement apartments. He longed to see men free and happy, which they cannot be without activity; but to be active they must be healthy, and, hence, he insisted that the pale little prisoners of the poor should be congregated in schools connected with gardens, that heaven's free air may have access to them and give them strength to act and to live. Next to bodily vigor, mental activity is requisite to a perfect life. The dwellings of the poor offer but little variety of impressions and yield but little food to the perceptive powers, the imagination, the will, the æsthetic faculty; and the social virtues have no chance at all in the isolation of the dwellings of the poor, where the dear little ones are not infrequently locked up as brutes in cages, while the parents are out to work.

That in England 408,461 infants of the ages between three and six years attend infant schools, or, according to the report of the Commission of the Duke of Newcastle, 12.17 per cent. of the population under 5 years, and in France 418,768 infants of the same ages are in public halls, proves sufficiently the practicability of infant schools, and that they could be made beneficial to the highest degree to the race by the training and direction given to the physical and mental activities of the young before they take the wrong direction, into which they are often pushed by vicious hereditary tendencies.

The progress of the Kindergarten schools in the last few years is a guarantee of their ultimate success. There were but twelve in the United States in 1871. The following table, taken from the Commissioner's late report, shows their growth in the last few years:

	1873.	1874.	1875.	1876.
Kindergarten, . . .	42	55	95	130
Teachers, ...	73	125	216	364
Pupils, ...	1,252	1,636	2,809	4,090

St. Louis has made a lively beginning of incorporating the Kindergarten system in the primary department of public instruction. Boston has entered upon the same experiment.

The Kindergarten demands the highest capacity

in the teacher, shows clearly the object of Education, and how to reach it; the teacher studying and developing the pupil, as books do not step in between the two and defeat the true object of Education.

Once the presence of the father assisted the mother in the government of the children; to-day the factory or the business house calls him away from his home; and the mother, burdened with additional cares and labors in and out of the house, can impossibly attend with an even temper to the difficult task of properly training her children. The generality of mothers have to do their own work, their cooking, washing, sweeping, mending, nursing and taking care of babies; and shall they be made also to train and educate our little children? Is it a wonder that women are weakened, break down in body and mind and transmit their feebleness to their children?

We insist upon it that the father's absence and the increased responsibilities and cares and labors of women to-day, together with the irritability of our excited nerves, make it a necessity—both for mothers and children—that the latter are managed by infant schools, which would thereby much improve the health of overburdened mothers, and, in consequence, improve the race.

As the house is dead and empty without the

presence of the blessed little ones, so is the nation without its public nurseries, in which alone our children can be properly trained.

Oh! what bliss is in store for the race, when juvenile processions of sweet children will on festive occasions brighten the careworn brow of the workers of the nation. The lamb-like innocence, beaming from the angelic little faces, will do more toward purifying the moral atmosphere of the land than all opposition parties.

Far from being an innovation, we find that Boston had already in 1823 an infant school of 130 children.

The growing difficulty of attaining success in the complexity of our modern relations, the advantage a cultivated intellect bestows, and the continuous exercise of this faculty, render it superfluous to dwell upon the necessity of mental training at school.

In proportion as men will be expected to do something well in life, the development of their faculties and energies, and, hence, their early training will become more important. The infant school, therefore, must be something different from a mere play or singing school; and, least of all, must the children be crammed.

Infant schools cannot but become worse than useless when children are taught in them in the manner of:

G, is for Goshen, a rich and good land,
H, is for Horeb, where Moses stand.
I, is for Italy, where Rome stands so fair.
J, is for Joppa, and Peter lodged there.
K, is for Kadesh, where Miriam died,
L, is for Lebanon, can't be denied.

Froebel's games must not be allowed to become monotonous, but the individuality of the teacher and the pupil must endow them with a daily freshness, which renders them a delightful exercise to the minds and bodies of the children. The teachers of infant training-schools do a most noble work and must have warm hearts and active minds.

Race Education, aiming at permanent qualities and fixed tendencies in the race, cares more for infant training than collegiate teaching. The latter may give us masters or commanders, who have neither the will nor the disposition to practice the laws they lay down for the regulation of others; it may make diplomats disposed to take advantage of the ignorance of the multitudes; but infant training makes men who are a law to themselves, and who succeed not by the folly and faults of other men, but by their own skill and industry.

It is a sort of malign providence in the state to educate the citizen just sufficiently to make him responsible for the law which he may be able to read, without developing in him the power to conform to it.

The culture of the disposition in the young, which is mostly effected by living example, is a grand school for the adult generation. But, alas! just here is the rub. It costs little or nothing to lecture. To give the example, we have to become learners and workers ourselves, and, hence, the preference of barren teaching to fruitful training.

If a person well trained in childhood strays from the path of rectitude, he is easily redeemed from his error through the early instilled sentiment, which, as it were, waits but for an opportunity to be aroused from its dormant state into full power, swaying again the life and action of the soul and purging it from vice and crime.

Race Education lays most stress upon the cultivation and development of a sound body, for where health and vigor are wanting, nothing great or good can be achieved, neither intellectually nor otherwise, and nations as individuals lose their hold upon success and pre-eminence with the loss of physical energy.

Still, though our main care in dealing with infancy is the attainment of bodily health and strength, we may and must lay the foundation to intellectual greatness already in the nursery. It has been observed by Beale that fixing the attention steadily upon one object, or the complete concentration of mind, makes the Newton or Leibnitz. And this faculty may be cultivated in the nursery by riveting the attention of a child to whatever he is doing, until he comprehends as much of it as his age permits before he passes to anything else. Children are so apt to fly from one thing to another with too much rapidity to thoroughly acquire a knowledge of one thing before they begin to examine another.

By a wise control over the appetites and propensities of our children the foundation is laid to that self-command in them, without which no real happiness in life is possible.

Let children observe and learn facts, storing their minds with material for a later age when the higher faculties will begin to combine and compare ideas.

We take only notice of what a child learns by set lessons, forgetting how much he learns by observation of innumerable facts and the acquisition of language.

Premature decrepitude and death are often the fruit of forcing the mind and neglecting to strengthen the body.

Proper digestion, perspiration, exercise and respiration are requisite to the proper action of the brain. Lessen the quality of the blood by impure air, or the quantity by insufficiency of food, and the brain lacks its proper stimulus.

Race Education aiming at permanent effect

through organic improvement seeks to ascertain in the nursery the temperament, constitution, idio-syncrasies of the various organs and their functions, morbid affections, hereditary tendencies and habits of those trusted to its charge. It being ascertained that the child we are to manage is of a bilious, san-guine, nervous or lymphatic temperament, of a weak or powerful constitution, scrofulous or phthit-ical, with a hereditary tendency to insanity, habits, surroundings and a mode of living are to be chosen opposing the development of the evil tendencies feared.

It is in the nursery that the habit must be estab-lished of conforming to the hygienic laws of our being, a habit that determines the whole of life, and is positively of itself sufficient to insure our success and happiness in life; and punctuality as regards food, sleep, temperature, evacuations, cloth-ing, etc., affords a constant opportunity for the establishment of this habit of conforming to the hygienic laws of our being; and this opportunity begins with our existence, and will do more for us than all later precepts and exactions.

The brain of the young, soon over-worked, dis-turbs the functions of nutrition and produces indi-gestion so common among us, as we over-task our children at school and ourselves in whatever enter-prise we may be engaged in

It is the excess that injures. A proper amount of physical and mental activity promotes the nervous activity requisite for the healthy functions of the human system.

Temperance and exercise of body and mind must be insisted upon, without which health of body and mind are impossible and life becomes a torment.

Though all faculties are to be trained, still they are to be subordinate to the intellectual powers, which must, above all, be called into active exercise, especially as we are naturally prone to yield to our animal propensities.

As the formation of regular habits, self-control and order are of the highest importance, a good nurse will lay the foundation to all these habits, and secure at the same time the health of the child by invariable order in the periods of feeding and in all other matters.

Much can be done for the future happiness of the child by a cheerful nurse, who avoids harsh tones. A discordant voice and ill-tempered mother are sure to beget moroseness in the child, and lay the foundation for future misery. Gloom and depression, says Taylor, during childhood debilitate body and mind. A sorrowful child, full of unkindness and misfortune, develops among the lowest class a ferocity, which startles from the commission of no crime. An unhappy childhood is often the cause of a wrong life, for it perverts the judgment and natural feelings of man; depression impairs the functions and lowers the tone of body and mind.

Bearing in mind all the time that the physical growth and development is at this tender age important beyond every other consideration, we still say, more can be done for the future mental development of the child in the first two years, than at any future period, for the child's powers of observation can be steadied and its curiosity strengthened, while we can weaken the one by discouraging the other, in order not to be annoyed by the child questioning us and exposing our ignorance besides trying our patience.

As light, air and exercise are the first requisites of the young citizen, we will remark that the fading of the carpet must not be allowed to interfere with free access of the rays of the sun, neither must the possibility of soiling clean garments stand in the way of free and easy out-door play, and as a properly warm and active skin is the foremost preserver of good health, we will add here our protest against children's bare arms and legs.

It is a shame, our factories interfere even with infant schools. But can we not by stringent factory laws, like Switzerland, keep little children out of factories? Or are our western prairies not as

7

fertile as the ice-fields of Helvetia, and can the American republic not as well provide for the future citizen, as the mountainous land of Tell does for its children?

EDUCATION A SOCIAL SCIENCE.

Providence, that gives the bird its beautiful plumage and teaches it to sing, that joins suppleness to strength in the tiger, gives antlers to the stag and fleetness to the hare, will it not provide for the suffering masses a way of escape from their miseries? The physician studies but one side of human life—the physical—and that in its abnormal state. The lawyer considers man in his legal and hardly in his moral or physical relations. The divine is almost wholly absorbed by the world to come, and the suffering masses themselves, and their hungry leaders, are too much in the thickest of the fight to direct with judgment the details of the battle.

May we not look reasonably to the teacher for the deliverance of humanity from its present troubles?

Great educators are not mere cipherers. They are lovers of the race, and sorrow with its sufferings. Luther, Franke, De la Salle, Rousseau, Basedow, Zinzendorf, Pestalozzi, De Fellenberg, Oberlin, Wichern, in short, all who have revolutionized old barren systems, or applied well-known principles

on a grand scale, were deeply exercised about the
social miseries of the people they yearned to relieve
from the burdens that were pressing upon them.
Vehrli, in Switzerland, was so strongly convinced
of the necessity of the teacher's sympathy with
the people, that at his normal school at Constance
the future teachers had to work as hard and live as
poorly as the commonest of the people, with whom
they were to be united in heart and feeling; and
the success of this system had become so manifest,
that it has been copied in numerous normal schools
all over Europe, and especially in those which had
the good of the people at heart as the great and
good V.ehrli.

The teacher is no theorist, but a practical worker.
He has the best opportunities for observing human
nature and for acting upon it when it is most susceptible and least prejudiced. He has but one
desire—the good of the race—and the world trusts
and confides in him to-day more than ever. Who,
then, of all men is more suited for the priesthood
of social reform than the teacher and educator?

The proper division of the sciences and the
assigning to each of them its proper work is the
very foundation and beginning of their successful
cultivation. Medicine was for long ages but a part
of theology and was practiced by the miracle working and healing divine, and astronomy was left to

the fortune-telling astrologer; while the chemistry of society, or social philosophy, like the chemistry of nature, was left to the goldmakers, and shared the same fate of never rising in such hands to the dignity of a science.

Remove social science from political economy— vulgarly speaking, the art of making money—to Education or the art of improving man, and social philosophy will experience the same change as the science of the heavens did when removed from its ancient quackery to the serene science of astronomy, or chemistry from the goldmakers to the schools and laboratories of the Berzelius and Rose.

As long as social philosophy was made the adjunct of political economy, man was made subservient to wealth, just as wealth will be made subservient to man when political economy will be made an adjunct to social philosophy.

Like law, medicine or theology, social philosophy must be put in keeping of some working profession; and there is none, as we have seen, more proper for the cultivation of this noblest of all departments than that of the educator, who has in his hands the formation of humanity almost from the very cradle, and whose work is the improvement of man. Of course, the educator will make man and his improvement the centre and circumference of social philosophy. But is there any serious objection to this?

Only in the union of social science and Education lies the success of both and the future of humanity.

Like the mills of the gods the educator grinds slowly, but surely, and equals all in the end. He does not convulse society with revolutionary measures; but neither are counter revolutions possible where he has prepared the ground for the onward movement of a progress in keeping with the conditions of time and place.

Race Education puts a new emphasis upon Lord Brougham's celebrated "the schoolmaster is abroad," and endows it with the force of an almost new inspiration. The suffering masses, humanity, need not despair, the schoolmaster is abroad. He is intelligent; is in daily contact with the children of the poor; his labors and aspirations are for the poor; their welfare is his success; his worldly prospects are modest; the prosperity of the poor is all he works for, and this is the highest reward of his most ardent labors. To the teacher the poor must look as to their most trusty friend, who will yet conquer for them the sphynx, answer her queries, and solve the problem that presses hard upon a suffering world to-day.

To fill this, his mission, the teacher must study the whole of man. He must understand the genesis of physical debility, morbidity and of excessive rates of mortality ; he must understand the genesis of pauperism, of drunkenness, of insanity, of vice and of crime ; for Education is the dietetics by which all these abnormal developments are to be prevented, and the race and the individual are to be preserved and improved.

But if Education is a social science, it certainly cannot teach, as it does to-day teach, everything save the principles of this science, which is the most useful of all to man.

Horace Mann has successfully urged upon common schools the study of human physiology. But is the physiology of society or political economy less essential for our social existence than common physiology is for the animal economy ?

Ignorance cannot interfere with the motion of the stars, but it does with the movements of industry. Passions and narrow interests blind us as to the facts and principles of social science, and make an impartial study of the same a double necessity.

How natural it is for a laboring man to believe that labor is the only factor in production ; that wages can be raised or lowered at option ; that what is gained by capital is taken from wages, and that to curtail capital is to improve wages, and the like sophisms, which form the stock in the conflict between labor and capital and which sound economical teachings must help to clear away.

England, with its extreme centralization of wealth, real and personal, would not enjoy to-day the peace and prosperity it does, had not its Broughams, its Robert Peels, its Chalmers, its Chambers, Charles Knights and Chadwicks worked as assiduously for the spread of sound economical doctrines as for the improvement of the condition of the masses.

Education, or race preservation, cannot overlook the laws of production, exchange, currency, distribution and consumption, which can no more be violated with impunity than any other laws of nature.

The aim of Education, says Mr. Blyth, before the National Association of Social Improvement, is not to make reading and calculating machines, or manufacturers of Greek and Latin verses, but steady, intelligent and thrifty men, practicing regular industry, beneficially to society, and, therefore, profitable to themselves; men who possess self-restraint to abstain from wasting or misusing the product of their industry; forethought to store a portion of that product against sickness or old age; honesty and trustworthiness, the prevalence of which qualities in society enables confidence to be felt that their savings will be enjoyed, and a sense of parental duty inducing them to seek to implant in their children a disposition similar to their own.

There are plenty of opportunities in school life

to follow up the lessons of industry, self-restraint, forethought, equity and the like duties with their practical application.

The mischief caused by the economical ignorance of the merchant class can only be imagined when we consider the universal calamity of our financial crises, which are as periodic and destructive as the pest formerly was.

If men of science do not teach at school correct principles of social science to the advancement of social order, peace and general prosperity, disorganizers will spread doctrines subversive to society and civilization.

Whoever will succeed to arouse the nation to a proper realization of the danger that threatens our future, from the neglect of the duty of teaching the people sound principles of social science in our common schools, will prove himself a public benefactor.

INDUSTRIAL EDUCATION.

The preservation and improvement of the race requires a certain degree of general well-being, which depends to-day chiefly upon the productiveness of the industrial arts, which, therefore, must form the chief concern of the school. Our whole course of instruction looks to general culture. The adding of practical science and industrial training, far from materializing the schools and rendering men machines, would only join practice to theory, and executing to planning, which humanizes us by the inter-penetration of thought and action. Science and industry are both gainers when they are united. Once the soldier held the scholar in contempt; to-day the school and the scholar avoid the contact with the workshop and the mechanic; and yet, if Lord Bacon is right, the workshop is the vestibule to real knowledge, and its methods are safer than those of Plato or Descartes.

The school should omit nothing in theory or practice to make men more productive, saving, forethoughted, just and moral. Science, in its practical application, the history and description of raw materials and the fashioning them into articles of industry, the management of tools, domestic and political economy and social science, form all-important parts of the workingman's course at the industrial school. The industrial colleges of the United States should graduate annually a thouand mechanics and artisans, models of skill, efficiency and reliability. How much more such graduates would be worth to the country than the graduates sent out by our Latin and Greek schools, the relics of the middle ages.

We are no more satisfied with verbal alterations. The abstract formulas and rules of science are of

7*

no more practical use than the fine points of the schoolmen of the middle ages. Our infant schools must build us up by their training; our common schools must use us to experimental ways by their constructive method of instruction, and our industrial schools must give us opportunities for applying that spirit to the practical arts of life.

A sensible people will as well submit to compulsory industrial training as to spelling and grammar, especially as many trace their miseries to the want of such training. One-half of the people are out of work, because the other does not know how to work, and has nothing to give in exchange for the labor of the other.

Or is this idea of compulsory industry a dream? If it is, it was sober enough a dream for the eminent jurist Lieber to have dreamt it forty years ago.

Against the spirit of the age Education is impotent. Joining with it, Lieber remarks, it yields a permanency of results attested by the stability of the Chinese Empire, in which the Education of the schools and the spirit of the country are of a piece. Wild speculation and industrial activity are the double tendency of this age; the school may reinforce the first and lead to extravagance and ruin, or it may sustain the latter and promote universal well-being.

In antiquity, lessening human wants was lessening

the double barbarity of slavery, which supplied
labor, and of war, which furnished the markets of
the world with slaves. In modern times, the increase of human wants is the foundation of a civilization in which labor is supplied by brains, directing machinery. Only when labor will be coupled
with intelligence and taste, and will be efficient, and
the capacity for consumption will be universally increased by the enhanced productive power of the
masses, will over-production cease to be a periodic.
calamity, distressing alike to labor and capital, and,
hence, the necessity of associating art instruction
and industrial training with the common Education
of the people.

Or must the children of the industrial classes
be pauperized before they can get into industrial
schools?

Is it just or wise to make industry the exclusive
feature of pauper schools? Is not this degrading
labor and sliding back into the foul spirit of slavery
and indolence, and the contempt of poor humanity?
Is it not undermining the foundation of national
wealth and public morality and manhood?

There are two sorts of culture, a traditional, oc-
cupying itself with the opinions of the past, and a
common, acquainting itself with men and things as
they are. The first is as barren as endless, and inaccessible to the masses, for whose wants public

Education ought to be suited. The second is suited for the people, whose Education must be such as will make them healthy and well balanced men, gaining a comfortable living by their skill and industry; and with health of body and mind, and industry, comfort and manly culture will not long be missing. To be plain, our schools are not to furnish us with young ladies and gentlemen shining in society, but to fit men and women for useful work in a 'world of toil and labor.

Our encyclopædic Education makes of everybody a superficial judge of everything; thorough universal elementary art and technical training make men skilful performers of useful things. We want workers and not everlasting talkers. We are all critics, but where are the artists?

Once schools were only attended by the clergy; and, hence, they were engrossed by Latin. Later, they were frequented by the wealthier classes and became commercial in character. To-day, when the working people crowd them, they must become essentially industrial. Drawing, geometry, science applied, technical instruction and industrial training must develop taste, skill and inclination for a variety of mechanical pursuits. As long as five millions of youths are annually unfitted upon our school benches for the plough, the shop and the factory, neither this, that or any other administration will relieve us of the misery of our times.

Who can count the direct and indirect victims of a half a million of dens of iniquity in the land? Who can measure the depth of their misery and degradation? What an army of paupers, drunkards, criminals, insane and idiots! What sorrowful batallions of the blind, deaf and dumb, who come into the world loaded with other men's sins. And the vicious, the proud, the avaricious, slaves and oppressors greatly swell this sad list.

When men have once been saturated with sin and shame, benevolent societies may pitying follow them to the grave.

The common schools must bring up the people for work; and a gentleman who thinks his children above such an Education, must have the dancing master come to the house.

Education alone can safely guide us through life. But Education must start us on the very way we are to travel through life. It must make us, when children, feel, think, live and act as we are to do through life. To pass our young years upon school benches entirely, prepares us for passing our lives in the school and not in the world. There are hours enough in the day for exercising a child in all the parts of life.

William Penn, the founder of the commonwealth

that bears his name, framed the following provision, which was adopted by the Provincial Council in 1683: "That all children within this province of the age of twelve years shall be taught some useful trade or skill, to the end that none may be idle, but the poor may work to live and the rich—if they become poor—may not want."

Our Education, says the State Superintendent of Pennsylvania, seems faulty in this, that too many young people are seeking a livelihood without working with their hands. Of 240 convicts, received at the Eastern Penitentiary of Pennsylvania, only twelve had a regular trade, and of the criminals of 17 prisons in the United States in 1868, 79 per cent. were without a trade.

Mr. Edward Winslow, of Boston, insists upon joining mechanical and industrial training to our common school exercises. So does Prof. J. W. Burns, of Philadelphia. Commissioner Eaton decidedly uses all his resources to direct the minds of the teachers of the United States to the want of a more practical Education; and aptly quotes, in introducing the subject of Education and Labor, the words of Humboldt: "The time is not far distant when science and manipulative skill must be wedded together, that national wealth and the increasing prosperity of nations must be based on an enlightened employment of natural products and forces."

Man's whole make of body and soul, his wants, and the whole structure of society, call for the perfecting of our industrial occupations, especially today, when the competition among unskilled laborers is so great, and the power of steam takes the place of muscle. But under our system of division of labor, when a man, making a twentieth part of a thing, can earn however scanty a living and doing it all the time, does it expeditiously and to the satisfaction of the employer, technical schools become a necessity, in which apprentices are taught every part of a process, and the theory as well as the practice, in order to become superior workmen.

Neighborhoods and countries blessed with such industrial institutions have distanced in the great markets of the world all the competition of the imperfect products of other countries, which by this sad experience have been awakened to their commercial danger.

Muhlhousen, Creuzot and Besançon, with their celebrated industrial schools; Belgium, with fifty such institutions and fifteen thousand apprentices, who have attended these schools with great satisfaction to themselves and the manufacturers; France, with its twelve thousand of industrial scholars; and Germany, with its 52,127 apprentices in fourteen hundred and fifty industrial schools, are sufficient proof of the practicability of such institutions.

Scott Russel shows the actual cost of the technical Education of a workman is no more than $125, and the surplus earning of educated over uneducated labor of one single year amounts to as much.

England is almost carrying on a crusade against the ignorance arising from want of like institutions for the technical training of her people. It recognizes the utter failure of a general Education, that is not followed up by a special Education and training in some particular industry.

A practical Education for useful life is hereditary; for, as it is all work and training, it enters the very make of body and soul, while superficial scholarship profits very little at present and nothing at all in the future.

Modern governments are expensive; and if they do not assist the pursuit of industry, especially when the scientific information and the technical skill necessary for the complete mastery cannot be secured without the assistance of public institutions, they will soon find empty the pockets of the people they so often rifle.

Why should the government not as well provide for the highest mastery of the occupations of the work-people as for the learned professions?

Solon freed children from all obligations toward their old parents, who neglected to teach them a trade.

Massachusetts made this duty obligatory upon parents by statute laws as early as 1642, and Connecticut in 1650.

Almost forty years ago, Lieber said in his "Ethics of Politics," that all his investigations lead him to the conclusion that modern crime is very much due to the want of fixed occupations. Among 358 convicts in one prison he found but 52, or one in seven, who had a trade.

In Belgium, in districts in which industrial schools are in operation, vagrancy, the hotbed of crime, has entirely disappeared, and at Creuzot, in which industrial instruction has been in vogue since 1841 though a city of twenty-five thousand inhabitants, crime, and even misdemeanors, have almost disappeared, and three policemen form the entire force sufficient to give the people the feeling of perfect security.

Education, without industrial training, starves the masses, breeds mutiny and ends in national suicide.

Race Education most stringently insists upon industrial training as the most effective preventive of pauperism, vice, crime, insanity, and, in fact, of every wrong from which society suffers to-day.

THE PROGRESS OF INDUSTRIAL EDUCATION.

The progress in the industrial arts in England, France and Germany is not by any means the result of mere manufacturing routine, which has but slowly advanced the arts, until the government has, by the creation of schools of design, of art, and practical science, spread the taste and the principles requisite for the advancement of a higher industry.

If we are to advance in the industrial arts for the sake of our commerce, our hungry masses, the purification of taste and the delights of a higher civilization, we must likewise found industrial schools. Our late national exhibition entitles us to say that with the same art and industrial training, France, England and Germany possess already for many years, we would soon be more than their equal in the manufacturing arts.

As far back as 1835 the House of Commons has appointed a parliamentary committee for ascertaining the state of art in England and other countries, the best means for extending a knowledge of and a taste for art among the manufacturing classes, and the state of the higher branches of art and the best mode for advancing them.

The want of instruction in design and the absence of public and open galleries containing approved specimens of art was pronounced by this committee the chief cause of the difference between the artistic feeling of the English manufacturing districts and that of similar districts of France and other countries. A normal school of design was, therefore, determined upon, and the Government School of Design opened at Somerset House, in 1837. Every student had to devote himself to the advancement of the interests of manufactures and ornamental trades. The course of study embraced—

1. Elementary instruction, as outline drawing of ornaments and of the human figure, shadowing, drawing from plaster, modeling and coloring.

2. Instruction in design for special branches; the study of fabrics and of such processes of industry as admit only of the application of design under certain conditions; the history of taste in manufacturing; the distinction of styles of ornamentation, and such knowledge as was calculated to improve the tastes of the pupils and acquaint them with art.

In 1841 the first common local schools of art were opened at Spitalfields, Sheffield, Manchester, Birmingham, Coventry, Nottingham, Norwich, Stoke, Hanley, Leeds, Huddersfield, Newcastle, Glasgow and Paisley, with 2,241 pupils.

Technical art instruction was given; museums were established; artistic anatomy, practical construction, wood engraving, painting on porcelain, decorative art in all kinds of woven fabrics, paper staining, furniture and jewelry, all were treated with the greatest attention.

In 1863 these schools of art have, through the continued care of Parliament, and the central institution, the Chamber of Commerce, and the general interest of the public, risen to 90 with 16,480 pupils under instruction, and 79,305 children of poor, and other schools were taught through their influence; and to-day 117 schools of art give instruction to 20,310 pupils, with 309 night classes, having 11,747 pupils and 148,256 scholars in poor-schools all over the country under instruction in design.

That these establishments have materially raised the character of the designs in all descriptions of English manufactures nobody doubts.

The opening of the trade schools at Bristol, Worcester and other places, in which building, mechanical and engineering trades and chemical manufacturing have made great progress since 1852, has been successfully followed up, until in 1870, 799 have been in full operation with 34,283 pupils. And it is universally admitted that these science schools had a lasting effect upon the scientific Education of the working people throughout the country.

In 1861, 82 classes submitted to public examination, such as entitles to government support; in 1870, 2,204 science classes were examined not only in mathematics, mechanics, drawing, physics and chemistry, but in practical work, testing the power of using the ax, saw, plane, chisel, file, forge, smithwork, turning, pattern making, moulding, etc., the

rule being that unless fully one-half of the science
students are practical workmen the school has no
claim upon the government for support.   What
an excellent example for our imitation.   A school
that does not aid the world in its work has no
claim upon its assistance.

The following table will best illustrate the importance attached by England to these practical
institutions.   Industrial instruction was given in

1860 . . . in	9 schools, with	500 pupils.
1861 . . . "	38	"	1,300	"
1862 . . . "	70	"	2,543	"
1863 . . . "	75	"	3,111	"
1864 . . . "	91	"	4,666	"
1865 . . . "	120	"	5,479	"
1866 . . . "	153	"	6,835	"
1867 . . . "	212	"	10,230	"
1868 . . . "	310	"	15,010	"
1869 . . . "	514	"	21,000	"

Enough has been said about the industrial, art
and science schools of England, which have made
it great in the industrial arts, to show how much
can be accomplished in a few years by a government, which has at heart the commerce of the
nation and the welfare of the masses.

In France, national schools of art and common
industrial schools have been fostered with the same
care as in England and with the same results.   The
schools of arts and trades at Chalons, Angers and
at Aix sent out every year 300 young men perfect

in theory and practice in a number of trades. Paris, Lyons, Muhlhausen, Rouen, Nimes, Dieppe, Rochelle and other places, have excellent practical schools of industry. In 1862, 79 cities had industrial schools, attended by 32,000 pupils.

France has two great national agricultural colleges, seventy farm schools, practical schools for draining, etc.; three mining schools, the central schools of arts and manufacturing at Paris, also the famous Conservatory of Arts and Industry, three national schools of arts and manufacturing in the provinces; in Savoy, a famous school for watch-making, the renowned Polytechnic School at Paris. In 1867, there were in France 250 special smaller technical schools, 21 schools of design, 12 of arts and trades, 5 of hydrography, 4 of the technical sciences, 4 of design for textile arts, lace, wall-paper, furniture, etc.

Germany, which ranks high in the industrial pursuits, swarms with thorough practical technical schools, of which Austria has 45, Bavaria 36, Saxony 76, Baden 50, among which are some for watch-making, weaving and straw plaiting. Switzerland has, besides its great polytechnic institutes, 29 industrial schools. Belgium has 15 technical schools and 68 national workshops.

Enough has been said to show the necessity of organizing industrial schools for our success in the

practical arts, commerce and the self-support of
the masses, who must live by their labor. We
have done more; we have shown by the example
of the foremost nations in art and industry that
these institutions are not only possible and thoroughly practical, but do actually exist in great
numbers and fulfill all that is expected of them.

Every lover of America cannot but look with
pleasure at the following table, which shows the
growth of schools of science in the United States:

	1870.	1871.	1872.	1873.	1874.	1875.	1876.
Schools,	17	41	70	70	72	74	75
Teachers,	144	303	724	749	609	758	793
Students,	1,413	3,303	5,395	8,950	7,244	7,157	7,614

These schools of science are an almost infinite
improvement upon the old Greek and Latin schools,
which in the vast majority of cases do more injury
than good; and as these schools of science grow
older, they will become more practical and teach
more science applied than pure science, with which
a graduate leaving the college cannot profit the
world sufficiently to get in return for his services
a modest meal. We have hardly any schools of
industry; and drawing, as useful, and even more so
than writing, to every artisan, is but slowly making
headway in our common schools, the only ones the
masses are able to attend.

It is often expressed that technical pursuits hardly merit the attention of men seeking a comfortable living. If this was really so, and an efficient artisan could not make a decent living, communism, incendiarism and every disorganizing scheme against a society, which refuses men a living for the labor it requires of them, would find almost an apology in such an unjustifiable condition. The fact is, we live in a crisis, in which a fat bank account or even plenty of real estate is no more security against want than labor is. An average importation of $500,000,000 to $600,000,000 worth of manufactured goods is evidence that we want more skilled men. The association of industry with the school and science, will raise it to the character of art and infinitely vary it. No matter how much machinery produces, as long as men work and exchange their products, they are benefited. But that they may all have work, industry must take the character of art, which admits of an almost infinite variety and demand ; for, of course, with a gigantic producing machinery, men cannot find employment in a few rude manufactures. An Arabic enameled glass lamp set up in the Louvre, became the support of hundreds of artisans modeling after it.

An industry raised to the character of art not only gives bread to the masses, but in purifying the taste of the people it improves their morals, for the beautiful and the good are but different expressions of the same thing.

Congress has manifested great wisdom in initiating the practical and scientific tendency of our higher institutions by its munificent grants for the establishment of agricultural colleges. That it put foremost agriculture and mechanics next, is eminently proper, as the promotion of agriculture is every way more to be desired in this country than the cultivation of manufacturing industry.

The National Bureau of Education, under the able superintendence of John Eaton, contributes its full share to rendering the educators of the land more practical. It does all in its power to show the need of the organization of infant schools. It acquaints us with the progress of technical Education abroad. It makes plain by statistical investigations the bearings of Education upon the various relations of the nation as well as of the individual. It brings face to face the theories and practice of the great educators of the land, which are thus corrected or supported one by the other. The influence of the National Bureau of Education is immense, and forms an epoch in the educational activity of the United States. It lifts the educator to a plane where he discerns all that is advanced the world over by the leaders of thought in his line, and where he beholds Education in connection with all the great interests of humanity.

The prospected delineation of our centennial history of Education by the National Bureau is simply stupendous.

INDUSTRIAL EDUCATION IN THE UNITED STATES.

In the beginning of the century, before the full tide of emigration had set in, when land was new and cheap, work hard and plenty and help rare, the farmers' sons had to do the work; and when they had grown into manhood and felt the want of an Education, the colleges and seminaries were glad to give it to them in exchange for their labor. Thus the condition of the country prepared for manual labor schools, and here, as everywhere else, has theory perfected what practice has roughly initiated.

Between 1820 and 1830 public opinion had taken a decided stand on the utility and feasibility of manual labor schools, which were introduced everywhere at the end of this period.

The democratic men who cleared the woods, broke the ground and made this country and government, did a good deal of hard working and hard thinking; and they thought their children most likely to do the same if they handled at college as many tools as books. They wanted their sons to work for their Education, and work while they were at it, as they deemed thought only valuable when work rendered it effective. They did not want polish got at the expense of health and vigor, which labor alone can give and preserve. Neither did they want the poor, who could not pay, but could work for their Education, to be excluded from the schools. But, above all, were they unwilling that their sons should lose at school their taste for working, while they acquired a taste for thinking. And, then, they believed nothing was gained when independence was lost ; and so, again, they wanted their sons doubly to work for their Education, that they might feel independent while they worked for it, and feel independent after they got it ; as they could live by the plow or the anvil—if they could not by their profession—and be true to their convictions.

The eminently industrial people of Pennsylvania took the lead in this matter. The Manual Labor Academy near Philadelphia, opened in 1829. "The hours of recreation are employed in useful bodily labor, such as will exercise their skill, make them dexterous, establish their health and strength, enable each to defray his own expenses, and fit him for the vicissitudes of life," the record reads.

In 1830 every invalid student, who resorted to the Manual Labor Academy and spent there about a year, was restored to health. "When thought shall need no brain," the report continues, "and nearly four hundred organs of motion shall cease to constitute the principal portion of the human body, then may the student dispense with muscular exertion."

The House of Representatives of the State of Pennsylvania, by a resolution passed in December, 1832, directed a committee on education to inquire into the expediency of establishing at the expense of the state a manual labor academy for the instruction of teachers for public schools. · The committee made out a report as the result of a very careful investigation, of which we will briefly state the following points:

1. That the expense of Education, when connected with manual labor judiciously directed, may be reduced at least one-half.

2. That the exercise of about three hours' labor daily, contributes to the health and cheerfulness of the pupil, by strengthening and improving his physical powers and by engaging his mind in useful pursuits.

3. That so far from manual labor being an impediment in the progress of the pupil in intellectual studies, it has been found, that in proportion as one pupil has excelled the other in the amount of labor performed, the same pupil has excelled the other in equal ratio in his intellectual studies.

4. That manual labor institutions tend to break down the distinction between rich and poor, which

exists in society, inasmuch as they give an almost equal opportunity of Education to the poor by labor as is afforded to the rich by the possession of wealth ; and

5. That pupils trained that way are much better fitted for active life, and better qualified to act as useful citizens than when educated in any other mode; that they are better as regards physical energy and better intellectually and morally.

This report was accompanied with an act to be passed by the Legislature establishing a State Manual Labor Academy.

New York City had a Society for Promoting Manual Labor in Literary Institutions, the principles of which were expressed by Mr. Wild, the secretary, in the report of 1833, in so solid a manner, as to command our attention even to-day. Our muscular system and bony structure, he says, does not look as if we were made merely for reading and writing.

The influences which body and mind exert upon each other are innumerable, incessant and all-controlling; the body continually modifying the state of the mind, and the mind ever varying the condition of the body. Not the body alone, not the mind alone, but both united by mutual laws make man. The mutual laws form the only rational basis for a system of Education. A system based upon anything else is wrong. The body is the house, the instrument, the reflector and the servant of the mind; and if it is rendered dark, dull and crippled, what is it worth, and of what use is it to the mind? And what is then the state of the mind?

The body and the mind must be educated together. We must preserve the body in the condition which will most favorably affect the mind. As the best condition of the mind always attends the best condition of the body, must not a system of Education, which expends all its energies upon the mind alone and surrenders the body to chance, be fundamentally defective? Is not a system false, which aims solely at development of mind and yet overlooks those very principles which are indispensable to produce that development, and transgresses those very laws which constitute the only groundwork of rational Education?

The mental part of Education has been vastly improved. But what has meanwhile been done for the body? What provision has been made for the daily wants of its muscles and nerves? What aids have been furnished to the organs of digestion, secretion and circulation? What means have been provided for preserving the body in its best condition, or for giving healthful energy to its functions, best securing to the mind that permanent vigor which results from such a condition of bodily organs? We have neglected the Education of the body, and with the sound body the sound mind has become rare. This is no new discovery. Milton has, two centuries ago, urged the connection of physical and mental Education. Locke has done the same. Jahn, Ackerman, Salzmann and Franke have done the same in Germany, and Tissot, Rousseau and Lond in France.

As far back as the end of the last century, Dr. Rush, of Philadelphia, recommended at length the connecting of agricultural and mechanical labor with literary institutions, saying, "The student should work with his own hands in the intervals of study."

President Lindsley, of the Nashville University; Professor Mitchel, of the Medical College of Ohio; Professor Harris, of the Medical Institute of Philadelphia; President Fisk, of the Wesleyan University, and Professor Hitchcock, of Amherst College, have all earnestly advocated the union of manual labor with intellectual culture.

Mr. Wild closes his very able report with the apprehension that the want of the element of physical work in our system of Education will make of us just as degenerate and sinking a race as the higher classes in France were before the great revolution, or as the noble families of Spain are to-day. But reports and speeches were the smallest part of the work. Manual labor schools sprung up North and South, and East and West.

The Society for the Promotion of Education of the Episcopal Methodist Church organized a number of manual labor schools. The Baptists were not less active in the cause of establishing like institutions.

The Governor of Pennsylvania recommended in his message the adoption of the system of manual labor in seminaries for teachers. The Governor of Georgia recommended the introduction of manual labor schools. The Legislature of North Carolina has passed a bill incorporating the manual labor schools of the State.

In the United States Senate, in 1836, the resolution was offered proposing the Committee on Public Lands to be instructed to inquire into the expediency of making a grant of land to our colleges in each State for the Education of the poor on the manual labor school system.

We may, by way of illustration, mention but few of the many manual labor schools which resulted from this discussion of principles and legislation. Connecticut had manual labor schools at Suffield, at Worcester and Haddenfield. Georgia had manual labor schools in Camden county, at Lawrenceville and Covington. These institutions were in successful operation, and paid the students at the end of each term, $14 to $30 for the work done in three hours per day.

In Kentucky, Cumberland College, at Princeton, was conducted as a manual labor school. Another labor school was at Lexington.

In the State of Indiana manual labor was introduced at Wabash College; and at the Teachers' Seminary at Madison the students paid entirely by their labor for all necessary expenses, without being put back in their studies.

Dr. Blyth, President of South Hanover College, in the same State, and organized on the same principle, says: " Such schools give birth to enterprise, create or perpetuate habits of industry and economy, generate and keep alive a feeling of self-support and independence, preserve health and create genius."

Massachusetts introduced a manual labor school at Lexington and at Andover Seminary.

In Missouri, Marion College required every student to work in the shop or field three hours daily, which enabled the student to pay a considerable part of his expenses.

In New Hampshire, at the manual labor school, straw-plaiting was carried on as a trade.

In New Jersey, we find manual labor introduced at the Stockbridge Academy, in Madison county.

In the State of New York, we find the manual

8*

labor schools practically introduced by the noblest of her sons, Gerrit Smith, at Peterboro.

In North Carolina, the Donaldson Manual Labor School gave poor young men an opportunity of getting the best Education by paying for it in labor.

Ohio seems to unite the industry of the East with the snap or go-aheadativeness of the West. It had a manual labor school at Granville, prepared teachers on the same plan at Marietta, and had another manual labor school at Dayton. At Lane Seminary, on Walnut Hills, near Cincinnati, the committee state that the combining of three hours daily labor in some useful and interesting employment with study, protects the health and constitution of our young men ; greatly augments their physical energy ; furnishes to a considerable extent or entirely the means of self-education ; increases their power of intellectual acquisition ; facilitates their actual progress in study ; removes their temptation to idleness ; confirms their habits of industry ; gives them a practical acquaintance with the common employments of life ; inspires them with independence of character and the originality of investigation, which belongs peculiarly to self-made men. Printing was followed. The students got sufficiently skilled in three weeks' practice to earn $2.54 per week, working daily three hours. They followed also cabinet making with the same good results.

The Western Reserve College, at Hudson, had shops and tools provided for those who wished to engage in labor. Some have gained, says the college report, only health of body and vigor and elasticity of mind, enough to pay, one would think, for two or three hours daily labor, while others did much toward defraying their expenses. Oberlin was never backward in the spirit of genuine reform, and required the students to do daily three hours of manual labor, with marked results as to the health of the students, which was made an object.

The Keystone State has already occupied our attention. The manual labor school near Pittsburg had 440 acres of land and a three-story building sixty feet long. Chester county was the seat of a very active association for the adoption of an improved system of Education, recommending the establishment of a model school combining agricultural and mechanical labor with literary and scientific instruction.

At Bristol College, in the same state, manual labor in school was found highly useful as well as economical, and the *Episcopal Recorder*, at Philadelphia, says, with reference to this institution: " We hope to send forth trained and strong men, no diluted manhood, who associate vulgarity and meanness with all manual labor, or young men blighted with college diseases. Sedentary invalids of every description demand that systematic and regular labor be incorporated in the very framework of our new institutions. Manual labor and mental culture ought to go together, for, as Plato says, " A good Education imparts to the mind and to the body all the power, all the beauty and all the perfection of which they are capable."

In South Carolina the report of the Manual Labor School at Pendleton says that the manual labor system in South Carolina has been fairly tried, and that it is decidedly the most advantageous mode of Education which has ever been introduced into this or any other country.

Alabama, Michigan, Tennessee and other states have interested themselves equally in this cause, but enough has been said to show what our fathers have thought and what they have done for manual labor schools.

About the time of the agitation of manual labor schools, 1820–1830, the population of the United States, all told, was not 10,000,000. Labor was then mostly native and respected. The American laborer wanted a higher Education he could not pay for nor find free of charge. The pupil, who came from the plough or the shop, felt more the benefit of manual labor, which, indeed, all appreciated in all its blessed bearings, as the young republic was still full of democratic inspirations. With the change of these conditions manual labor schools lost in popularity; but physical labor is so fundamental a condition of human existence, that these institutions will never be superseded without detriment to society, though their methods may have to be varied to meet new wants and purposes. Our cities have in the last thirty years grown to the size of the largest cities of the Old World; land has become rare, and the foreign population— especially under the present system of manufacturing—is flocking more and more into these hives of human beings. In these days of steam and machinery, these masses must be aided and sustained to maintain themselves by an industry, skill and knowledge have elevated to the character of art, or we all end in chaos brought on by idleness, misery, vice, crime and a turbulent and despairing mob.

Enough has been said to show that our fathers have thought the union of labor and study at school eminently wise and practical as well. We do not ask to make of every school a workshop, but we insist, the most important years of man in which his character and habits are formed for life and the many millions which are spent on Education in

this country, must have something greater, better
and wiser to point to than a little grammar, spelling, arithmetic and geography.   Industrial Education is not a new crotchet.   It had many years ago
a most tangible existence in this country; it is to-
day organized on a great scale in Germany, France,
Belgium, Switzerland, and is making rapid progress
in England.   It has been urged upon the teachers
and legislators of the land by most practical men
for the last twenty-five years; and the modern
apostle of Education, Pestalozzi, held it sufficiently important for the school to help the pupil to sustain himself in the world, that he combined manual labor with school instruction.

We plead for practical scientific instruction, with
full application to the industrial arts and life.   We
plead for drawing that shall give the scholar full
exercise of the eye, hand and imagination, and
develop his taste and skill; for more geometry, the
science of form and color, and the history of industry and technology.   We plead for technical gymnastics in every school, which, besides promoting
physical development, shall give the scholar the
use of the common implements of the trades.   We
plead for special industrial schools of a nature to
assist in the progress of the trades peculiar to certain localities and districts.   We plead for the organization of industrial institutions of all grades

into one great system, with a national industrial university. at its head, that shall inspire our hands with great and useful works. We plead, in fine, for the cultivation of the industrial spirit in every normal college, which is to send out into the world teachers for the people, whose success as well as the success of the country depend on the cultivation of industrial habits.

In our pleading for industry we plead for agriculture—the noblest of all industries, and the most useful as well as the most elevating of them all—and the one in which more than in any other we have great nature as an especial ally on our grand and unequalled prairies and in the variety of our climes, which produce whatever will bless man.

How long still will teachers set before them with indifference of mind the vacant task of making children read and write, and, perchance, know a little geography, arithmetic and grammar?

It is time we spread the practical facts and principles of science, which would make of every laborer, mechanic and manufacturer a thinker and an inventor; a man, who by his skill would largely contribute to the pleasures and adornments of life, and add to his own happiness as well as to that of mankind. The capabilities of art and science for making of earth a heaven will not be known until pervading the masses, every child in the land will be tremulous with sensibility, and love of order and beauty. With the energy of thought peculiar to practical science and the sensibility attending art, every home will be the blessed abode of peace and plenty, of love, order and beauty, in which sadness and sorrow will be unknown, as all will be industrious and live in natural simplicity, hardly ever visited by sickness, want and misery.

Such is the future the union of science, art and industry is to usher in. But who has the heart to dwell upon the picture of the misery of the laborer of to-day, who, unaided by art and science, plods along in the old beaten path with but a poor return for his toil, and lives in squalid quarters made darker and more miserable still by the sight of cheerless, sick and dying children and a poor mother borne down by labor and care?

Industrial Education for the people is no theory. It is with them a question of life and death. It is a question of civilization. It is a national question, and touches the existence of the state. And the rich are as well interested in it as the poor, as the time is near when only capital turned over by laborers, skilled through the knowledge of art and science, will yield a return to its owner.

PART IV.

THE PROGRESS OF CIVILIZATION.

THE history of the world is the Education of mankind, and every step in the onward march of civilization is full of lessons and suggestions to the educator who aims at the preservation and improvement of the race.

Schoolmen take the wit and wisdom of books for civilization. They do not know what effort it has cost humanity to develop the industrial arts, which have made life possible and even pleasureable in a world that harasses man at every step.

Industry, or human activity applied to the arts of life, has changed us, and is changing us every day; and if Education is to become a civilizing power, it must improve and advance industry to a science and instrument for the mental and moral improvement of the people who are ever engaged in it.

Industry is the mother of the inductive method of reasoning from enlarged experience, and of the utilitarian philosophy, and both these, her daughters, are fast changing the life and mind of mankind.

It is a maxim recognized and acted upon by practical statesmen, that general progress is not influenced by abstruse principles or reasonings, which never penetrate the masses. Only as far as science mingles with the trades and occupations of the people does it become the property of the world and civilizes the age.

The decorations of a building are not the building, nor are they as important as the foundation laid solidly deep down in the ground. It is so with literature and the common arts of life, which sustain life. Civilization existed before prophets, poets, philosophers and statesmen appeared.

Long and laborious was the way industry had to travel before the present stage was reached.

Not only civilization as a whole includes many changes, but, as Tylor conclusively shows, there is not a tool, a garment or any other object of art, but it is the survivor of a thousand changes; and as every pebble is an epitome of all past geological changes, and mirrors the cosmos to him who understands its language, even so it is with every object of human ingenuity, as each is a volume of the world's history, stretching back from this our Age of Steel to that of Iron, back to the Age of Bronze, and the Flint Age, when man was the companion of the mammoth and the woolly rhinoceros.

Yes, the whole world of human objects is a library,

and nothing in it is so trivial, be it a spade, a knife or a hatchet, but it has to tell wonders of the thousand sires that preceded it, and whose history is closely interwoven with the history of the race.

Pedants see civilization exclusively in schools and books which exist but since yesterday, while the mechanic arts date back a hundred thousand years, and their remains are found to-day buried under thick strata, the work of myriads of years and in company with a fauna that shows the very skies and climate as well as the earth have changed, and are no more what they have been when the hands of men have formed these débris of another age and world. Such is the cycle of ages that was required to bring the mechanic arts to their present maturity.

Well says Gibbon, " The poet or philosopher illustrates his age and country by the efforts of a *single* mind, but these superior powers of reason or fancy are rare ; *many* may be qualified to spread the benefits of government, trade, manufactures, art and science, but even this requires the union of *many*, which may come to naught ; but the simple practice of the mechanic trades strikes an everlasting root into the most unfavorable soil ; under all changes and restrictions these inestimable gifts have been diffused ; they have been successively propagated ; they can never be lost. We may, therefore, acquiesce in the pleasing conclusion, that every age of the world has increased and still increases the real wealth, the happiness, the knowledge, and, perhaps, the virtue of the human race." Thus with the practice of the mechanic trades the progress of the race has begun and continued through unnumbered ages, and through them alone what has been acquired in the long struggle will be maintained and descend to new races and civilizations, when all else will be lost and become unintelligible.

Thousands of years the race roamed about before it stole the thunder from the clouds—learned how to kindle fire and how to keep it up. The Egyptians, the Phœnicians, the Persians, the Greeks and the Chinese have all preserved the tradition of the invention of this art by their ancestors, and to this day we meet with tribes who miss it.

To pluck fruit from trees was the first method of sustaining life. A long time passed before man made the first tool or instrument, the first step in his civilization—the arrow and the bow—which made the chase possible. Only as men multiplied, and the chase fell short of sustaining life, would men consent to tend flocks of sheep and herds of cattle.

When man succeeded in domesticating animals and throwing the burden and slavery of his work upon the horse, the ox and the ass, a great stride was made in the civilization of the race. In China and India but until a very recent date men were used instead of animals for transporting goods over roads; and an embassy from Holland to Peking required the service of a thousand men to carry the baggage. In the taking of Mexico by Ferdinand Cortez, fifty thousand Indians were employed in doing what five hundred horses might have accomplished.

It was no small matter when man discovered the chestnut and the like preservable fruits; and the cereals, as rice, wheat, maize, were still later discoveries, and became each the foundation of a peculiar civilization — rice in Asia, wheat in Europe and maize in Peru and Mexico.

Hunting, fishing, pastoral life, mining, working of metals and tool making had all to precede the plow, without which the proper cultivation of the cereals was impossible. It certainly is hardly deserving the name of agriculture when plowing was done with horns, the rib bones of cows were used for cutting the grain, and threshing was done by driving wagons, or rather sleighs, through the grain, or the wheat was gained and at the same time prepared for eating by burning the straw.

We find still, tribes not only preparing the ground for receiving the seed in such a rough way, but wholly ignorant of seeding. The plow is a great stride in the civilization of the race; for, by increasing food and making man secure against hunger, it gave him leisure to provide for his higher and nobler wants.

Bread, the first necessity of life, most aptly illustrates the slow and laborious progress of the arts of civilization. After the discovery of the cereals, seeding, and cultivation by the plow, the cereals were for long ages roasted and thus eaten. Next came the improvement of pounding them, and not until long after, were they ground on hand mills, and made into flat and brittle cakes, whence the Scripture expression of breaking bread. Bread, properly speaking, was a much later invention, and wholesome light bread raised by ferment, belongs to a still later period.

Let none think that these first steps toward providing for the race belong to the fabulous ages. Wheat bread was in England but a very few hundred years ago a luxury indulged in by the higher classes; fruit and vegetables are there but of a very late date; and even the consumption of fresh meat was restricted to the fewest.

Next to food is clothing. Here humanity had to learn curing or tanning of skins, spinning and weaving of wool. The preparation of flax cannot have been learned but slowly and is due to woman's

fine observation and painstaking; and language
has preserved the history of this art in the etymol-
ogy of *wife*, which means literally a *weaver*. How
inefficient was man before he understood the working of metals and the use of tools. It was the
plow that by a proper cultivation of the soil turned
nations from cannibalism.

The first houses were caverns, not as perfect as
the dwellings constructed by beavers. Ages passed
before the cave was improved by a hole at the top
for the smoke to escape.

The first implements of war were clubs, spears,
darts and arrows, and the latter were headed with
brass as early as the siege of Troy. The battering
ram was first used by Pericles. The first cannons
were made of iron bars held together in the shape
of a concave cylinder by rings of copper, and the
first cannon balls were stone.

The first vessels were beams joined together;
next trunks of trees were cut hollow, and at last
planks were joined in the shape of a boat. The
ship with a prow and a stern with a movable helm
and sails came after thousands of years.

Burning wood was anciently the only method for
lighting the house; torches came next; and even
at the time of Homer lamps and candles were unknown among the Greeks, so were spoons and forks.
Neither had their houses chimneys. Locks and

keys were unknown, and bundles were secured with ropes intricately combined ; and, hence, the famous Gordian knot.   Shoes and stockings are a late improvement ; so are shirts, which came into use in the last days of Rome ; and in modern Europe shirts were not common before the eighth century.

Hardly any commerce was possible before the discovery of the wheel, the wagon and the ship, which were rendered more effective by steam and the compass.

A new epoch dawned upon mankind with the discovery of letters, which, again, took thousands of years, and is not by any means perfect as yet.

The Egyptians used hieroglyphics.   It was a divine inspiration that first permanently fastened on any material the idea of gentleness by the picture of the lamb ; strength by the picture of the bull, or magnanimity by that of the lion.   The Chinese use to this day sixty thousand arbitrary signs representing as many words, the greatest scholar can hardly master in a long life, a method that much retarded their progress and made them stiff and conservative.   Our alphabet is the evolution of hieroglyphics and shows the outlines in its letters of the things from which they are derived.   The representation of the simple elements of sound by visible signs or letters was a wonderful process and one that had to pass through many stages ; and writing

was most probably but little known in Greece at
the time of Homer. Charlemagne could not sign
his name, neither could many of the bishops at
his time. Books were still rare at the time of
William the Conqueror. The Countess of Anjou
gave for a collection of homilies two hundred sheep,
a quarter of wheat, another of rye and a third of
millet, besides a number of marten skins.

To encourage the art of reading in England,
capital punishment for murder was remitted if the
criminal could read, which was expressed in law by
the phrase of "benefit of clergy." An English edition of six hundred copies of the Bible, when first
printed, was not wholly sold in three years. The
Emperor Rudolphus, in 1281, ordered all public
acts to be published in German instead of Latin,
as formerly. In France all public edicts were still
published in Latin in 1539, and in Scotland and
other European countries the practice continued
to the last century to the damage of the language
of the land and the common people, who were
thereby kept ignorant of the public law and cut
off from all contact with the higher classes, who
were jabbering hog Latin among themselves.

We find tribes who cannot count beyond five.
Our decimal system has early been learned from
our digitals. The Peruvians used knots of various
colors to designate numbers. Our ciphers were

invented in Hindoostance and were brought to France in the tenth century by the Arabs, who are also the inventors of algebra or the science of solving mathematical problems by representing numbers by the common letters of the alphabet.

Money was certainly a vast improvement upon barter. Cattle were the first general medium of exchange, as they could be driven from place to place, and as men bought their wives, a virgin was, for instance, held worth a dozen heads of cattle. The Lydians were the first who coined gold and silver money after the Trojan war, at which barter was still the common method of exchange.

Money is one of the mightiest instruments in the rise of civilization, as it encouraged industry by facilitating commerce through a universal standard of value and a portable and preservable instrument of exchange, which could be used as an equivalent for the greatest as well as for the smallest values.

It set man free; he could at any time liquidate his property and go where he pleased and thus escape tyranny, but it made man also greedy for so desirable an article, rendered him more selfish and also powerful for ill as well as for good.

The useful arts lead to the fine arts; and sculpture, painting, architecture, and, at last, gardening, rose into prominence one after another already in antiquity.

We have already remarked that civilization followed everywhere the introduction of the cereals. The Egyptians and the Chaldeans were the first cultivators of the cereals and the first civilized nations. The civilization of Europe dates equally from the introduction of the cereals, iron and the plow.

How much has common industry done for humanity by the cultivation or introduction of the cereals, the plow, iron, steel, the loom, steam and machinery, each of which marks a new epoch of civilization.

Little has the school achieved hitherto in comparison with this, neither will it in the future, except it makes its object the improvement of industry and effects thereby civilization.

Without iron, man is impotent, for he is then without tools. A hatchet, a knife, or even a nail, will buy almost anything among tribes who have not the use of iron, as they feel their power infinitely increased by it. Copper, brass and the precious metals have all been earlier discovered and used on account of their brightness and state of purity in which they are often found on the very surface of the earth, and as they are softer and easier worked. It is all otherwise with iron. At the time of Homer iron was still thought precious enough to rank with gold and silver as the price of the conqueror.   Every step in the improvement of the working of iron and the manufacture of steel is an improvement in civilization affecting humanity far more than the smoothest rhymes or the most acute system of metaphysics.

Herodotus mentions Glaucus of Chios as the first who smelted iron.   It was not before the Middle Ages that iron entirely took the place of brass. Think for a moment we lost the use of iron ; without a plow or a tool we should soon sink into utter barbarity ; and but few could maintain themselves even in that condition, but would perish.

Erasmus describes England at the time of Henry VIII. as a land of filth, every room full of " grease, fragments, bones, spittle, excrements of dogs and cats and everything that is nauseous." Madrid had not a privy as late as 1760, and the royal mandate to build such raised a storm of opposition. Iron brought the age of industry, which cast men into a new mould, and made of the English a people loving cleanliness.

In 1563 knives were first made in England. Pocket watches were brought from Germany 1577. In 1580 coaches were introduced.   A saw mill was erected near London 1633.   Coffee houses were opened 1652.   Steam flouring mills began as hand mills, horse mills, water mills, and, finally, became what they are to-day.   Striking clocks were not known until the end of the thirteenth century, and, hence, the custom of watchmen calling the hours of the night. Paper was first made in the fourteenth century. The eggs of the silk-worms were first introduced in Europe under the reign of Justinian from Hindoostanee.

With the progress of industry, food, clothing and all other means of comfort and luxury so increased, that the poorest man to-day has a greater quantity of them than fell to the share of kings or nobles but a few hundred years ago.

Queen Catharine could not command a salad for dinner until the king brought a gardener from the Netherlands. About the same time the artichoke, the apricot and the damask rose made their first appearance in England. Turkeys, carps and hops were first known there in the year 1524. The currant shrub was brought from the islands of Zante 1533. In the year 1540 cherry trees were brought from Flanders to Kent.

At the time of Henry VIII. there were but few chimneys even in the capital towns of England, and the smoke issued at a hole in the ceiling, the door and windows; utensils, forks, spoons, etc., were of wood. The people slept on straw with a log of wood for a pillow.

Henry II., of France, at the marriage of the dutchess of Savoy, used the first silk stockings that were made in France. Elizabeth, the great queen of England, had her reception room strewn with rushes or straw—as in our days half decent stables are ; she received in the third year of her reign a present of a pair of black silk stockings. The first stone bridge over the Thames was built in 1213, and over the Seine in the beginning of the six-teenth century. The first silk factory was built in Lyons in 1536. Glass windows were still rare in private houses in the twelfth century. King Ed-ward III. invited three clockmakers from Holland.

Gunpowder, firearms and artillery, with the new art of war, called forth standing armies, while the rest of the people remained at home and devoted themselves to the trades, which gained thereby such importance that they ruled the state and pretty much ended the old régime, which was one of con-stant war, and, therefore, barbarous.

The Saracens have spread a taste for chemical manipulation and the observation of nature and mechanical improvements. Roger Bacon has trod into this path, and prepared the way for the great Bacon of Verulam.

Men have never paid attention enough to the importance of the industrial arts. Glass was intro-duced into Britain 671 ; still it was not applied there for windows until the thirteenth century, was but in the sixteenth century manufactured there and did not enter into general use until the middle of the seventeenth century. Country houses in Scotland were not glazed until 1661. The manufacture of silk was more than a thousand years traveling from the shores of the Bosphorus to England.

Henry the Great, king of France, and his distinguished minister, the able Sully, have laid the foundation to France's eminence in the manufacturing arts. Under the great Colbert, the minister of Louis XIV., the since famous manufactory of Sevres china was established, the manufacture of glass brought from Venice, wall paper invented in France, the manufacture of fine cloth introduced from England; until, in 1685, the revocation of the edict of Nantes had driven away the Huguenots, the best artisans of France, with whom a great part of the manufacture and civilization of France have wandered to England, Germany, the United States and other countries.

In the Middle Ages all arts were debased through the spirit of feudalism, and all labor was considered slavish. Hence the slow progress in manufactures and civilization. All articles of furniture were rare, the same room was used for cooking and eating, and the ox often lived under the same roof with the farmer. Lords, even at the time of Elizabeth, would, like other movable furniture, take with them the windows of their castle on leaving for London and the court. Forks were unknown until James I.

Barley bread was the usual food of the poorer classes in 1626. In some portions of England, as late as 1725, even a rich family used but a peck of wheat in a year, and that about Christmas. Dry bran bread, mixed with rye meal, was commonly used by servants and laborers. Corn was mostly ground at home by the hand mill, even at the time of Elizabeth. Holland provided London with vegetables, and at the time of Henry VIII. not a cabbage, carrot, turnip or other edible root grew in all England. Natural enough, in proportion to the want of industry, barbarism and crime abounded, and 70,000 thieves were hanged under this prince in England.

Spectacles were introduced in the thirteenth century; needles were brought from France to England in 1543, and first made there in 1626. Umbrellas made their appearance in England in 1768, and their first use excited the jeers of the vulgar. The land was one waste and the mines poorly explored.

Take the quantity of iron smelted in the Middle Ages. It amounted to fifteen pounds at most, per hand. Using coke instead of charcoal in making iron, a furnace produces in our time thirty tons a day, or four hundred pounds of a superior quality per hand. A man accomplishes, therefore, thirty times as much as before.

When grinding flour was done by hand mills it took one grinder for twenty-five consumers. In our improved flouring mills one man turns out flour enough for 3,600, so that one man does the work of one hundred and forty-four formerly employed. Fourteen large mills, employing two hundred and seventy-eight hands, do to-day the milling of a city of a million population. In Rome and Athens the hand mills kept going 40,000 hands for an equal population.

In the manufacture of cotton one man does to-day what seven hundred could do before recent improvements were made. John Kay, of Bolton, introduced the fly shuttle in 1750, so that one hand can attend from ten to twenty shuttles. Mr. Hargreaves, of Blackburn, first introduced the spinning jenny in 1770. Mr. Arkwright built his machinery for carding and roving in 1771, and Mr. Crompton's mule was introduced in 1780; and about the beginning of the century Mr. Watts' steam engine came into use, the power loom began its work, and from that day the modern factory system dates. About the middle of this century 250,000 power looms were in operation.

The muslin exported from England in 1833 measured ten times the circumference of the globe. In

9*

1840 it was equal to thirty-five times the same length, or one milliard and three hundred and eighty-three millions of metres, and the whole export of cotton manufactures amounted to one hun-hundred and sixty-three millions of dollars. The cheapness has increased with the supply, so that it was in 1853 five times as cheap as twenty-five years back, and twelve times as cheap as fifty years back.

In 1740 England produced 17,000 tons of iron, in 1840, 1,500,000 tons, and in 1856, 3,000,000 tons.

But in transporting power we have gained per-haps most. One man with an efficient locomotive can carry 500 tons of freight. It would take 50,000 men to do the same carrying in the same time. All this was accomplished by the hard struggle and ingenuity of industry, hardly aided by the school.

Let the reader notice that we traced the progress of the arts before an earnest attempt of introducing universal Education was made. Solely by the nat-ural force of circumstances, by a continually spread-ing division of labor, and the devotion of the whole attention of the laborer to but a small field of labor, skill and invention have made rapid progress, com-forts have been increased, taste has been improved, and leisure has been gained, which has called forth the literature of the day, of which the arts and trades are the cause and not the effect.

Slavery in all degrees gave way in England in 1351 to the arbitrary power and stipulations of legislation, which settled the price of labor. And the trades were so backward that four-fifths of the people were agriculturists, and yet, as we have seen, the land was a waste.

The discomfort of the people may be seen from the fact that from the year 1075 to 1575 the population of England and Wales has but doubled. From 1600 to 1700, the increase was about 30 per cent.; from 1700 to 1750, the increase was 25 per cent., and in 1800 to 1850, the population of the United Kingdom doubled, besides furnishing a constant stream of emigration for this and other parts of the world.

Commerce had anxiously explored the sea to find a new way to the East Indies; and the maritime discoveries which were constantly making, kept the world agitated and enterprising.

The first attempt of manufacturing in the United States was made in 1608, only one year after the first effective English settlement at Jamestown, in Virginia. So early has the spirit of industry developed in this country.

In 1776 the first attempts of raising cotton in the South were made, and the cotton of 1790, 1791 and 1792 together, made one moderate cargo. At the end of half a century the cotton crop amounted to two millions of bales ; and to-day it reaches the figure of four and five millions.

In 1812 the first glass works were erected in Pittsburg. The first iron works were built in the United States in Pennsylvania, in Newcastle county, in 1726. In 1805 the population of the United States was 6,180,000; its manufactures amounted to $30,000,000, and its agricultural productions to $85,000,000. In 1870 the population of the United States amounted to 38,558,371, and there were counted 252,148 factories, with 40,191 steam engines and 51,018 water wheels, with a total of 2,346,142 horse power, and 2,053,996 hands, yielding a net product of $1,743,898,200, or, including the raw material, $4,232,325,442.

These sums are too large to realize their amounts. We will, therefore, take some of the great industries separately :

Iron industries	$346,952,694
Cotton goods	177,903,687
Woolen goods	178,064,453
Boots and shoes	181,644,090
Clothier goods	147,650,378
Leather	137,480,097
Furniture	57,926,547
Mining products	152,598,994

The agricultural productions of every sort amounted in 1870 to $2,447,538,658.

The United States had in 1873, 70,178 miles of

railroad, at a cost of $3,436,638,749 for carrying on its internal trade.

The foreign trade of the world amounts to $10,-000,000,000 per annum, and is carried on in 200,-000 vessels plowing the ocean with a cargo of 20,000,000 tons.

Of 2,500,000 tons of sugar—the yearly consumption of the world—the United States consume 500,000 tons.

How slow, uncertain and laborious was the progress of industry, feeling, as it were, her way in the dark for thousands of years, and how glorious and rapid was her march since she has caught sight of the rising sun of science! Let science, then, fully join her, and the effect on her as well as on her children will be immense, and a new era will rise for humanity.

But industrial progress does not merely mean so many bales of cotton and so many tons of iron or coal; it means the progress in the condition of the slave, serf or villain, and the free laborer; it means the moral progress of the chieftain or successful bandit to the privilege of birth; and, at last, to personal capacity and useful enterprise. With the increase of production the laborer gained in personal and political influence as well as in a material view. As slaves, laborers were crowded together without reference to health or decency; as free mechanics and small masters they occupied small properties; they became possessed of all the virtues and advantages attaching to property and well-regulated homes.

But, alas! the great industries under the régime of steam and machinery have centralized capital and population; and, again, laborers are crowded in tenements without regard to health and decency, ending in the formation of a permanent low, short-lived, stinted type of degraded humanity.

We cannot separate from our present form of industry the sanitary and moral relations of the people; they are all eminently questions of civilization, and find their solution in Education. Associate industry at all points with Education, and mind will control matter, and reason will bring order into the present social chaos.

The Education of the industrial masses into thinking men once achieved, further steps will best suggest themselves to the men most concerned, and who are the best judges of their condition, wants and means of relief.

But this Education must embrace the industrial, economical, domestic and social relations, and increase their efficiency as producers, their intelligence, their moral power, their health and their social consideration. Our all-absorbing great industries can find their only justification in the

union with art and science and in the spread of ·
taste, sensibility, fine feeling, knowledge, wisdom
and well-being among the masses engaged in them.
Industries which had no other end than the production of a million of trifles to satisfy the vanity
of their consumers, and left their producers unimproved and miserable, would be a most degrading
materialism, which could only end in universal
brutalization and in the downfall of the nation.

Every field and every factory throughout the land
and the wide world is a laboratory, and every laborer
producing profitable results is an experimentalist.

Where the hand and the brain work in unison
and shape nature's elements into angels ministering to the well-being of man, most is effected for
human civilization.

Schools, hardly organized for half a century, have
as yet done little for industry, which has progressed
by its own unaided exertions, until its advance has
aroused practical men to found polytechnic institutes and industrial schools, which promise to lead
industry to still higher development.

The unaided success of the industries is plainly
to be read in the greatness of the Italian republics,
the Hansas, Flanders and in France prior to the
persecution of the Huguenots; or in England in
our own day, where Education has been organized
but of very late.

We do not deny the importance of the school; but to advance civilization, it must prepare the people for their work—nice essays are for the philosopher. The nature of the civilization of an epoch is determined by the character of the people, which, again, depends on the work they are engaged in and on the manner in which they perform it. The tens and hundreds of thousands of fabricates they manufacture are their volumes; and, hence, the more intelligence and science is brought to bear upon them by an industrial and technical Education, the more the people will think and improve, and the higher a civilization will be attained. Industry has advanced to a science, and its theory must be taught as well as its practice, if it is to progress with the rapidity peculiar to all the movements of the age we live in. All the appliances of human ingenuity are to be set in motion to increase the quality as well as the quantity of our manufactures, to make the workmen consumers as well as producers, and to restore harmony between labor and capital.

With every new step industry increased the happiness of mankind, and made us wiser and better in proportion as the common wants were satisfied and the higher ones awakened and cared for.

How vast are the numbers engaged in the industries of the world and how great is the capital

—the whole earnings of the past—engaged in them. Can Education do anything worthier and more fruitful of precious results than by improving the industries, improve the great majority of mankind engaged in them, and by doubling the wages of labor and the profits of capital, and satisfying all, fill all with peace and concord, wiping out the sorrow and woe attending the present state of want, madness and crime?

In very deed science owes all to industry, and it is time it serve in its turn industry, that it may the surer serve humanity and the moral progress of the race.

The beautiful arts of architecture, sculpture and painting, clocks, spectacles, telescopes, air pumps, chemical manipulations and printing, were all developed before universal Education was introduced, and are all the results of the progress of the industrial arts, which furnished the tools and often the entire mechanism and the very observations which led to the principles some claim for the school.

When we consider the innumerable host of technical arts and trades furnishing the necessities, comforts and pleasures of life, providing science with her tools and developing the taste, mind and morals of the great mass of mankind engaged in them, the infinite observations, facts and combinations of ideas stored up in them as displayed in the great industrial exhibitions of the world, and especially in the magnificent one we have just witnessed in our own country, what an infinite world of mental activity they present to us.

And right here, speaking of the indebtedness of the world to past labors, we will express our obligations to scores of laborers who have preceded us in our field of inquiry, and especially would we mention the noble author of the "Sketches of Man," upon whose resources we have freely drawn. Little can man in his few days see with his own eyes; past labors are the genuine source of inspiration, and their honest recognition is the most befitting invocation.

In almost every trade qualities and relations hidden from the superficial observer, are made the basis of operations and applications. How mighty small is the sum of our little school learning compared with the thought and experience treasured up in a thousand skilful trades, each of which manufactures often a hundred different articles. The most complicated technical arts require as much mental force as any of the branches of school learning, which were only injured by metaphysical subtlety.

Bishop Heretius remarked that all the learning

down to the beginning of the eighteenth century could be put into six to ten moderate folios, to which we may add ten or even twenty volumes for our late scientific acquisitions. What a library, on the other hand, would it form, if every observation and every manipulation in every trade and art was written down! And, yet, these practical observations are unquestionably founded in truth, and useful much more than most of the learned trash of the schools.

Industry, more than science, has worked in the past under the guidance of practical observation— the main instrument of genius and the source of all invention—until Bacon has got his philosophy from the shop, which has done the world more good than the philosophy which Socrates has brought down from heaven.

The knowledge of the schools or abstract philosophy has done infinite mischief, by fostering religious prejudices and false political theories sustaining despotisms, false moral systems and standards; in short, it has caused much physical, moral, political and religious mischief, while technical inventions have saved and preserved mankind from much physical harm and have assisted in the moral and intellectual culture of the race.

The technical pursuits, by cultivating physical

and mental activity, developed the body and mind of the people, and thus materially increased their health, efficiency and well-being.

Industrial progress is continuous in its development; theoretical knowledge and literary culture are often inactive and dead for ages.

The labor of the world may be historically divided into the following epochs: The time of the first rude labors; the trades, with division of labor; industry, combined with science and art, or ornamental industry; and, at last, the highest technic, or union of strength and beauty. In the first days of the race, the same man was hunter, fisher, smith, carpenter, cabinet maker, tailor, etc. This sharpened his wits; but, of course, he brought it to perfection in nothing. However, as everybody was his own customer, he was easily suited.

As mankind increased and formed towns, each man was able to dispose of his surplus, he devoted himself, therefore, to one trade, produced a great quantity of articles of better quality, and got in exchange for his fabric a greater number of articles of higher quality than he could have made himself.

This division of labor led to almost scientific exactness and perfection in the trades. Competition among the producers led to ornamental industry.

At last, use, beauty and strength, with the greatest possible productivity and cheapness in articles of manufacture, were aimed at ; and what formerly seemed to be the work of individual skill, is now performed by a mechanism which replaces the dexterity and intelligence of the laborer.

In Greece as well as in Rome the trades were despised as fit only for slaves. In the world of to-day they are the very beginning of freedom, universal liberty and civilization.

It is the tradesmen who formed in the Middle Ages fortified towns and founded modern liberty, maintaining their rights against a fierce nobility and often against kings.

The Florentine republics, the Hansa League and Flanders have achieved wealth and liberty, not by their arms, but by their industry ; and to-day, the greatest of all modern states, as Germany, France, England and the United States, are founded upon industry, as the ancient states developed their strength in war.

How productive of great and noble qualities is industry by the independence it procures and the opportunities it gives us for developing our talents. Wealth develops power and dignity and health and well-being among the masses.

The industrial laborer is the soldier of the nineteenth century, making daily more conquests for civilization and humanity.

Industry creates commerce and new sources of maintenance, lessens idleness and vice, and improves morals by employing men. It was the want of industry that made the people of Rome and Greece accessible to the tricks of the demagogue and rendered them turbulent.

To the rise of the industrial classes and the consequent development of wealth, Europe owes its liberty and civilization, as the third estate, grown powerful, forced royalty and nobles as well as the clergy to respect the rights of the people.

Industry, through commerce following in its wake, gives rise to intercourse among men and nations, to interchange of ideas, mutual liberality, and peace and good-will among men. Commerce, which rests upon industry, is one of the main sources of modern civilization. Industry constitutes our superiority over the ancients.

Slavery and contempt of labor form the centre of the civilization of the ancients and of the military life in which their activity found the only outlet. Among the Bœotians, men who defiled themselves by commerce, were for ten years excluded from all state offices ; and Augustus condemned a senator to death because he took part in manufacture.

The slave system engendered ferocity. Slaves had to imbrue their hands in each other's blood as gladiators, and to engage in deadly combat with brutes almost as ferocious as their masters. They were often mutilated with atrocious cruelty; they were tortured on the slightest suspicion and crucified for trifling offenses. If a master was murdered, all the slaves were put to torture; and if the perpetrator was not discovered, they were all put to death. Tacitus relates a case in which not less than four hundred were thus slaughtered. Ladies of fashion amused themselves by the repeated infliction of painful flesh wounds on their lady maids with their own hand and dagger, and by ordering others to be crucified. Old and infirm slaves were exposed on an island of the Tiber, where they were left to die from starvation.

As a man's children could not be considered less his own than his slaves, and his wife is but part of his household, he had also over them the power of life and death; and as a man is not likely to be more tender with strangers than with his own wife and children, savage barbarism characterized all the relations of man with his fellows. Such was antiquity and such the models classical Education would force upon modern civilization.

Industry, or application to the arts and trades, led to the development of the spirit of observation and to facts; it led away from dreams, sophistry and dogmatism to genuine enlightenment and reasonableness; it led to the discovery of the inductive philosophy, or, rather, declared working the only true philosophy and the shop the best school, and thus laid the foundation to genuine progress and improvement.

It led to the development of the principle of utility, which is the safest test of truth and goodness. It led to peace and good-will among all men, as they all work for each other and exchange with each other the products of their labor.

Industry cultivates enterprise and caution, two qualities Hume calls the most important for success in life.

Industry, says Buckle, makes us conscious of our power. It is averse to superstition, as we daily feel that all depends on our own resources and how we manage them. It is the mother of wealth, and, hence, of civilization, and seeking for markets it leads to maritime discoveries. Industry gives men with competency and independence dignity and respectability, and thus cultivates a higher regard for humanity.

Industry, assuming the character of art, develops the taste for the beautiful, and, hence, the cultivation of industry and art leads to virtue and good manners, as the good and the beautiful are akin.

Industry strengthens the physical and mental capacities of man by constant exercise; increases his self-restraining power, the basis of moral excellency, and thus renders man better and nobler.

Industry, says Leckey, by providing the world with refining comforts, undermined the asceticism of the Church, its monastic spirit and ecclesiastic power; it secularized Europe and made it tolerant.

Industry led from dreamy philosophy and metaphysical speculation and dogmatic theology to the cultivation of science and the formation of a practical code of natural ethics for the regulation of man in his intercourse with his fellow, nature or with himself.

All the gold in the world flowing into a state cannot save it if industry leaves it ; witness Spain.

The main idea of Adam Smith's "Wealth of Nations" is *industry*, which all his measures tend to promote as the pillar of a nation's greatness. Labor, according to him, is the basis of value. Adam Smith employed his whole genius to show that industry must be freed from all its former shackles.

A new lesson we must learn—inasmuch as industry makes a nation great and prosperous—the school as well as the state must chiefly direct its efforts toward the promotion of manufactures and industry. For, as skill and excellency are only attained by habitual exercise, we must be trained to industry from early childhood.

10

Liberty, industry and peace are indissolubly linked together. Nothing but the enlightened self-interest of industry and commerce will eventually abolish war among nations.

But industry and commerce, which cement foreign nations, should they not draw closer to each other the different classes and conditions in the same nation by showing them the identity of their interests?

Industry, says Leckey, while it disposes nations for peace, makes them strong in war.

Under the industrial régime production gives rise to new wants, and wants to new exertions, and exertions to wealth, which again gives rise to refined tastes, finer perceptions of beauty and intellectual aspirations.

Industry produces capital, which gives opportunity for higher pursuits.

Slavery, war and despotism, all recede before industry. A law-abiding spirit, sobriety, integrity and a steady character are all in the wake of industry.

The old ascetic spirit destroys with human nature human energy. Industry strengthens human energies and unites all by an enlightened self-interest.

Human industry has connected oceans separated by continents; has drained lakes in low lands and created others in high places; has pierced mountain chains; has planted gardens in the wilderness; has built cities upon the waves of the ocean; has laid low ancient forests; has changed climates; has turned rivers from their natural course and has altered the face of the whole earth by changing its vegetable covering. St. Helena, when discovered in 1505, produced about sixty vegetable species, including but three or four known to grow elsewhere, also. At the present time its flora numbers seven hundred and fifty species. The flora of tropical America has been found by Humboldt and Bonpland to have been greatly introduced after the discovery of the New World. At the time of Aristotle the peach, that ripens to-day in England and Germany, could but imperfectly be raised under the Grecian sky; and many of the fruits that in the days of Pliny thrived but poorly in sunny Italy, do well to-day in northern Europe. The mulberry tree was introduced in southern France in 1500, and to-day it does well in much more northerly climes of Europe.

Who dares to deny but that tropical plants may ultimately grow in the temperate zone, by industry transplanting them gradually into countries more and more removed from their tropical home?

The changes effected by human industry in the animal kingdom are not less extensive than those in the vegetable world, and these changes multiply each other by their mutual bearings, until the final results assume a universal aspect.

Not to speak of the changes effected by the introduction of birds which live on insects—the agency of which is important in fertilizing plants—the ox, the horse, the sheep, the swine, so useful to man, have all been transplanted to the New World by human industry, as hardly any of the quadrupeds of the Old World were found in America. And in our own day the Cashmere or Thibet goat was brought but in 1850 to South Carolina and the camel to Texas and New Mexico, where they promise to do well.

The monumental buildings of the world are its true public libraries, seen and read by all, spreading in one or another style lessons of severe and chaste beauty or of spiritual grandeur, and imparting the spirit and civilization of one age to another; and this, too, is the work of industry.

With the increase of pleasure and refinement arising from the beauty and delicacy of an industry daily more assuming the character of art, human sensibility and kindliness of heart spread among men, and brought with them a higher state of civilization. As laborers, mechanics and manufacturers obtained wealth, they gained importance and achieved freedom, consideration and influence; the courts and the law had to do them justice, and thus changed all together; governments had to consult them and became representative and constitutional; and now, at last, schools have to suit their course to the practical needs of the laborer.

We best learn the nature of Education by studying it in the great style of Providence or universal history, which is the Education of the race. The Education of the individual must be in kind the same as the Education of the race, and must end in it. If educators find nothing in the history and development of the race that concerns them, the worse for their system ; as for us the Education of the individual must begin the very work the Education of the race will complete.

Draw closer the connection between the school and industry, science and the trades, and spread sound economical knowledge, and a humane disposition among employers and employees, and you reduce the mortality of the laborers of the land by at least 50,000, and the number of cases of sickness by 750,000 per annum.

There is hardly a department of science but its fundamental facts have been furnished by the observation of the practical men of industry. But how many of these observations are lost through the want of scientific knowledge in the practical workers of the world, and who can set a limit to future progress and improvement when practical workers will be scientific observers?

As long as labor is a drudgery, leaving the mind and the heart vacant, men will rather scheme than work. Join to labor science and art, and the venerated high priests of human industry, ministering in their laboratories to the comforts and necessities of mankind, will find their work a delight and a pleasure, they would no more exchange with the leisure of the elegant trifler than the toiling chemist or physicist would.

Labor is the physical aspect of moral power, and a nation cannot be free, powerful and truly great without being eminent for its industry. Rome and Greece possessed no industries, neither were they great, for their masses were slaves.

Industry, through constant exercise, bestows the freedom of the power of using our faculties for our own good as well as for the good of the race, and this freedom constitutes true liberty.

As long as war is tolerated, the spirit of rapacity, inhumanity and domination will pervade every sphere of private and public life, and men and nations will be barbarians. As long as men are fools and knaves enough to butcher one another, it is simply ridiculous to talk of civilization, which only can begin where war ends. War deteriorates a nation physically as well as morally. After every

great war—in Sweden and Germany after the thirty
years' war, in Prussia after the seven years' war and
in France after the great Napoleonic war — the
number of diseased, crippled and weak men had
increased to an extent that interfered with the
recruiting office. For, as the able-bodied men have
been taken from their homes, and have fallen in
the field, the weak and the sickly formed families
and humanity necessarily was physically deteriorated.

So, for instance, do we find in France exempt
from the service—aside from causes of sickness,
low stature or of being crippled—for constitutional
weakness, in

1816–1820 . . .	51.05 in 1,000 recruits.
1831–1835 . . .	79.04 " "
1865–1868 . . .	96.90 " "

In Prussia were exempt for all causes of sickness,
for being crippled, constitutionally weak and of low
stature, in

1831	345 in 1,000 recruits.
1854	382 " "
1858–1862	423 " "

In Saxony, were exempt from the service for all
causes in

1832–1836	33 in 100.
1850–1854	50 "

The steadily diminishing number of long-lived persons is another incontestable proof of a deteriorating humanity. There were in Sweden over 90 years of age in

	Women.		*Men.*	
1751 . .	10.4 in 1,000.		6.6 in 1,000.	
1763 . .	7	"	4	" (1766)
1780 . .	4.4	"	3.4	"
1790 . .	5.3	"	2.7	" (1775)
1800 . .	2.7	"	1.3	"

We dare not enter upon a recital of the social, moral and economical disorders which follow wars, neither is it necessary, as we all keenly feel them just now.

Our armies are slaughter houses. The killed in the field are the least. The barracks and the camp do the work of destruction. Though the soldiers are picked men, the mortality among them is double that of the entire population.

Balfour shows the mortality in England in a 1,000 population at the age of

	20–25.	25–30.	30–35.	35–40.
Civilians . . .	8.4	9.2	10.2	11.6
Soldiers . . .	17.0	18.3	18.4	19.3

The mortality of colonial troops in warm climates is a real slaughter, and amounts among the English troops in

The Bermudas . . . . : to 52.1 in 1,000.
St. Helena . . . . . " 33 "
Jamaica . . . . . . " 128 "
The Small Antilles . . " 82.5 "
Ceylon . . . . " 75 "

In the Russian army the regular mortality is 38 in 1,000, almost four-fold what it is among the common people at the same ages.

In Algeria, during the war, the French lost 100,000 men, of whom 3,400 died from wounds, while more than nineteen out of every twenty were the victims of camp diseases.

During the first seven months of the Crimean war 38.5 per cent. of the English troops died from camp diseases.

In the great Russian campaign Bonaparte lost two-thirds of his magnificent army, before he reached Moscow, in camp diseases. The great Russian army of 209,800 men that opposed him counted, after five months, 40,290 men.

In our own great war we had from June 1, 1861, to June 1, 1863, 53.2 deaths per annum for every 1,000 men in the field, of whom 8.6 died from wounds and 44.6 from camp diseases.

We know the slaughter in the battle field was great, and yet the slaughter in the camp was more than five times as large as that by ball and powder. The slaughter from suicide is not less remarkable in the army, and compares with the number of suicides among civilians in

Saxony	as 177 to 100.
France	" 253 "
Prussia	" 293 "
Sweden	" 423 "
Austria	" 643 "

And Christian governments foster military organizations and parade with them on occasions of great religious solemnity. Russia is carrying on a war of aggression against Turkey with a prospect of another war fifty years hence for the enslavement of the whole of Europe. Has the press a word against it? Is our plea, then, for the sacredness of human life out of season? According to an article in the *Lancet* of April 10, 1841, the mortality in the English work-houses was 207 in 1,000!

But we need not go so far back. It amounted in 47 work-houses in

London, 1851–55	227.2 in 1,000.
Berlin, 1852	142.8 "
Massachusetts, 1861–67 .	133.7 "

The wantonness of these mortalities among the state poor appears in its true light when we consider that even in hospitals, which only take in the sick, the mortality averages in the smaller 150 in 1,000 and in the larger 100 in 1,000, and that on an average there is but one death for fifteen cases of sickness, so that a sick man entering a hospital has a better chance of life than a poor man entering the almshouse. Among prisoners averaging 30–40 years, 30–50 in a thousand die per annum, while in the outside world the mortality among men of the same ages is but 10–20 in 1,000.

If the mortality in our public institutions, right under the eye and control of the government, surpasses the general mortality — which already includes all sorts of vicious and criminal classes— must we not conclude that sacredness of human life has not as yet the supreme influence it ought to have even with the guardians of public order and safety?

Or is this fearful mortality in our public institutions due to the deep-seated deterioration in the classes gathered in them? We do not deny it partly is, and this establishes our position of the prevalence of deteriorating tendencies in society, which, again, have very much for their basis a general disregard for human life, which allows causes unfavorable to human life to accumulate and gather strength until they settle in a permanent deteriorated type of humanity.

No, the sacredness of human life does not as yet find the recognition it calls for. We occasionally suspend hostilities to give a chance to the natural increase of population and to the industrial savings of a few years of peace to fill the gap made in the ranks and in the pocket by Krupp's eighty-ton guns, the improved implements of destruction of an advanced Christian civilization.

War organized and carried on openly by governments established mainly for the protection of the lives of the citizens, is the most flagrant outrage upon God, man and nature; and, as long as it is tolerated, justice among men will be but a mockery. For, if governments indulge in direct murder for the sake of self-aggrandizement, why should not individuals commit indirect murder for the same purpose? And they do, as the slaughter of factories, railroads and tenement houses proves.

Dr. Parne finds scrofula prevalent in the industrial district of the department of Aude. Bossard ascribes the physical debility of the inhabitants of the Ardennes to their industries. In Haute Rhin, Muller tells us that the agriculturists are fine men, while the operatives are pale and sickly. Poter finds in the department of the Rhone the people, exclusively devoted to manufacturing, physically degenerated and furnishing the greatest number of exempts from the service.

Dr. Engel showed for Saxony in 1852, 1853 and 1854 unfit for the service,

In cities . . . . 56 in 100.
In the country . . . . . . 51 "

Repeated recruiting gave the following results as to unfitness for the service :

Farmers	46 in 100 recruits.	
Cabinet-makers	51 "	"
Operatives	57 "	"
Artists	63 "	"
Merchants	70 "	"
Scholars	80 "	"
Domestics	83 "	"

A higher civilization must protect us against the insiduous attacks upon life growing out of the conditions of a lower state of civilization as well as against the open violence of the savage state. It must deal with causes, and not with isolated flagrant acts, which like weeds spring up from the old stock.

The higher civilization is greatly hygienic and improves the race in its highest aspects by improving its physical basis and its very genesis.

Our industries create a new sort of barbarism in the very midst of our much boasted civilization by their stolid indifference to the physical and moral condition of the millions engaged in them.

Several years ago the average age at death in the weaveries of Leicester was eighteen years! For every one agriculturist, who dies from lung diseases, 2.63 die from the same diseases in the manufacturing town of Manchester. Of women engaged in lace making 617 die from the same terrible malady to every 301 men otherwise occupied in the same district. At the age of thirty-five to forty-five the mortality of the London tailors is 57 per cent. and the mortality of the London printers 117 per cent. higher than that of the agriculturists. At the age of forty-five to fifty-five London tailors have twice and London printers more than twice the mortality of the agriculturists.

The enumeration of the various pests making havoc among the workmen in many industries, and against which a higher civilization must protect the masses, would fill not one, but many volumes.

Of 1,078 children who worked in English spinneries 22 reached the fortieth year and but 9 the fiftieth. Of 824 young hands in six spinneries 183 enjoyed good health, 240 were in delicate health, 256 were sick, 43 were puny, 100 had tumefactions of joints, 37 had curvatures of the spine. Trades with excessive labor cause inflammations, curvatures, ruptures and hemorrhages.

According to Dr. Friedlander one-fourth of the workingmen of England and one-eighth of Germany are ruptured. France, England and Germany keep an exact inventory of the work-people reared with the treasure of the nation. The time is coming when we shall have to raise our laborers, and then we shall at least take as good care of them as we do of other chattel; but until then the friend of humanity can study only abroad the effects of modern industry upon the lives and health and morals of the work-people.

Considering the army of martyrs among the hands engaged in the manufacture of fine clothing, Ruskin says of the wearers of these articles: " They have literally entered into a partnership of death and dressed themselves in his spoils. Yes, if the veil could be lifted not only from your thoughts, but from your human sight, you would see—the angels do see—on those gay white dresses of yours, strange, dark spots of crimson patterns, that you know not of—spots of the inextinguishable red that all the sea cannot wash away; yea, and that among the pleasant flowers that crown your fair heads and glow on your wreathed hair, you would see that one weed was always twisted which none thought of — *the grass that grows on the grave.*"

In our chase for gold we have become reckless as to human life, and so various are the ways in which men in our day are got out of the world that fully half the people die by a brother's hand. This murderous spirit so perfectly possesses this age, that men snap the cord of life before their sands are run. The increase of suicide has been fearful in the last hundred years. There were committed in

Paris, 1794–1804, . . . 107 annual suicides.
"   1804–1823, . . . 334   "   "
"   1830–1835, ... 382   "   "
Berlin, 1758–1775, . . . 45   "   "
"   1784–1797, . . . 62   "   "
"   1797–1808, . . . 126   "   "
"   1813–1822, . . . 546   "   "

The average annual suicides in France were

1826–1830	1,739
1831–1835	2,263
1836–1840	2,574
1841–1845	2,951
1846–1850	3,466
1851–1855	3,639

While during 1826–1856 the population has risen from 31,858,937 to 36,039,364, or in the ratio of 100 to 113, suicides have risen in the ratio of 100 to 209, so that while the population has but little increased, suicides have more than doubled.

In Denmark the annual number of suicides were

1835–1839	261
1840–1844	300
1845–1849	330
1850–1854	389
1855–1856	414

The proportion of suicides has thus risen from 219 to 392 in every million of population.

In Prussia suicides have increased in 1823–1858 from 510 to 2,180.

In general, suicides have increased, taking most European countries, 3 to 5 per cent., while the average increase of population has been 1.64 per cent.

The proportion of suicides in

Denmark . . .	is 388 in 1,000,000 pop.		
Saxony	" 215	"	"
Scandinavia . .	" 126	"	"
Germany . . .	" 112	"	"
France	" 105	"	"
Spain and other .			
Romanic nations	" 80	"	"
Slavonic races . .	" 47	"	"

The annual ratio of suicides to every million population is for

Berlin	212
Rural Districts	123
Geneva	250
Copenhagen	477
Rural Districts	488
Paris	640
Rural Districts	110

According to Legoyt the proportion of suicides in a million population is in France among

Farmers	90
Industrials	128
Liberal Professions	218
The Poor	569

These figures speak volumes. For only a deteriorated humanity can act contrary to the natural instincts of self-preservation, and the increasing ratios of a suicidal mania prove, therefore, a progressive deterioration of the race. And as like insanity suicide is most prevalent among civilized nations, in the large centres of the world, and among classes of men who are mostly drawn into the vortex of civilization, the falsity of this very civilization is the unavoidable conclusion.

The social relations of a people are the main factors of the prevalent suicidal mania, the amount of which is the guage of its prosperity, health and soundness. In our extravagance, luxury makes of the one a blasé, and misery crushes the other, until both lose their mental balance, and neither the one nor the other cares for living. This demoralized condition loudly calls for a more solid Education and training in our youth, and for an industrial system and laws in consonance with the physical and moral elements of our nature, which only a government based upon hygiene can give us.

Pauperism, crime and human degeneracy in its various forms, treated in other parts of this work, lead by various routes to self-destruction, the final judgment of nature, events and of the individual upon himself.

Murder, insanity and oppression beyond endurance culminate in suicide, the most tragic catastrophe in life in which man wrecked in his mind and all else makes the fearful plunge. Yes, suicide is but one of the many forms of social murder, which must be stayed, that something may be sacred beside gold—and that is human life.

Do we give an uncertain sound? We trace on every page of the history of our age the spirit of social murder and insist upon an honest regard for human life. We insist upon an unflinchingly sanitary government, that will protect the life of the poor and his children as much as the property of the rich.

The ages of war have not slain more men than this age of industry has. The ages of war have spared at least women and children. This age of industry has fastened its fangs deepest even in the flesh of women and children.

The stolid indifference with which industry sees the life of the poor waste away, nurses among the masses an apathy that must become dangerous to society.

In the name of God, humanity and the future peace of the world, let industry lesson the people in other sentiments than contempt of life and a disregard of humanity.

The adjustments of an infinite Providence may turn to profit the slaughter of wars and revolutions, and death may feed life in decaying organisms, but it is madness still to destroy life that out of its ashes it may rise again.

Already Pinel noticed the immense points of contact between the diseases of men and the world's history. Let statesmen study less politics and more pathology. They will thereby prevent diseases physicians vainly endeavor to cure. By acquainting themselves with the special tendencies of certain classes and ages to suffer from leading diseases, statesmen learn how they may preserve the health and strength of the nation. That there are general social relations under which death and disease single out whole classes and ages for their special victims we have established by facts, reasonings and authorities.

The diseases of a people and the degree of their sufferings are the truest index to the culture, the moral and social condition as well as the prosperity of a nation. " History," says Virchhow, " has more than once shown that the destiny of a nation depends upon its condition of health and energy, and it is plain the pathological history of a people is inseparable from its civilization. Fearful rates of mortality are writings on the wall in which the statesman of capacity can read the disturbing element which has invaded the life of the nation, and which even a careless government cannot afford to overlook."

There was a time when the wrath of the gods was looked upon as the source of disease ; later the stars had to bear the blame; to-day it is the occult forces of nature and what not, instead of tracing the main cause of disease in the food we eat, in the water we drink, in the air we breathe, in our occupations and their deleterious influences and cares, anxieties, over-exertions and ensuing debility.

Civilization is the conquest of nature and of our-selves through obedience to the laws of being. And, certainly, a people cannot be said to be civilized which is greatly wrecked and diseased, body and soul, by slavery, want and misery.

We understand the significance of prevailing rates of mortality. We know they greatly vary in the different industries and may be swelled or lowered by measures taken or neglected; and still the government, which alone has the power of enforcing such measures, takes no notice of this matter, involving as it is the lives of tens of thousands. England has long ago shown its wisdom and humanity by its factory legislation, which is being imitated by every other government, as local legislation is too much under private influence, and the self-help of the work-people is liable to run into excess.

Moses, Lycurgus and Numa have knitted together slaves and brigands into nations loving liberty, order and virtue, through institutions embodying immortal principles; and to-day great nations are threatened with dissolution through the all-disintegrating selfishness of a self-seeking age. There is a mutinous war of the masses the world over, in Germany, France, England, Belgium, Holland, Italy, Spain, Scandinavia, Russia and in America. This is no more a prophecy. It is history for all who can read.

Never were the conditions more favorable for the building up of a great and beautiful humanity than to-day. Prejudices of race are dead, and we are all brothers; slaves no more work for us, but we delight in industry and live by it; the ignorance of former days has passed away, and science illumines and directs us all.

Humanity, industry and science incorporated into public institutions, established for the preservation and the improvement of the race, and based upon an unflinching regard for human life and whatever touches man and his rights, duties and entire nature, may still give rise to a grand and beautiful humanity, such as the past has neither known nor conceived of, and this consummation will be achieved when hygiene, the law of life and health, will control the individual as well as the nation as the supreme law of a grand and a complete humanity.

It is not bread for the stomach, but regard for humanity, the life, the mind and the position of the masses the age demands.

But the right of the masses to this regard implies their duty to exercise it themselves toward others, which unless they do, can never become a universal sentiment, as is desirable for the good of mankind.

Self-sufficient capital may delight in the strife of competition, which by itself would reduce the social world into conflicting atoms; and labor may consider paramount association, by which it sustains itself in its weakness. We acknowledge both these principles as necessary and natural complements to each other; still neither competition nor association are the highest elements of civilization; they are both but means to an end, and this end is humanity itself, and the highest principle is, therefore, regard for human life or the preservation of the race.

The oddity of our position does not escape us. Setting aside the high considerations of philosophy and literature, we treat the life, health and well-being of the masses as *the* question of civilization. And this our subject not suffering us to turn from it for the sake of making apologies, we will only say what needs no further proof, that the health and well-being of a people are its wisdom and its virtue, and its honor and its greatness among the nations, as its weakness and its poverty are its folly, and its crimes and its downfall and its shame among the nations.

It is clear to every historical student who casts his eye observingly over the world, that a most fearful revolution is imminent, one not to be put down with the baton of the police nor with the bayonet or cannon of the regular army. We would, therefore, inspire a sacred regard for human life, such as would lead to peaceful reformation and improvement. But if the fates, or, better, the folly and inhumanity of man, have decided upon revolution and violence, may the lesson of the sacredness of human life, repeated on every page and almost in every line of this volume, help assuage the wrath of man, and stay in some degree the fratricidal hand of man raised against his brother man.

There is no other foundation for peace, prosperity, freedom, concord and equity among men than the sacredness of human life; it is our only security against oppression, injustice and grinding rapacity. The sacredness of human life means educational opportunities for all; it means the integrity of the family, the bulwark of civilization against its dissolution and moral chaos; it means sobriety, temperance and moderation against all that leads to drunkenness, madness and human decay; the sacredness of human life pleads for the fallen criminal, who is after all a man, and against his further brutalization and the gallows; the sacredness of human life pleads for the good of all, be they rich or poor, strong or weak, wise or foolish, aye, be they good or bad, as all are men and all are more or less erring and all in want of more light and more love.

The sacredness of human life alone is the harbinger of the reign of justice, love and peace and of God's kingdom among men. But there is a new school of reformers who, discarding every noble sentiment that dwells in the human breast, feign to make us believe that might is right and brute force is the highest divinity. These self-styled Darwinians say the struggle for existence is nature's method for weeding out the weak and improving the race. The old practice of destroying feeble children is approved of; hospitals are discarded; wars are deemed useful as mowing down the less vigorous; no quarters are given to the weak, and the gospel of war and selfishness is preached in the name of Darwin and his principle of the " survival of the fittest."

Humanity revolts against this slaughter - pen civilization, which is not less false in principle as it is cruel in practice. Though the law of heredity is true, still the law of the dissimilarity of children and parents is not less true than the law of similarity, and the law of deterioration is often corrected by the natural tendency of reverting to the normal type, which is effected by children taking after the healthier organized of the two parents or even after a remote ancestor ; and, hence, a father mean in body and soul has often children of finest quality. We must not push inferences to an unreasonable extent and preach in the name of Darwin indirect murder, already too prevalent.

We are not to join the blind elements against a brother, but rather avert from him their fury. We must instruct the ignorant, strengthen the weak, lead the fallen back to virtue's ways, and thus use all gentler means for the improvement of the race ; and if death and destruction are to come, the earth has her volcanoes and the skies are armed with thunderbolts. But let not man volunteer to be a minister of death to his brother man, directly or indirectly, either by what he does or by what he omits to do.

Only when the sanctity of human life will determine our Education and industry, will our progress in civilization be genuine. The history of the world is as yet but the history of humanity suffering death under a thousand forms at the fratricidal hand of man.

The Spartans hunted down their slaves, occasionally, as if they were the meanest animals, to keep down their numbers.

The Greeks butchered in war in cold blood, sparing neither age, sex nor station.

The Romans, as we have seen, were no less cruel at home than in war. Cicero, having been beheaded by the order of Antonius, and his head having been brought, Fulvia, the wife of Antonius, struck it on the face, drew out the tongue and pierced it with a bodkin.

The delight of the Romans in the combat of wild beasts with slaves shows their bloodthirstiness. Turkey never showed such barbarity.

Clotaire, King of the Franks, 559, burned alive his son with all his friends, because they rebelled against him. Queen Brunehaut, being condemned by Clotaire II., was dragged through the camp at a horse's tail till she gave up her ghost. The Goths were extremely prone to blood. The Scythians made use of the skulls of their enemies to drink out of. The Gauls deposited the heads of their slain, brought from battle, in chests as trophies. The scalping of enemies by Indians is too well-known.

The French peasants, in the civil wars in 1358—sorely oppressed by the nobles warring against each other—hung a knight, after they had violated in his presence wife and daughters, whom they forced to eat of the flesh of the husband and father they had roasted upon the spit, and terminated that horrid scene by murdering the whole family and burning the castle. The nobility treated the peasants no

better. The Dutch, in Amboyna, deprived the natives, if they were found guilty of theft, of their
ears and nose, and William Funnel, who was there
in 1705, reports to have seen 500 of such ear-and-
noseless wretches in one gang.

Poisoning and assassination were most commonly perpetrated as late as the seventeenth century in England. For a score of trifling offenses
people were hung in England as late as this very
century. For treason or lisping a word against the
King of England the prescribed punishment was
to cut up the criminal alive, to tear out his heart,
to dash it about his ears, and to throw it into the
flames.

The torturing and burning of the Jews, the knight
templars, heretics and witches are well-known.

The treatment of the Mexicans by the Spaniards
shocks us ; so does the infecting of the Peruvians
by the Portuguese with the clothes of smallpox
and scarlet fever patients, or the shooting of
the Tasmanilians by the English to feed their
dogs on the flesh of these unfortunates, or the
poisoning of wells with strychnine by the ———
to get rid of the redskins. Of course, we would
not do these things, and yet we are but a refined
set of anthropophagi and let but exceedingly few
of our fellows die a natural death, and the victims
of indirect or social murder are more than a thou-

sandfold the number of those who are cut down bluntly by the armed hand of the undisguised homicide.

The story of Madame Lapouchin has but too often repeated itself. She was the most admired at the court of the Empress Elizabeth at St. Petersburg. Suspected of plotting against the government, she was condemned to undergo the punishment of the knout. As she appeared at the place of execution, every feature in her face plead for her innocence. Her youth, her beauty, her life and spirit pleaded in vain for her; she was deserted by all and abandoned to the grim executioners. Her cloak being torn off, modesty made her start back, she turned pale, and burst into tears. One of the executioners stripped her naked to the waist, seized her with both hands, and threw her upon his back, raising her some inches from the ground. The other executioner, laying hold of her delicate limbs with his rough fists, put her in a posture for receiving the punishment. Then laying hold of the knout—a sort of whip made of a leathern strap —he, with a single stroke, tore off a slip of skin from the neck downward, repeating his strokes till all the skin of her back was cut off in small slips. The executioner finished his task with cutting out her tongue; after which she was dispatched to Siberia, the land of Russian mercy.

Our theme is humanity, and were this the history of an individual only, we should not have told it here; but it has repeated itself so many times that it has become the history of humanity, and we have no apology to make for its recital.

Not only pagan Rome was profuse in shedding human blood in constant party strife, as the names of Marius and Scylla, Cinna and Octavius will call to everybody's memory. Not only religious fanatics have caused human blood to flow in torrents, but even in the name of liberty and human rights men have been butchered.

According to good authority, 18,613 persons have been guillotined in the madness of the first French revolution. In the Vendée have been killed:

Women	15,000,
Children	22,000,
Killed of all categories	900,000,
Carnage under the proconsulate	
Carrier at Nantes	32,000,
Carnage at Lyons	31,000.

Neither does the great French revolution form an exception to the rule.

Has the French government not fusillated forty thousand citizens in the name of order as it was but yesterday?

And what is every war organized by we care not what government, but public murder sanctioning the killing of our fellow-men in one or another way under one or another pretext, whenever it suits our own private advantage or public cupidity, national glory or what not.

The murdering of wives, husbands, children, slaves and old men, the avenging of imaginary offenses in the duel, political assassinations, have all been sanctioned in their turn, and the want of the unconditional recognition of the sacredness of human life has marked every century with another form of bloody mania. At one time husbands trembled for their lives as women could not resist the temptation of poisoning their natural protectors. At another time tyrants were smitten with fury, and every free thought was expiated on the gallows. Priests have more raged than all other madmen put together, knights challenged and fought everybody for their love's honor sake, red republicans did their part, and when there was none against whom to turn a bloody hand, men ran in companies to drown themselves, and laws prescribing the dishonorable treatment of the dead bodies had to be passed to stop the suicidal mania.

Give but one page to the sad story of every unfortunate individual, who fell a victim to fratricidal rage of one or another sort in the last five thousand years, and they would fill volumes outnumbering the books of all the private and public libraries of the United States.

The lesson for which more than ten thousand times ten thousand have paid with their dear lives can be nothing else and nothing less than THE SANCTITY OF HUMAN LIFE.

Men, nations and periods have excelled in religion, poetry and philosophy, and have at the same time been inhuman in their dealings. Herein, even, has the past failed. It has treated humanity as a circumstance, but not as the corner-stone of civilization.

None of the civilizations of the past has declared man sacred and inviolate by any and every power, under each and every pretence, be it of a private or public nature, in the name of justice, religion, God, country or anything else.

It is time man and his well-being are declared the paramount object of the state and civilization. Wealth, science, philosophy, religion, were all made for man, and not man for them.

Some put knowledge above man. But most of the knowledge of our age is only the present error that replaces the error of the past age, to be in its turn replaced by that which is to come. In Education as well as in religion, the good of mankind has hitherto been sacrificed to barren opinions. We plead for man, his life, his bread, his freedom, his happiness. His civilization will take care of itself.

In spite of the prophets, poets and philosophers of the past, ignorance, misery and injustice have cursed and oppressed the race. There is but one principle, that proclaimed in all its absoluteness, can save and bless the race, REGARD FOR HUMAN LIFE, FOR ALL THAT PRESERVES, PROLONGS AND SAVES HUMAN LIFE, AND AN ABSOLUTE CONDEMNATION OF ALL THAT WORKS DESTRUCTIVELY UPON HUMAN LIFE, WEAKENS, SHORTENS OR RENDERS IT BURDENSOME.

No man, or government, or institution has a right to sap directly or indirectly human life, the very foundation of all rights and duties, and whatever is sacred in human rights and institutions.

As the sanctity of human life is the foundation of civilization, so it is also the cardinal priniciple of Education, which must aim at the preservation and improvement of the race through the preservation and improvement of the individual.

We maintain civilization means something different than a little gloss here and a few sophisms there. It means a people at work for its own good and doing well; a well-to-do people; the foundation of a free and perfect manhood, that will in its own way work out the problem of civilization.

Industry will do more for mankind than all the

11*

Iliads.   Greece has excelled in philosophy, Rome in jurisprudence, and the Middle Ages in religion, and each has oppressed the masses.   Human life, despised by them all, must become the corner-stone of a new and altogether different civilization, philosophy, jurisprudence, religion and industry, such as will usher in a better and happier age than the world has yet seen.

A straggling piper, fiddler, rhymer or dreamer are but poor evidences of a high civilization.   A good government patterns after nature; it builds up the body, and the mind will take care of itself; it looks after the seemingly trivial things of to-day, which bear in them the germs of the great things of to-morrow; it sees the future culture of the masses in their health and strength and bread and butter of to-day, and goes for it with a will.   This is civilization.

PART V.

THE PROGRESS OF EDUCATION.

The progress of Education in the United States, as everywhere else, establishes our proposition that it is the tendency of the age to improve the condition of mankind and to solve the great social problem by making the world a schoolhouse, in which humanity is not taught letters, but is taught and trained in the art of living and acting.

At the close of the last century we had but twenty-three colleges and thirty-seven academies and no common school system in the United States. In 1813, the State of New York appointed the first superintendent of common schools. Normal colleges, school journals, high schools, and, at last, the erection of agricultural and industrial schools, are all of a late date, and the National Bureau of Education is still more so. To-day the common school property of the United States amounts to $173,838,545, the yearly expenditure of the common schools reaches the sum of $88,618,950, and the teachers number 249,262! The entire property of all sorts of schools, exclusive of orphan asylums, houses of correction, etc., amounts to $340,601,718.

The following table of the Commissioner shows how deeply and rapidly the conviction is spreading that through the school we are to solve the great social problem, and, hence, the erection of normal colleges, which shall provide us with professional teachers devoted for life to the art of educating men :

	1870.	1871.	1872.	1873.	1874.	1875.	1876.
Normal Colleges in U. S. . .	53	65	98	113	124	137	151

As the world relies upon the school, the school must study the problem it is to solve. The teacher must understand the cause of every deviation from the normal type of humanity in the pauper, the criminal and the insane ; he must strive to lessen human misery and weakness as far as physical, mental, moral and industrial training enable him, and that will quite suffice to regenerate the world.

It is but a couple of centuries when the doors of the better institutions in England were slammed in the face of the common people, who had the impertinence to aspire after a gentleman's Education. It is hardly a hundred years when in Scotland, foremost in Education, the usual deficiency of the schoolmaster's budget had to be made up by cock-fighting displayed in the school-room—the victims of the feathery tribe being adjudged the teacher's—

who was sure to put into the field a most valiant fighting cock.

It is not yet forty years that the schools of the people in England had to be provided for by all sorts of charitable tricks, of which one pretty common was clubs meeting every Saturday at the beer houses and taking up collections to pay the schoolmaster, who was a member of the club and was bound to spend part of his dues in beer. The teacher was very frequently drawing pauper rates, and by teaching for the consideration of four or five shillings a week kept out of the working house.

No wonder teachers did not feel sweet-tempered, who, as Friedrich Richter informs us, had in Prussia an average salary of two hundred dollars per annum, while many had but from five to ten dollars, and some got one cent per week for each scholar, upon which they could but poorly subsist, but recuperated during the half of the year when they drove out to pasture their bovine friends, whom they treated to less blows than the scholars who kept them lean. John Jacob Häuberle, more punctual than the rest, kept a School Flogging Journal, in which he informs us of having administered during his schoolmastership of fifty-one years and seven months, 911,527 strokes of the cane and 124,000 of the rod; also 20,989 blows with the ruler; not only 10,235 boxes on the ear, but also 7,905 tugs at the

same member; and a sum total of 1,115,800 blows
with the knuckles on the head. He imposed besides 22,763 fines in the shape of chapters in the
Bible and catechism and parts of grammar to be
learned by heart. He threatened 1,707 children
who did not receive it, made 777 kneel upon round
hard peas and 631 upon a sharp-edged piece of
wood, to which are to be added a corps of 5,001
riders on the wooden horse. Such was the treatment of scholars by John Jacob Häuberle, who
thought the floggings the children received of sufficient importance to keep account. What must
have been the treatment of helpless children at the
hand of less scrupulous teachers?

To Lord Brougham belongs the glory to have
aroused the Parliament of England by his position,
his learning, his eloquence, his humanity and states-
manship to the danger that threatened the country
from the gross ignorance of its population; and
mainly through his exertions a Committee of the
House of Commons to inquire into the educational
condition of London, Westminster and Southwark,
was appointed in 1816. In 1818 Mr. Brougham's
Committee on the Education of the People generally, was appointed. In 1820 his first bill was
brought before Parliament. In 1834 the first Parliamentary vote for Education was passed, and a
select Committee of the House of Commons ap-

pointed to inquire into the means for establishing a national system of Education. In 1836 the first Parliamentary vote was passed for the erection of schools of design, and from this time one Parliamentary act after another laid vividly hold upon general, industrial, scientific and art Education, until the most comprehensive of all, the Elementary Act of Education, passed in 1870.

As late as 1850 half of the people of England and Wales were illiterate, and half the children were without school attendance. The teachers were poor, miserable men, not to be trusted with the commonest work. The schools were kept in unwholesome cellars and garrets, without maps, blackboards, books, apparatus or playgrounds, and, of course, without rooms for classification. Many parishes were without any schools at all. Among the teachers we find blacksmiths, tailors, colliers, cooks, hatters, hucksters, some of them continuing their trade.

The noise in these school rooms was usually such that a person could not hear what was said. These wretched, miserable schools, with a few worm-eaten benches and tables for their furniture, were often hovels in ruins or over stables, with small windows, poorly lighted, with damp earth for their floor; and among 692 of these schools, 364 had not as much accommodation as anything in the shape

of a privy. Parliamentary grants for Education
were for the primary department in

1833	$100,000
1840	150,000
1850	900,000
1862	3,873,715
1870	4,573,605
1872	7,757,800

In France, of 38,000 communities, 14,000 were in
1833 without schools ; in 1870 only 800 very small
communities were without schools. In 1832 one-
sixth of the French people were educated. In
1856 almost one-half of the people were educated.
Upon 10,000 in the army of France could read in

1828	3,518	men from 21–40 years old.
1846	5,331	" " "
1860	7,000	" " "

The primary department in France counted in

1830	1,000,000	scholars.
1848	3,530,135	"
1850	3,784,710	"
1868	4,442,421	"

The appropriations for primary instruction in
Paris were in

1852	1,300,000	francs.
1859	1,700,000	"
1866	5,207,000	"

In 1862, France had 1,833 school libraries, in 1866 it had 10,243 !

Belgium had in 1830, 293,000 children in the primary department ; in 1848 it had 462,000 in the same department.

The progress of Education in the past and present is very much the same everywhere, and not only proves that the world came to the conclusion that its improvement must come from the school ; it also shows that if the misery of the masses has been very great hitherto, so has been the neglect of their Education. It further proves that scholars and philosophers, while they indulge in the delights of the intellect and the imagination, are, as a rule, to their own reproach, unconcerned about the brutality, ignorance and misery of the masses. But the weightiest lesson of all is that private means and efforts are insufficient to provide for the Education of the masses. England, with its state church, and mutually jealous sects and its public-spirited men of wealth, proved by the miserable failure they made of the Education of the people, that the power and wisdom of the state alone are to be trusted with this great work and responsibility.

The more the masses equal in moral and intellectual grasp the rest of society, the more it must be admitted that they are the most important factor in the production of wealth, and are, therefore, entitled to the best wealth can give—a good and substantial Education ; and this is also all they can claim from the state without detriment to themselves and without confusion of ideas and principles ; and whoever endeavors to deprive them of that, under whatsoever pretext—public economy, or what not—his name ought to be loathed as that of Arnold, the traitor.

Reforms should commence so imperceptibly as to be sure to escape the opposition of opinions and things, and the capital invested in them should only grow with our experience in managing them. We should then be sure of meeting with success and of finding imitators. " Do not pitch your improvements too high," is the instruction of the Prussian Minister to his Commissioner of Education.

Connecticut feels the necessity of combining industrial training with school Education, as the people in many localities visibly suffer from want of occupation, and she refuses $100,000 of a testator, bequeathed for the purpose of inaugurating that improvement, as the committee appointed for the investigation of that matter reports an industrial school requires a capital of $500,000.

We should open our industrial school with two dozens of needles, a half a dozen spools of cotton and sixty yards of muslin ; and if, in an evil hour, we should allow our ambition to run away with us, we might open in two branches at a time, and put into the students' hands two dozens of knives, and commence wood carving with a stock of 200 square feet of walnut lumber. Anyhow, we should begin with a capital of not over $50, and be sure of success; but the Connecticut industrial school cannot start on less than $500,000!

Our philosophy as how to open industrial schools applies to infant schools, obligatory evening schools and every new movement.

Train the children to profitable employment, and every parent will hurry his children to school and keep them there, until the morals of the school accompanying the work of the muscles will become assimilated, fixed, organic and hereditary.

The cultivation and improvement of the few favorably situated for a time is lost with their opportunities in the unimproved masses in which they soon sink back; only the culture and improvement of the whole people can become hereditary; and, hence, Race Education, or Hereditary Culture, implies universal culture.

Luther, the reformer of the schoolhouse as well as of the Church, and Pestalozzi, are beginning to tell on Germany.

After the Austrian defeat at Sadowa, a high Prussian official having been asked, "Who was your biggest general?" answered, "The school-master."

It was the lack of this sort of general that beat France. The Polytechnic Institute of France is the best in Europe—its primary instruction is the poorest.

The Protestant leaders, as early as 1560, asked for an obligatory school law; they were crushed; and to-day, after three hundred years, the French government is still wrangling over such a law. Germany, having taken possession of Elsace and Lorraine, March 1, 1871, introduced compulsory school attendance the 18th of the following month, and made an annual school appropriation of 6,562,427 francs. The French government, under the Restauration, made an annual appropriation of 50,000 francs for the primary Education of the whole of France.

That England appropriated for primary instruction in 1841, $150,000, and in 1872, $7,757,800, and France, in 1828, for the primary instruction of the nation 50,000 francs, while Paris appropriated for the primary instruction of its own population in 1873, 11,132,046 francs, is a guarantee of progress and gives us faith in the future of humanity.

Prussia, with 12,256,725 population, had already in 1825, 21,623 primary free schools, with 25,000 teachers and 1,664,218 scholars under attendance,

while England, as late as 1841, had an annual appropriation of $50,000 for the primary schools of
the whole country; and, as a natural consequence,
expended during the same period for the suppres-
sion of crime, $3,224,845.

COST OF EDUCATION AND OF CRIME.

An Education that trains, teaches and fits us for
usefulness from our earliest childhood may be expensive. But is a quarter of a million of drunkards,
as many criminals, paupers and defectives, less so?
A half a million of men consume, waste, depre-
date and not only produce nothing, but absorb the
labor of one army watching them, and of another
that is administering to their vicious propensities
in a hundred thousand haunts of vice, shame and
drunkenness! The wages of these idlers, at the
low rate of $1 per day, would amount to $150,-
000,000 per annum. But the difference between
the production of a nation of forty million industrially and morally trained and one that is without
such influence, does not count by the hundred, but
by the thousands of millions; as the result of every
producer would be enhanced by increased efficiency
and economy.

The habitual criminals, of whom we have about
40,000 in our state prisons, cost the state each, for
detection, apprehension, conviction and mainte-

nance, $500. The depredations of each, during an
average criminial career of five years and a half,
amount to $2,750, which gives a total cost to so-
ciety of $130,000,000. Drunkenness costs the nation
four and five times as much, and the same may be
said of the idle pauper class and the defectives.
For pauperism and its misery nearly double the
rate of death and disease in the land. But we may
multiply tenfold the damage to the nation from
pauperism, drunkenness, crime and every sort of
defectiveness, and these miseries assume vaster proportions still, as they are hereditary and multiply
with every generation in a geometrical ratio.

The Juke family thus yielded in seventy-five
years in

Adult paupers	280
Criminals and offenders	140
Habitual thieves	60
Common prostitutes	50
Women specifically diseased	40
Men contaminated by these women .	400
Aggregate of children who died pre-	
maturely	300
Cost of crime, pauperism, depredation,	
premature death, specific disease and	
loss of wages, etc.	$1,308,000

This is the fruit borne by the cheap Education
of a family of four sisters in the State of New York
during seventy-five years.

Charles L. Brace has proved the wholesome influence of industrial schools on crime. But does our common Education prevent crime?

The criminal class is, naturally enough among other things, also illiterate; but, certainly reading and writing have in themselves but little restraining power over crime. Prof. John W. Draper, who is very guarded in his statements, positively asserts in his treatise on Physiology, that our common Education has rather the reverse tendency. The same position has been taken by Herbert Spencer and other investigators.

DOES EVERY EDUCATION PREVENT PAUPERISM?

It has equally been established beyond a doubt, that a common school Education is not proof against pauperism. Thus, the counties lying between London and the south coast of England are by far less illiterate than the North Midland counties, and have yet a great deal more of pauperism.

Only an Education that develops from early infancy all the powers of body and mind, fosters good habits, imparts practical information and trains men to active and skilled industry, is a preventive against pauperism and crime; and, in fact, against every other deviation from the normal type of humanity.

It is time the sham of our illiteracy statistics be made clear to the comprehension of everybody. The fact that most of paupers and criminals cannot read and write is used as a conclusive argument, that all Education has to do to diminish pauperism and crime is to teach people how to read and write. In truth, however, illiteracy is not the cause of pauperism and crime; but, like pauperism and crime, it is a symptom of want, misery and a general deterioration and degradation, which are the real causes of illiteracy as well as of crime.

The detection of this fallacy is of vast importance, for it teaches us that to impart a knowledge of reading and writing does not touch the cause of pauperism and crime. To effect this, we must remove want, misery and congenital deterioration, which can only be brought about by the prevention of the development of inherited evil tendencies through correct early training in infant schools and the cherishing of active habits in the industrial school, developing skill and capacity, promoting well-being, health and comfort, where degraded tendencies, left to themselves, would have produced want, misery and degradation.

INTELLECTUAL PLEASURES.

An increased outlay and effort for educating the masses is our greatest security for the future. It

has long ago been observed by prominent economists, whenever intellectual pleasures are in the
ascendant, civilization progresses, and when sen-
sual pleasures predominate, civilization is on the
wane. It certainly shows in our favor that we
spend a hundred and fifty millions per annum for
the culture of the young, and, besides this, vast
sums taken out of the fund of material gratification,
lessen by so much luxury, ruinous by its effeminat-
ing tendency, and add so much to the virtue, force,
intelligence and efficiency of the next generation.

Water, air and earth make the wheat and cotton
plant, which, in their turn, are made into food and
clothing. So does under the process of an advancing civilization matter enter into the production
of mind. Our spiritual wants increase daily, and
their satisfaction is attended with least waste. One
loaf can feed but one stomach, and one coat can
cover but one back; but one idea may feed a thousand minds. The production of mind is, therefore,
the most profitable investment, and the progress
of the race, of manufactures and of values lead all
to it, and, hence, our increased educational efforts.

EDUCATION AND THE STATE.

Lycurgus has already said, the business of the
legislator resolves itself into the bringing up of
youth.

12

Plato has said, man cannot propose a higher and holier object for his study than Education and all that appertains to it.

Nothing, says Auguste Comte, can give stability to a government but a great principle, to which under every change or revolution of opinion all the people will hold and around which they will rally; and an Education that will teach them the submission of their desires to the will of all.

Race Education, or the subordination of the individual in each and every act to the race, gives us the principle and the Education, which of all others trains for this wholesome subordination.

" It is most natural for the individual," says Aristotle, "to be educated for the nation, of which he is but a part, as the limb is of the body and for the body." We admit the criticism, that antiquity sunk the individual in the state. But do we not fall in the opposite vice, and err on the side of meanness, as the ancients did on the side of nobleness, by running individuality into consummate selfishness? Race Education deepens and unites both elements in educating the individual for the race.

EDUCATION AND OUR FINANCIAL CRISIS.

Too dull and listless to learn in the school of thought, nature's laws will make themselves heard at last by speaking to us in pinching want, ruin, misery and bitter disappointment attending the upheaval of commercial crashes, and, at last, in revolutions and national ruin.

Witness our present crisis, aggravated by our false Education. War has demoralized the industrial habits of the land; the late discontent of labor has materially lessened its results, and production was thus doubly cut short; still mislead by an inflated currency, the people were sure of getting rich, and spent more than ever. How could we but get poor, losing at both ends by a decreased production, and an increased consumption when labor and saving are the only sources of wealth? From the firing of the first gun at Sumter we got poorer as a nation, as we produced less, or what we produced were not means for further production, but destruction. We were piling up fences, farm implements and the wealth of cities and states, and made of it a great and fearful conflagration. And even this is not all; we destroyed a million of producers, made the living worthless through habits contracted in the camp or the extravagance and the gambling spirit at home. What a strange way of getting rich! From Adam Smith down to Mill, McLoid, Jevons and Cary, economists have taught us differently.

When we felt flush, the crash was coming; for we were indulging in a dangerous delusion.

Our future will never be secure until our children are trained from their fourth to their seventh year to be active, skilful and creative, and thus a lasting foundation for industrious and moral habits be laid ; then to their twelfth or thirteenth year they must be intellectually trained and instructed, and after that to their eighteenth year industrial employment must be combined with the highest technical and scientific instruction.

We are wofully deficient in industrial and moral habits, as also in the knowledge of the plainest principles of economy. We have to overcome the financial fiction of honestly getting something out of nothing, when, in fact, labor and saving are the only factors in the production of wealth.

If we bring up our children for work, we bring them up for the country and for the production and the cheapening of the first necessaries of life, the increase of which increases the well-being of the masses. If we raise them for idleness, we raise them for the city and for chance stakes, which tend to unprincipled transactions. It is the lack of the element of work in the popular Education that swells the movement of the population toward the great cities, where everybody fishes for his prize, and one wins while a hundred sink beneath the wave.

Our Education is at best a hunt for charming

information, but the power of producing our necessaries to sustain life must precede the delightful.

Our defeats as our victories come from the schoolmaster, and the school is at the bottom of our
financial disasters. "Nonsense," says my critic,
"it is the time." But, pray, who makes the time
but we, and who made us but the school?

ERAS OF CIVILIZATION.

Our present development of the understanding
must be followed by the reign of reason, as it has
been preceded by the dominion of the imagination.

The creation of language and the fine arts formed
the dawn of civilization; now science absorbs the
age. Only the perfect state is the consummation
of the highest reason.

THE SCHOOL THE MINIATURE OF THE WORLD.

It need not be repeated that to instruct is not
to educate. But it is not enough realized that
knowledge is not always saving, and that the downfall of empires has mostly been attended by subtlety of intellect and universal skepticism.

To educate the young is to make them live long
enough the life we wish them to live, that they
may continue it from habit. It is not to show
them at a distance the way they are to walk in,
but to train them in it. The school must be a

miniature of the world with all its work and duties, in which the young must be exercised. And this simultaneous training of every part of man's nature is the more necessary as each has its modifying influence on the other, and none can be cultivated to advantage separately.

THE PERIOD OF CRIME AND OF EDUCATION.

The greater amount of crime is committed between the ages of twenty and thirty years. By increasing the industrial usefulness of Education, which enables scholars to support themselves, parents are more induced to send their children early, long and continuously to school than by compulsory school laws, and thus prolonged school attendance influencing those years of vicious tendencies, will lessen crime by one-half.

THE HALF-TIME SCHOOL SYSTEM.

Race Education divides the scholar's time between instruction and industrial training, which is acknowledged to yield better results than the long hours of our common schools, in which, however much talking the teacher may do, the jaded scholar receives but little.

The half-time system, not interfering with the acquisition of a trade, enables the student to prolong his period of Education, to become acquainted with the theoretical acquirements of his especial trade and their use; and having for years combined work with study, his success as an artisan and inventor is assured.

The leading educators of England agree with Mr. Chadwick in pronouncing short school hours a success; that prolonged attention is impossible for a young child; that school hours are wasted because they make impossible demands upon a child's immature powers; that short lessons, with bodily work, produce better intellectual results than lessons twice as long, without the relief bodily exercise gives to the mind.

Dr. Norris says, before the British Association, he has confronted this subject on all its sides, and found that children who studied half the school hours, and worked the other half of the day, studied and worked more efficiently than children who worked or studied all the time.

OUR WORDY EDUCATION.

Let our scholars have less to do with words, the shadows of things, and more with the things themselves, and they will prove as energetic and successful as our self-made men. Teachers and parents often think that children must learn all the words Johnson, Walker, Richardson, Worcester and Webster did not know how to spell and pronounce;

that they must know by heart every third and fourth rate river in Africa, soon to be forgotten; and that their heads must be filled with Rs, Xs and Ys until they are turned themselves into unknown quantities.

Who will deliver us from the yoke of the letter, and permit us once more to have a soul and to act an honest part in the world!

Our schools teach too much, educate not enough and train men for labor not at all.

Our information is too general, which means especial ignorance as far as accomplishing anything in particular is concerned. We want science adoing, as life and nature are. The word must become flesh, and not the flesh word, says Richter.

EDUCATION AND INDUSTRIAL LABOR.

Locke treats what the schools call learning in comparison with physical, mental and moral habits with a most hearty contempt. How strenuously this philosopher, eminent above all others for his great good sense, insisted upon combining one or several mechanical pursuits with intellectual Education even in the highest classes of society, of which practice he cites many examples among the ancients. Cato and Cincinnatus were but illustrations of what was most common among the great men of Rome. Spinoza does not stand alone in modern time. Luther made a good hand in several trades, so did the great Lord Brougham, and so did other men of like eminence.

Industrial universities, receiving their pupils from industrial common schools, would be of infinite more advantage to the country than our present colleges with their Latin and Greek pretences. It is the Central College of Arts and Manufactures at Paris, the pupils of which are in great demand among the manufacturers of France.

But not only Locke, the father of the modern sensational school, but as we have seen Leibnitz, the author of the monadology, and Fichte, the transcendentalist, all equally insisted upon the necessity of joining handicraft to mental culture. Froude, the realistic historian, instills the same lesson. And our own great dead of but yesterday, was not his parting tragic enough, that we so soon forget his life and his teachings? The destruction of slave labor was but half of Mr. Greeley's lesson. The union of Education with free labor was the other and more important half; and half the utterances of his life we should have to cite were we to repeat all he so forcibly said upon this score.

Solon made labor binding upon all men; our Puritan fathers legislated it; philosophers of all schools enforced it; Germany, and all Europe, more or less, introduced it in its schools more than a

12*

hundred years ago. We may turn a deaf ear to the teachings of lawgivers and philosophers of other nations and our own, but the ruin of our industries, labor failing to feed the people, and giving way to dishonesty, corruption and anarchy will at last force us to concede to labor its place in the Education of the people.

Labor, says De Gerando, is the great educator. Labor means wealth, power and civilization. Labor means character, duty and nobleness. Labor prevents disorder, ennui and dissipation; it inures to action and usefulness. It is a school of sobriety, cultivates attention, perseverance, precision and method. It allays the passions and brings inward peace and health to the soul. Labor gives vigor, a sense of dignity and the power of self-restraint. It restrains inordinate ambition, and accustoms us to estimate reality above empty applause.

All honest work, says John Mill, is for the universal good, and as honorable as any public function; and by doing perfectly whatever we do we perfect our character.

Froude sets handwork before headwork. The first business of Education, he says, is to assist us in honestly supporting ourselves. A man must work, steal or beg. The practical necessities precede the intellectual. As long as society does not mind the common wants of humanity and

give this sort of Education, it has no right to condemn the rogue or mendicant.

Miss Nightingale has well said, that without industrial training the three Rs are most likely ending in a fourth R—Rascaldom.

Mr. Pearson, in his report before the House of
Lords, says: I am satisfied that the cause of juvenile crime is not the absence of Education, and
that any Education of the children of the laboring
masses unaccompanied by industrial training and
actual employment in manual and useful labor,
will entirely fail in checking the growth of crime.

And what opportunities have the people for engaging in profitable trades? says another well-in-
formed authority. Owing to a variety of circumstances it has become almost impossible to procure
for children such educational training as will make
them skilful artisans. The public school must fit for
work. European nations are competing in establishing schools of art, and we must shape our public
schools in the same direction or fall behind the civilized world in our industries. European countries
swarm with schools for drawing and technical training. Little Wurtemberg alone has four hundred
drawing schools. The United Kingdom has eight
hundred schools of art. Every country and every
great city in Europe has a grand school of arts and
industries. Whatever time and expense has been

devoted of late in England to drawing has richly been repaid by the improved industries.

New York, Boston, Philadelphia and a few more cities have a few such schools as any German province is swarming with.

The Superintendent of Education of the State of Rhode Island says, our motto should be "the best Education to the largest number." The present course of study is arranged for those who intend to complete the whole course in the high school and not for the masses, who are growing up in ignorance, vice and youthful crimes, which multiply in a geometrical ratio.

Hundreds of orphan asylums, industrial schools and reformatories, in which many industries have for years been successfully taught, prove the practicability and utility of teaching and training the masses in skilled labor. Massachusetts has the honor of having passed an act in 1872 providing that the city council of any city or town may establish and maintain industrial schools and raise the money necessary to render them efficient, and prescribe the arts, trades and occupations to be taught.

The Cooper Institute of New York City, founded by the munificence of the eminently good and wise Peter Cooper, with more than two thousand students, mostly mechanics, crowding its courses in engineering, mining, metallurgy, analytical and synthetical chemistry, architectural drawing and practical building, schools of telegraphy, wood-engraving, photography, design and painting, proves the eagerness of the public to benefit by schools of art and industry, and is a reproach to public remissness in not following the lead of this great benefactor in giving the masses in similar institutions opportunities for combining labor with study, that they may rise from their unprofitable drudgery to remunerative technic art.

The Institute of Technology at Boston, the Worcester Institute of Industrial Science and Cornell University, under the able lead of President White, are all hopeful illustrations of the combination of labor and study.

It is pleasant to mention the noble beginnings made by the Women's Educational and Industrial Society of New York City, who train and instruct thousands of women in a variety of occupations. Long Island has a Printers' training school. The Hebrew Orphan Asylum of New York and the Episcopal Orphan Home of Brooklyn teach several trades, and so does the Wilson Industrial School of New York to girls, the Brooklyn Female Employment Society and the Young Ladies' Branch of the Women's Christian Association completing the list. A model for future institutions of healthful labor, is presented to us by Girard College, with its extensive arrangements for type-setting, printing, book-binding, type-casting, stereotyping, turning, carpentering, photographing, electroplating, telegraphing and shoemaking.

By refusing labor a place in the Education of the masses, we practically tell them "we will not teach you anything useful, but even that will make you paupers, criminals and orphans, and soon enough bring you to our industrial pauper schools, reformatories and orphan asylums where you shall be taught some trade or other." But must we burn down the house to roast the pig? Must the people pass through pauperism, crime and orphanage to get into industrial schools? Would it not be more sage to engraft industry upon our public school system, and rather prevent pauperism, crime and premature orphanage than make them the bridge to industry?

Women suffering nearly twice as much from poverty than men prove by the consequent deterioration of the race the failure of our present Education.

As long as in the absence of a great national system of Kindergartens women are not employed in what is peculiarly their work—the Education of the race—only a varied industrial Education can save them from being crushed by a competition they are bound to meet with in a few overcrowded employments open to them. By giving women a reasonably extended industrial Education, we curtail by one-half prostitution, crime, woman's slavery to man, widowed misery, the idiocy of orphans starving with their pining mothers and other innumerable evils, all flowing from woman's helplessness.

A proper industrial training would enable woman to provide for herself and for those depending on her whenever she should be thrown upon her own resources.

In 1859 women in New York City made and pressed stylish caps for two shillings per dozen. In London about the same time fifty thousand females were working for under sixpence per day, and above one hundred thousand for under one shilling a day. Shirt-makers made a dozen shirts for two shillings. Waistcoat-makers earned only from three to four shillings a week; workers for the army clothiers received eight cents a piece for jackets and trousers, earning thereby two shillings a week. Shoe-binders worked eighteen hours a day, and earned one shilling and sixpence a week. The mantilla-maker, working from nine in the morning till eleven at night, made four shillings and sixpence a week in the busy season.

At a meeting of one thousand female slop workers in England the curious result was obtained, that none of that number had earned more than five shillings a week. Ninety-nine had earned only one shilling, and two hundred and thirty-three had had no work at all during the whole of the week.

In 1867, the New York *World* informs us, there were in the metropolis 70,000 women and girls, beside domestics, who worked for their living, of whom 7,000 lived in cellars, and 20,000 were in a constant fight with starvation and pauperism. Since 1860 establishments doubled employing these haggard creatures at the top of princely merchant houses.

The New York *Times* in December, 1867, informs us of thousands of women in the city working from seven in the morning to midnight getting seventy-two cents for the making of a dozen of shirts. Six cents for a shirt! And pay for drawers, undershirts and blouses in proportion. But flannel shirts carefully made brought 12½ cents a piece, best white shirts 87½ cents, a dozen best drawers $1.25 a dozen. A soldier's widow, with four children to support was getting $4.50 for embroidering a cloak, two weeks of toiling! the cloak selling at $50 to $75, the woman being told, if she will not do it plenty others will do it.

The average labor for 1866 was for

Cloak makers . . . . $8.00 per week.
Shirt   "   . . . . 9.00   "
Cuff and collar makers . . $8.00 to 9.00   "
Umbrella   "   . . . . 5.00   "

Button hole makers	3.00 per week.
Fur-sewers	.$4.00 to 7.00 "
Machine operators	4.00 to 8.00 "

In Boston we read there were in 1868, 20,000 women working at starvation rates, 8,000 workers at 20 to 25 cents per day, 12,000 workers for less than 50 cents, and even at these rates there was little work. These women lived at times on one cracker a day for breakfast, dinner and supper. American wives and mothers work in Boston from dawn to dawn to get one mouthful of food, making shirts at eight cents a day! Some women take shirts at 50 cents a dozen, and operate sewing-machines at $2.50 a week. Dr. Dio Lewis says: "These operating girls run the machine from one and a half to two years, and their backs give out, and their spines give way. When they give out they are pretty well spoiled, and are then thrown out to pick up what they can get, until God in his mercy shall take them hence."

In 1868 one of the best informed journals reports, 30,000 girls struggled in New York City with starvation and cold, six cents for the making of a shirt and furnishing the thread!

In 1869 the New York *Herald* writes: "The working women live in nasty tenement houses, in cellars unfit for human habitation, in pools of foulness, where every impurity is matured, and every vice flourishes, with no air, no light, a rickety bed, a broken-down stove and second-hand cooking utensils. Such is the condition of 75,000 working women in New York City."

A room of 12 by 14 feet, ceiling 8 feet high, paying $8 a month and earning $6 a week, working on an average 12 hours a day.

The *Economist*, in 1869, said: "The maximum average of female labor was $5 per week. The surgeons of Bellevue and other hospitals, who investigated the subject, assert that much of the sickness and mortality of females in the city of New York results from insufficient food and clothing, exposure and cold. The ranks of shame and death are recruited by thousands of unfortunates, who would never have strayed from the path of rectitude if they had obtained honest employment."

Does all this not loudly call for an industrial Education? Is it a wonder that with such mothers the race deteriorates? Who is there but takes good care of a valuable mare, and have we become so debased that we do not value our mothers and our race as much as a farmer does his stock?

Woman in her great misery, involving the ruin of the race—in more than one way—is the condemnation of our impracticable system of Education, which does nothing for the preservation of the race or for the individual, and the stolid indifference of which for human weal or woe betrays an appalling degree of barbarity.

The answer of Agesilaus, the Spartan king, upon the question, what was best for boys to learn? "What they will practice when they will be grown to be men," is as sensible to-day as it was then.

The masses of the people must be skilled in industrial labor; they must be used to the application of knowledge to work and must be industrious, and, hence, the importance of training them early to these requirements of their mature years.

Nervousness leading to a variety of affections, ending often in insanity, is one of the most serious symptoms of the general degeneracy of our age; and all great physicians pronounce moderate labor the most remedial agent in cases of insanity. Cabanis fully proves that muscular activity lessens nervous excitement; hence, physical labor is most wholesome in this our age of nervous affections.

The fostering of honest work would certainly have a good effect on the insanity of mammon worship or the madness of speculation.

The life and motion of the stars is kept up by the opposing centripetal and centrifugal forces; the adjustment of the inner and outer conditions is maintained in organic life by assimilation and dispersion, and social life consists in progressive adaptation and conservative institutions.

The conservatism of China is known, so is its intellectual culture. The code of the Jews is "study the law and observe it," which includes research and steady adherence. And both these nations have outlived all others. The Romans were warring and progressive tribes; but, as we have already seen, the mothers grown up under the shade of domestic habits, had charge of the Education of the children, and supplied it with the conservative element. The Greeks conbined the culture of the physical and intellectual element as no other nation, and, hence, their perfect health and beauty of mind and body.

The hard toiler is slow, patient and conservative, while the student is progressive, as thought will impatiently outrun the slow march of stubborn reality. By joining study with labor, we combine the spirit of progress, development and adaptation with the spirit of conservatism, both so necessary for the historic development of a nation.

Nothing but the union of intellectual Education with physical labor can save us from corruption of every sort and bring us back to the perfect culture and natural simplicity of the Greeks. Or, is there any reason to contradict the statement, that with culture, honest labor and simple living the simplicity of the Greeks is more likely to come than with musty Greek grammars and dictionaries?

Our schools, instead of developing in us a taste for technical pursuits equal to that by which England, Germany, and, above all, France excel, force us to speculate on each other's hide. If, of a hundred scholars leaving school, ninety-five engaged in useful work, and five scrambled for the profits of their labor, that might do; but of the hundred, ninety-five scramble for the questionable profits of the unwilling labor of five, and, hence, the murderous competition, which leaves the five and ninety-five dead on the field.

The clergy have started our Latin schools, the commercial classes have organized our grammar schools. The laboring masses of to-day call for industrial schools.

The famous Dean of St. Paul says, before the British Association: "Whether we have advanced as far as we wisely may, in blending the useful with the ordinary Education, may well occupy the thoughts of the reflective and practical men. I am at a loss to see, why exercise of the faculties may not be combined with what will be applicable to the future employment."

Dr. Fitch, one of the foremost educators of England, says, before the same Association, the children of the masses want more than reading, writing and arithmetic; they want to be put in possession of the mechanic arts; they want right habits; they want to be taught to think about their work, to feel an interest in inquiring and observing for themselves, and to know how knowledge is acquired and applied.

We badly want schools and appreciate them; but they must not devote themselves exclusively to teaching us how to talk about things, but to do the things and do them rightly.

We appreciate the teacher's difficulty. He tries to make the pupil what he is; and as he is an everlasting talker, talkers he will make. But the world is getting tired of words. What it wants is doing, and to this the school must make some sort of an approach or the world will stay away from it.

The State of New York has a right to expect a better return from thirty millions school property than five hours spelling and geography five times a week. The school must form the home and the shop as well as the school of the youth of the land during eight or nine hours of the day. A nutritious but simple meal, not costing over five cents, a simple dress, earnest work and a generous conduct upon the playground alone can educate the nation to simplicity, industry and universal good-will. Moral teachings, enforced by such habits, must regenerate the nation that, though young, has already entered upon its period of decadence.

As we have already quoted, learning forms our

speeches, but habit our inclinations, after which our actions take. Learning is not the end of man, for we can but little know at best; character and achievement, or what we are and what we accomplish, are much more important; and, hence, the organization of the school must develop our nature in infancy, and not dismiss us until we are ready to do our work in the world intelligently. The science of life and the art of living are the main object of Education, as leading to the preservation and improvement of the race.

Once the phenomena of nature have been deemed unworthy the attention of the schoolmen, and the fancies of men have been dignified with the name of philosophy. To-day learned men have but half parted with their conceit, and despise the knowledge of the common things of the world. But who can take an intelligent survey of the international exhibitions of the world without being struck with the amazing variety and grandeur of the works of common men when compared with the smallness and paltriness of the most elegant words of literature.

What is Homer, Virgil, Horace, Dante, Milton or Shakespeare in comparison with half a million of intricate mechanisms, each doing the work of dozens of men, and one hundred million articles of use and beauty? Well may Herbert Spencer say, what is stored up in books is but the smallest part of the knowledge of mankind.

We disavow every intention of disparaging science, but as emphatically declare that practical work, which has furnished science with the great facts underlying it, must be taken again into the service of science and must be treated more graciously by the new mistress.

Our abstruse scientific treatises may be excellent for scientists; the masses who must work must be initiated into the principles of science by studying and working them out in their application to industry. We need no more be ashamed of affiliating the school with the workshop than with old dame nature. To be plain, the school must become considerably a workshop, in spite of literary fops and word-mongers. Science and life will be gainers by the change.

A person of a practical turn of mind may not care about electricity, caloric or the common properties of matter, but will take interest in electroplating, the steam engine and the strength of building materials.

Let every school district have a library not of the battles of England or the wars of Rome, but of every treatise on every branch of industry carried on in the said locality, with a museum containing every article manufactured in different countries and ages of the same nature and the tools used in the process, and the saloons will be less visited, and inebriety and pauperism will receive a check, and every industry flourish as never before.

From our primary and secondary departments of instruction to the college and university all is verbal, culminating in Latin and Greek, which is a very fraud, not one in ten scholars going through them ever being able to read these languages, save the few text books, parrot-like got by rote. Every town ought to have its industrial schools, every county its industrial college, every State its industrial university, and the whole country its national academy of the industrial arts and sciences.

The whole land must become a bee-hive, in which each works for all, and all work for each. Then, and only then, will all be sound in body and sound in mind, sound in government, sound in finance and sound all over.

Education must not begin and end in generalities, but must branch out in different industrial institutions, in keeping with the pursuits of the different sections of the country, to which they must give a higher impetus.

Since religion has ceased to be a state power, binding men's consciences and hands, too, a rational discipline must school men from very childhood up in useful activity and severe simplicity.

13

The industrial training of a long line of generations must become an instinct with the race. Production is characteristic of civilized, as destructive-
ness is of savage life, and our social instincts make
daily more the preservation of the race as dear to
us as the preservation of our own life. Only when
the world will be all work, will vice, fraud and war,
and every other species of wrong and oppression,
disappear from among men.

Let any one judge in the light of the recognized
principle, that Education should enable us to avail
ourselves of all our powers to our best advantage,
and teach us how to learn and improve through
life—if our schools are serving this double purpose
—teaching and training, as they do, the people in
nothing that bears directly on their future vocation,
which is mostly industrial.

"The circle of knowledge through which every
man in his own place becomes blessed, begins
immediately around him from his own being, and
from his own relations." Such are Pestalozzi's
words. Instruction, foreign to a man's pursuit, is
soon forgotten, while the science that discovers
to a man the philosophy of his daily work, renders
it to him an opportunity for constant mental growth
and satisfaction, besides the practical advantage he
derives from the thorough understanding of his
business.

To fit men for duty and the labor of life is the paramount work of public schools. Do they either?

We are beginning to feel the effects of crowding even upon this continent, especially in the larger towns; and nothing but Race Education, insisting with equal stringency upon physical, mental, moral and industrial training from earliest infancy to full maturity, can bar the door to pauperism, and prepare for us a future in which none will be so poor as to suffer want; none so vicious as to inflict wantonly an injury upon his neighbor; none so ignorant as not to know his duty and none so unmanly as not to practice it.

RACE EDUCATION DESCRIBED.

After we had penned down these our thoughts on Education, Dr. E. Seguin's masterly contribution to physiological Education came to our hand. Our standpoint is the practical forced upon us by the study of the unspeakable misery of the masses and their deterioration, leading us to Race Education, or Hereditary Culture, which at every step is an ethical as well as a physical problem.

The principle of Race Education, or Hereditary Culture, combines physical, mental, moral and industrial elements; it satisfies the highest requirements of science, answers the common ends of human life and society, recognizes the claims of the individual, the nation and the race ; the ends of life and the means for attaining them evolve from it. It warns us against every possible mistake, and commends itself the more as the common degeneracy of mankind is studied. Practical necessity leads to it ; the general demand for universal Education finds its fullest expression in it ; the latest biological results are formulated in it. It is highly realistic and idealistic, or a complete synthesis of both ; and, finally, history shows us our ideal system of Race Education in execution with results, the most exalted imagination could not equal as far as the realization of the beautiful in man is concerned.

THE EDUCATION OF THE OLD GREEKS.

The ancient Greeks, who were but small in numbers, have furnished the nations of the earth ideals in every manner of greatness, unsurpassed, yea, unapproached. It is not the sky, it is not the race—for these still exist—but the great men have not come again since the Education of that race has changed. Lay it not to the age, sky, race or God ; give us the Education of the Greeks, and God, nature and the race will give us Greeks again.

We take issue with the absurd method of the schoolmen, who think we can model after the

Greeks by turning the pages of musty Greek grammars and lexicons. If we are to excel as the Greeks excelled, we must adopt the same training and spirit of Education, only improved by the experience of later ages.

While we protest against forcing Greek grammar upon a hundred thousand youths of the land for the sake of one hundred, who will make a successful study of the noble literature of that language ; we insist, however, upon the propriety, the possibility and the necessity of giving every child in the land the same Education the Greeks gave their children. It matters little if we read Greek, especially as it is commonly read, or not. What we want is to excel in action as the Greeks did, and this the like training alone can give.

All branches of Education were comprised by the Greeks under the terms of gymnastics and music, wonderfully expressing thereby that like these, they must all be practiced in a manner as to produce strength and beauty of body and soul.

A perfect life is a work of art, and is not attained by reading about it, but by acting, by living, exercise and steady training, and in this we must model after the Greeks, if we are to equal them in beauty and harmony or rhythm of action.

THE EDUCATION OF MASSACHUSETTS.

Massachusetts more than any other state has made our system of common schools what it is. We love study and admire that state for the tenacity with which it labors on its historical institutions and develops and improves them. But if we oppose the common school system of Massachusetts of to-day, we point with preference to Massachusetts two hundred years ago—the stand it took then on industrial training ; and if we insist on early Education, it is Boston fifty years ago that gives us our argument.

Mr. Phillips, one of Massachusetts' most favored sons, said : " The fact is that many young people, graduates of our public schools, are not capable of doing any work for which any one should pay a dollar, nor can they write a decent letter at fifteen, nor even read a newspaper well. The old New England system, which made a boy work six months by his father's side on the farm or in the workshop, after he had been six months at school, was better than the present one. From such a system it was possible to get such a man as Theodore Parker. Now the public school hands a child to its parents with no means of earning its bread."

Mr. E. Washburn, another favored son of Massachusetts, admits that the Education the mother must give the child is a thousand times more important for society and the state than the Education our schools give. This admits our whole position so far as the indispensableness of national infant schools are concerned. If to watch over and nurse a baby every hour and minute night and day, to cook, wash, mend and keep a home neat and clean, and attend to a hundred other household duties, if all this is as much as one unaided young mother can attend to, the state must give us infant schools to attend to that Education of the heart and character of young children, which Mr. Washburn admits to be a thousand times as important to society and the state than the later Education, but which hardly one mother in ten is situated to afford her young children.

THE DEMANDS OF RACE EDUCATION.

The demands of Race Education are not unreasonable. It condemns the present system, which is purely intellectual, and gives rise to an intellectual strife and to a remorseless competition in life, which sends millions to insane asylums, poor-houses, jails and early graves.

Race Education simply insists that the intellectual culture of the present common school system be preceded by the still more important culture of the character, morals and faculties of the young children in national infant schools, and be followed by industrial training indispensable for self-support, general usefulness and the development of national wealth and the prevention of pauperism—the pest of modern states.

We may sum up the practical points of our system as follows :

1. Education must aim at the preservation and improvement of the race.

2. Many causes at work contribute to a race deterioration, which manifests itself as

    a. An excessive infant as well as adult mortality;

    b. Nervous derangement and frequent insani y ;

    c. Habitual criminality ;

    d. An inactive pauper temperament, and a va-
        riety;

    e. Of congenital defectiveness, weakness or deformity.

3. To lessen human deterioration in all possible forms is the great aim of Education.

4. The development of low hereditary tendencies must be counteracted by the formation of opposite habits in its very infancy, and thus the foundation must be laid for desirable hereditary tendencies, and, hence, the all-importance of infant training schools.

5. Information must be spread among the people about the hereditary nature of morbid tenden-

cies, and the duty of parents to their children in whom their own passions, drunkenness or weakness, assume the shape of madness, homicide or idiocy, blindness or deaf-mutism.

6. A knowledge and observance of the laws of hygiene by the parents will lessen in the children weakness, the cause of every sort of defectiveness and an excessive infant mortality.

7. Race preservation being the end of Education, no woman's Education is finished until she has acquired practically the art of raising children in the infant training school.

8. The laws of health, domestic economy and moral government are woman's first studies, as upon them depend the life and health, the economical success and the moral tone of the family.

9. As the masses must live by their physical exertions, and as rude labor cannot successfully compete with machinery, men must be trained to industry and art in childhood by infant training schools.

10. The tendency to nervous derangement and insanity, so prevalent in our age, can only be corrected by inuring men to physical labor.

11. The spreading of technical industry alone can infuse into our age a spirit of simplicity, moderation and honest dealing, and thus counteract the present extravagance and fraud ending in ruin.

13*

12. The school, science and Education must be brought in closer relationship with the factory, and lessen the dangers accruing to life from deleterious processes.

13. In the people's school technical skill and proficiency must form the acme of man's Education, as domestic proficiency must be the end of woman's Education ; and the school must provide for each, and dismiss neither the one nor the other until this is accomplished.

14. Education must, above all, prevent pauperism, which through want and misery leads to every form of moral as well as physical depravity, by fostering chiefly what is useful, and making man an efficient and self-supporting producer.

15. Every part of Education must practically as well as theoretically be based upon the devotion of the individual to the race.   Our present Education is neither practical nor moral.   It is all literary foppery, and too trifling to be borne with in an age of hard common sense.

RACE EDUCATION AND A RATIONAL IDEALISM.

The preservation and improvement of the race are the plummet line of every part of our system of Education.   The hygienic and economic relations of the individual are ever present to us, as morbid juices lead to morbid desires, and an empty stomach is dull of moral comprehension, and health and bread are important factors of virtue, and are both secured by labor wisely and moderately performed. But, though our aim is tangible, it is comprehensive, and by no means excludes the ideal ends of all schools, which we only use as means for the improvement of the race, which to us is the highest goal of Education.

It has been most truly said before us, Education must help us to help ourselves, not so much impart as draw out. It must train us to learn from our own observation, or to get our knowledge at first Hand from nature. It must inure us to freedom without license, for chains are as galling to the mind as to the body, and lawlessness is debasing.

The whole of Education must be a process of unfolding, a gradual revelation of what is in man. Education, in developing the faculties and capacities of the human mind, always commences with what is nearest to us, and leads us gradually by our own exertions to do and to comprehend by our own power and energy what seemed but shortly beyond our capacity. It begins by naming to the child the external parts of the body, and leads it gradually to the knowledge of the most complex functions of the human system and the laws we must observe if we wish to live a healthy and happy active life.

Education, beginning with the simple relation

of the child to its parents, leads it on to the knowledge and obedience of the laws which govern men and states, and selfishness gives way as the child feels its dependence upon its mother, father, brothers, sisters, the community and humanity.

Education makes the child feel and act in unison with nature, humanity and the infinite. While it cultivates individuality, it develops the consciousness, that it is but part of the great whole, in harmony with which it must seek its own growth.

Education must embrace the activities of the body, which give energy to the mind. It must assist us in giving shape and form to our ideas with our own hands. It must make us creative as well as intelligent. We must realize our thoughts in the world without us as well as form correct ideas in our minds of things external. In man the ideal and the real blend and take coloring from one another, and, standing as mediators between the two, we are at peace with all.

Education must ever work under the inspiration that the child it directs is part of nature, humanity and the infinite, for which it must be educated fully as well as for itself.

We must be educated for intelligent work, for virtue, for freedom, for progress and for humanity.

The development of the capacities of man secures his highest usefulness, and the bringing his passions under the rule of reason, bestows the truest happiness—peace of mind.

Education embraces the cultivation of the heart as well as the development of the intellectual powers, and the science of the duties and responsibilities of human life is the paramount knowledge of mankind and must form a part of his instruction, adapted to the various stages of Education.

Education must train us to the highest activity in the service of humanity, truth, justice and goodness. It must train us to take the right for our guide and to be content, and have internal peace when we have done our best.

Education must train the body, enlarge the understanding, develop the affections, give clearness to our perceptions and energy to our thoughts. It must free us from narrow-mindedness and lead us to reason and justice, to the infinite and the absolute, in which alone there is rest.

Education, by properly watching over and developing every faculty, physical, mental and moral, assists in the revelation of our God-likeness, which consists in living not in and for ourselves, but in and for all things. It cultivates thoughtfulness, kindliness and industry, a hand ready in execution, a quick eye, an inventive imagination and whatever else renders man effective, is in its scope.

While Education works up to the general ideal

of a universal humanity, it fosters with particular care what is original in every single man, and constitutes his individuality.

Education leads us to know ourselves and to comprehend the times we live in, to move with it and to live not for the present, but for the future, not in the narrow limit of our own self, but in the whole. It trains us to subordinate selfish desire to universal principles and the good of all. The noble passions must be inflamed by examples of nobleness, patriotism and self-sacrifice studiously held up to them, as fire kindles on fire.

Education brings the child up to the ideal of the educator and fits it for the world it is to live and act in; showing man his destiny, it assists him in fulfilling it. It is the lever by which we act upon the future of the race.

Education trains man to submission to the infinite, to the love of man and to a self-determined activity in the service of the true, the good and the beautiful, in all his relations to man, nature and the infinite. It imparts to him true human culture and a character, as far as possible, independent of external influences and in full accordance with reason.

Education trains us to be true to the relations of things, and to act upon general principles, so as to earn the approval of our own conscience as well as that of an impartial world. It cultivates the æsthetic faculty and renders the will effective, promoting thereby the good and the beautiful, and making us perfect.

Let us hold up the sacredness of childhood, humanity and the eternal laws of mind and its relationships, as reflected from this rapid sketch of the nature and work of Education, and compare with it the dead materialism or aimless routine work of our schools. What wonder that the generation it brings up is as indifferent as men brought up according to the mandates of eternal reason would be glorious. Mankind ought to resemble a blissful family, a haven full of rest ; but, alas! it is all a pandemonium full of unrest, in which every one is at war with everybody else and with all that is good in himself.

THE CLAIMS OF CLASSICAL AND SCIENTIFIC EDUCATION.

More than one battle has to be fought before a great cause is forever won. For upward of two hundred years the contest between the Old and the New Education has been going on ; and only induced by repeated recent attempts to introduce Latin into the highest grades of our common schools, do we enter upon an argument that we should have considered settled long ago by the popular verdict.

We combat the introduction of Latin as the adoption of a false principle, which vitiates our whole system of popular Education.

Once, when Popery and Cæsarism swayed the world, institutions had to take the line of authority, the rule of life and the norm of their culture from Rome; and the effects of this conspiracy still blight our system of Education. Latin and Greek grammar, we are seriously told, are better suited for the formation and development of the human mind and its faculties than God's infinite universe. Latin and Greek grammar usurp, therefore, the place of science, which alone gives us power over nature for our own good and the benefit of mankind.

Even our purely English Education is vitiated by putting grammatical pedantries and verbal trash before, the practical knowledge of things real and useful.

It is comparatively a short time when Latin was the only written language of modern Europe; next, an English book was hardly thought decent without being interspersed with crumbs of Latin; and even to-day the sciences useful to the common people are inaccessible to them by barbarous Greek and Latin names without number. Scholars naturally over-estimate their little Latin and Greek, but this magnifying of a deceitful sort of half-knowledge is hardly decent or honest.

Already Comenius, born 1592, clearly saw that nature and industry are more properly instruments of mental development, observation comparison and judgment than mere words and phrases are.

John Locke, born 1632, insisted upon the same principle, and, hence, laid stress upon drawing and the principle of utility, deprecating the loss of time bestowed upon a miserable little Latin and Greek.

Herman Francke, born 1663, the founder of the celebrated Orphan House and many other public institutions at Halle, was equally eager to give to the common course of instruction a more realistic tendency.

J. J. Hecker organized as early as 1747 the first *real*, or high and technical school, at Berlin upon practical and scientific principles. Men of common sense have since opposed the senseless routine of Latin and Greek grammar; until to-day, in Germany, the land of thorough scholarship, the old seminaries are fast giving way to *real* schools, teaching drawing, mathematics, science, technology and modern languages instead of the old Latin and Greek jargon.

The national budget necessitates the government to favor *real* or industrial and technical high schools, which are building up the industry, commerce and financial condition of the country.

But science and industry are not only to be recommended on the ground of their utility, they are every way superior as instruments of thought or educationally than Latin and Greek.

The school must make men think. How is this end best to be attained? The new method answers, by early acquainting men with nature as a system of thought, law, and spiritual relations; so that, wherever men may be, the air they breathe, the water they drink, the sky they see, minerals, plants, or whatever may meet their view, may bring to their mind the physical, mathematical, chemical or physiological relations underlying them, and thus exercise their thoughts and keep their minds active.

Next to nature, industry occupies men's thoughts, which, therefore, combined with science, is of great educational value through life.

But as the individual is rooted in the nation in which it finds his·spiritual home, the national literature forms another important element in the Education of the individual.

Thus the new Education builds its system upon nature, industry and nationality, to which the old Education opposes its miserable pittance of Greek and Latin.

Undoubtedly Petrarcha, Reuchlin, Erasmus and the like men, who penetrated into the genius of Greek civilization and its realism, or perfect union

of spirit and matter, which they opposed to the re-
vilings of nature by the old Church, were highly
favorable to modern advance; but, alas! our fourth
and fifth rate classical scholars know nothing of the
old Greeks, and their miserable little Greek grammar and parrot-like learned few detached pieces of
Greek or Latin stupefy them, and make them intol-
erable through the ill-founded conceit with which
it fills them.

Emerson says, that he has not met in all his travels in America with half a dozen of men who could
read Plato profitably. This whole Greek and Latin
scholarship is an imposture, the writing of miserable verses in these languages included. There is
not one teacher in ten who has sufficient knowledge
of these languages to derive from them a higher
culture. The learned apparatus requisite for their
thorough understanding requires the study of a
lifetime. Must hundreds of thousands of students
in the land throw away their years and opportunities for the sake of a few hundred Latin and Greek
roots, which can be learned by any English student
with the help of an etymological handbook in a
few weeks, if not days?

And, as for the historic value of Greek and Roman civilization, a few parrot-like learned detached
pieces of Latin and Greek, forming a classic course,
have nothing whatsoever to do with this sort of

study; and any English reader can find most competent information about it in the great writers on the subject; and as to an original familiarity with antiquity, not a half a dozen of men ever attain it in any country.

A noted Oxonian scholar, in his address before the British Association, says that educators complain of the indifference of all classes for educational opportunities offered them in all sorts of higher and lower institutions. And true it is, he continues, university professors would lecture to benches literally empty, were it not that the pensions attached to scholarships attracted students to the universities. But educationalists forget that, though parents esteem Education, their chief care is to bring up their children that they shall be able to provide for themselves; and, hence, if schools will not teach and train scholars for their future vocation, but insist upon making the critical, grammatical and literary feature of the old schools the ruling tendency of our present Education, the hard-working, matter-of-fact world of to-day will entirely turn its back upon them.

Classical students pretend to be a privileged class of scholars, and use Latin and Greek as the badge of the aristocratic order, when, in fact, their Latin and Greek amounts to little more than nothing.

Would we pardon the arrogance of a German or Italian, who maintained that we cannot be men of culture without studying his literature? And is it less stupid in a Latin or Greek scholar to maintain that we cannot be men of the finest culture without going to school to Rome or Greece?

Is the book of nature written by the hand of infinite power and wisdom, and is our own history and literature not instructive, refining and suggestive enough for us, and every way more useful and full of great issues, than the half-understood crudities of Greek and Latin books?

Has our modern civilization developed no new ideas and principles to which the ancients were strangers?

Is humanity so poor that it cannot develop itself on nature, industry and nationality, but is utterly lost without Latin and Greek? And still men will boast upon the superiority of Christian civilization!

Is it not enough that we are denationalized by a constant stream of men of all nations flowing in upon us? Must the school, too, tear us from our own soil and take us to Rome and Greece to make of us anything but what we are by our own past history? Should not our public schools deepen our national feeling and nurse our souls with the life, work and words of our own poets, authors and statesmen?

Or are we so poor that we have none good
enough in our own history and nation who could
serve as models to our children? People, of course,
will study Sanscrit, Zend and Arabic, and so they
may Latin and Greek; but the imposition is to
force any of these languages upon our children as
a thing indispensable to culture, and deprive them
of the study of science, industry and their own,
perhaps equally excellent, if not superior, literature. By introducing Latin into our high schools
we exclude practically from them the industrial
classes, who have neither leisure nor taste for such
studies.

Latin has for ages, like an impenetrable barrier,
separated the educated class from the common
people. Do we want to build up this wall again?
Is it not more in keeping with our civilization to
make our own tongue the sole medium of science
and literature, that it may be the harbinger of culture and refinement to the lowliest hut in the land
as to the proudest palace?

That the Greeks had a monopoly of ideal culture,
which is only to be acquired by the study of their
literature, is simply preposterous. Ideal men had
never any more an existence than ideal trees or
animals.

Only science, or the knowledge of the laws of
nature and of common things and the literature

of the land, can reach all and be the means of universal culture and prosperity; and, hence, the importance of schools of science and industry, which are nurseries of national intelligence and greatness.

Whoever wishes well the cause of truth and humanity must be in favor of the advancement of science, which has always aided general education and the improvement of the masses, as it is in the whole course of human history attended, as Buckle has noticed, by a widespread culture and a social reform fostering the material interests of civilization.

General principles and philosophy are also a very unsafe guide, and even a dangerous one, if they do not rest upon the safe basis of scientific knowledge and practical observation.

Beside, we cannot understand the spirit of our own time nor choose the right means for achieving our own purposes without a knowledge of the elements of science, industry and social philosophy.

The Church fashioned our old institutions, and as she is the only road to heaven and the saints lived in her early days, so is Latin the only way to human culture and only the ancients were perfect. The modern culture, with its new elements of freedom, industry and commerce, is the mother of our new schools of science and industry for the masses,

and their deliverance from ignorance and its thral-
dom.

It ill becomes the realistic Greek student to
charge science with materialistic tendencies. It is
through matter the spirit manifests itself. Material
elements have often a great moral significance.

What would become of modern civilization if it
were deprived of coal, cotton or iron? Industry is
to culture and civilization what the body is to the
soul.

Industry, far from materializing us, forces us to
the study of the laws and relations of nature, her
products, the methods of gaining, treating and preparing them for the wants of men, and fosters the
knowledge of the laws and conditions of nations
with whom we are brought in contact.

There is not an occupation—and if it were breaking stones on the road—but affects ultimately the
state and the very constitution of society.

Industry, through the creation of wealth and the
distribution of property, becomes the mother of
civilization.

Industry is progressive, promotes peace, favors
labor—the condition of order—and science—the
basis of its progress—as well as the higher arts,
which alone satisfy increased wealth.

Schools of science educate us for life and industry. It is hard to say what Latin and Greek edu-

cate us for. Or are we to take this very uselessness for ideality?

The achievements of science and industry are countless. Every day is marked by some new discovery, be it the compass, the telescope, the spectroscope, the telephone, the power-loom, the steam engine, the locomotive, the sewing machine or the mower and reaper. Chemistry opens the way to the very heart of nature and leads to every profitable manufacture; its elements are the alphabet by which we may read every page in the book of nature. Geology discloses to us the past, as astronomy does the future. What has Latin and Greek to put beside all this? We admit that the very remains of the ancient life of man are imbedded in old linguistic strata, and that the history and . development of language are the history of the race and of the human mind. But what has the miserable Latin and Greek of the schools to do with the science of language and its history?

Almost seventy years ago Sidney Smith scourged classical pedants with his caustic wit, and said, they bring us up as if we were all to become village school teachers and spend our lives in declinating nouns and conjugating verbs. They despise the science of things and the knowledge of human affairs, and dignify their Latin and Greek stuff with the name of erudition.

14

The learning of a language, beside the vernacular, may bring clearly and distinctly before the mind every idea expressed in human language, assist in clear, exact and vigorous thinking, and develops the highly important power of abstract thought. But all this may be achieved just as well by learning a living language, and even much better than by a dead one.

Once the privileged few sought in school a sort of diplomatic shrewdness; and the impenetrable Latin fog made them appear to the masses like demi-gods. To-day, when the people rule, and private as well as public expenditure is large, something more than mere shrewdness, make-believe and grand phrase—science, that increases and improves production, is looked for in schools.

The masses cannot bend over books. The general fine taste of the Greeks was due to the element of culture in their public institutions; and universal culture among us is only possible if the industries in which we all are engaged assume the character of art and science, and become thereby a school of culture for us all, as public life was for the Greeks.

Once life was monotonous and the imagination needed a stimulation word-culture afforded. To-day life is only too exciting, and nothing but sober science can bestow what is wanted—prosperity, the basis of universal civilization.

We, too,—had for many years neither eyes nor ears for anything but the poetry of the ages and the dreams of philosophy. Arabic and Sanskrit trifles, like Latin, Greek and other literary trash came all in for their share of our attention. And to-day we freely confess, had we less indulged in idle curiosity and literary vanity, but by washing and combing a few forlorn boys, made of them decent members of society, the world would have been the gainer, and we should have lost nothing by it.

Men seem to escape one error only to fall into another. We have no more faith in the jargon of the creeds, but put our trust in the jargon of the schools, and men neglecting to do the good work at their door think to lay the world and civilization under obligation by talking about Arabic and Sanskrit.

Our classical students have much to say about a formal ideal culture and the beautiful. But are these grammatical pedants not notoriously awkward in their taste? And is the genius for art and the beautiful not rather an inspiration than a scholastic acquisition?

Is not the flood of grammatical, archæological, mythological and literary notices accompanying every line of the classics sufficient to destroy all poetic charm? And what can a tyro in the ancient

languages know of the beauties of an author of
whom he has read but a few scraps?

We leave it to the judgment of anybody, what is
more apt to develop formal ideal culture, a heap
of arbitrary grammatical observations or the study
of nature, which is a systematic series of interde-
pendent relations and an organic whole, every part
of which is the embodiment of a beautiful law.

Or does the formation of the root, branch, leaf,
bud and flower in a plant and its contemplation not
contribute as much to the ideal and formal culture
of the student as the memorizing of the prefixes
and suffixes of declensions and conjugations?

How utterly false is the assertion that the study
of the material world is less rich and suggestive
than the so-called humanistic studies.

The simplest mineral, beside its physical properties and uses, leads us to the contemplation of its
chemical composition and geological relations, and
thus carries us back to the past history of the globe.

But when we consider that nothing in the state,
religion or life of the ancients, their slavery, gladiators, unmentionable vices, cruel tyrannies, etc.,
comport with our taste and civilization, can it be
wholesome for the heart and mind of the student
to attach himself to the classic phrase which, whatever its form may be, is substantially ignoble?

How infinite, rich and real are the laws and ob-

jects of nature and its kingdoms and their relations
to man. What a study, and what an opportunity
for culture, for observation, reflection and self-improvement !

Science and industrial schools use nature and the
living present as educational means, as the Greeks
made use of their own day, who, verily, did not
trouble themselves with the grammars and literary
remains of a still more remote antiquity.

Mathematics, astronomy, physics and chemistry
are said to deal in definite quantities and relations,
and the process of reasoning in these branches is
too much in a straight line, while in human affairs
we must be on the outlook in every direction. But
does not the past history of the globe and the formation or upheaval of mountain chains, the formation of seas and rivers, the change of climes, the
migration of plants and animals—does not meteor-
ology, does not political economy, the philosophy
of history and a host of other highly useful sciences
afford infinitely superior instruments for the development and culture of general reasoning than musty
Latin and Greek grammars and vocables ?

Physical nature is not a stranger to moral relations. Columbus, Copernicus and Newton have by
their physical discoveries revolutionized the world
of human relations. And Humboldt, Oersted and
Darwin have changed the whole tenor of human

thought in our own day. Watts, Stephenson, Arkwright and Morse have by their discoveries of steam, the railroad, the jenny and the telegraph thrown humanity into an altogether different mould and created a world of new moral relations.

Science and industry are not by any means purely materialistic, but rather highly humanistic in many of their relations and tendencies.

The wealth and prosperity of nations depend upon their exploring the laws of nature; and the knowledge of the true, beautiful and sublime in nature is wonderfully linked with the useful, aptly remarks Humboldt.

Nothing, says Oersted, is more elevating than the knowledge of the ever-constant laws of nature. Science, says the same savant, a help to industry, leads to work, while a fanciful culture leads man away from his work.

That the classical studies, which are hardly anything else than grammar, cultivate the moral feelings, hardly deserves a refutation; while, certainly, the study and contemplation of the physical universe in more than one way cultivate the finer feelings of man.

Everything, says Guyot, is order and harmony in the universe, because it is the thought of God. This sublime unity in the infinite variety of things is one of the many voices of nature audible to a susceptible heart.

The collegian may melt into ecstasy at the beauty of a landscape ; the scientific student is led by the observation of a pebble or a piece of chalk to a thousand facts and relations past and present, from which he construes a landscape, or an order of things that existed millions of ages ago.

The observation of nature is a school for the senses, which the linguistic student uses but very poorly, so that he can hardly be said to see, hear or smell with correctness.

What stupidity to maintain that we can better form our minds by reading the words of Homer or Sophocles than by reading the eternal thoughts of the infinite Spirit written in flowers, rocks, trees and milky ways ! The Iliad is but a syllable—if as much—in the great book of existence.

Not languages, but science, was the password to Plato's academy, over the entrance of which we read the inscription : " Let none ignorant of geometry enter here."

The utter dissimilarity of antiquity has been made an argument in favor of its study by us moderns. We have learned to be surprised at no sophistry. How much nearer the truth is the argument that antiquity being entirely dissimilar to our own world, whatever we learn about it is, for want of analogy or association of ideas, forgotten as soon as we lay the Latin and Greek books aside and enter upon this new, modern world.

Man is but part of nature, and to know himself and the laws which govern him, he must know nature. To know nature is to know himself.

Prof. Youmans says very significantly, the simplicity in the structural elements and the complexity of the whole in nature as well as in the brain, are such as to make the phenomena of the one the fittest instrument for the development and culture of the other.

What wonder that, as Matthew Arnold confesses, young men at the university exhibit a slackness, a sleep of the mind, a torpor of intellectual life, a dearth of ideas, an indifference to fine culture, a disbelief in its necessity, spreading through the bulk of our highest society and influencing its rising generation.

Train our young men in the love of the race, and teach them what appertains to our own life, culture and happiness and not fragments about Greece and Rome, and their attention will be at tiptoe.

It is too absurd to study Latin and Greek for the sake of understanding English; for, then, we should have to study the Sanskrit and the Zend also, and, with still more reason, the Anglo-Saxon, Old English, the French and the Provençal. But where have we the guarantee for living to an old age sufficiently advanced in which we might perchance get at our own mother tongue?

Did the Greeks so study their language? Why, then, should we ours? To know a language is one thing, to know its philology is quite another thing, and as a rule men who know the one are ignorant of the other. The greatest grammarians are the poorest writers, and Homer, Sophocles, Dante, and Shakespeare have written before a grammar or dictionary of their respective languages was in existence.

Political culture, parliamentary eloquence and patriotism, we certainly can derive as well from our own countrymen as from the Greeks and the Romans, who are hardly intelligible to us at a distance of more than two thousand years; and modern nations, like France and England, so much nearer and comprehensible to us, are more instructive because more applicable to our condition, which is not unlike theirs. Or must we go to Greece and Rome to learn to be Americans?

There is unquestionably beauty in the severe simplicity of the works of art of the Greeks, but the immaculate nature of the Greek ideal and its inapproachable excellence and perfection are dogmas akin to those of the old Church and the infallible Pope. The Greeks were no more ideal men than we or any other can be. We all are one or another thing, we are Greeks, French, Germans, English, Americans, etc., and ideal men exist only in the imagination.

14*

The world has not stood still in art no more than in any other thing, and poetry, sculpture, painting and architecture have advanced beyond what they were in ancient Greece, nothwithstanding the assurance of men who would make us believe the ancients were infallible and immaculate in art and in matters of church and religion.

But let us look a little closer at this would-be ideal world of the ancients, to which we so anxiously send our sons and daughters for examples. Let us look at Athens with its narrow, filthy streets, mean dwellings, public halls and temples. Slaves meet us at every step, the temples are reeking with the blood of victims, the state is filled with party strife, revolutions follow as fast upon one another as thick clouds in stormy weather; the great patriots are rewarded with ingratitude; the party that wins murders the party that loses, and plunders it; the sweetness and sacredness of quiet family life is hardly known, neither the amenities of modern life; newspapers, picture galleries, or our quiet places of amusements are not known; boxing, prizefighting and the like pleasures, are national; war is almost incessant, and the taxes are very high. In Rome the abominable combats with wild beasts or men in the arena of the colosseum are the great delight. Education is left to the slaves; public information is at a low ebb; industry supplies but poorly the wants of men; a well-regulated state or religion is not known; superstition reigns supreme, and the flight of birds and the mutterings of an epileptic priest decide the most important political events involving the existence of the state.

It is hard for us to emancipate ourselves from the old Catholic superstition, that there is no soundness in us, and that truth and beauty lived and died with the ancients, though the masses were slaves and women were treated not much better, and infants worse. Strangers were called barbarians, and on all possible occasions sold into slavery. There was but little humanity in the general arrangements at Athens and Rome. National pride and barbarity even rose to the bloody infamy of human sacrifices. Passion and ambition did not recoil from civil war and oppression, and rich as well as poor were corrupt and venal. And from the literature of such nations our sons and daughters are to learn humanity and ideal culture?

If there is any such ideal in their literature, the tyro, bewildered with the ten thousand difficulties besetting the reading of a language dead for two thousand years, cannot find it.

Does any one seriously contemplate that nature, painting, lithographs, and drawing cannot develop our æsthetic powers and fill the place of heathen mythology? If the gods of Olympus were really so potent, we ought to recall them by all means, and become pagans again.

Modern nations need not go for patriots and statesmen to Rome, with its bloody Cæsars, or to Athens, with its demagogues.

But even if antiquity had unequalled politicians and historians, they would naturally be beyond the comprehension of youngsters, and would, therefore, be without educational value to us.

Homer, Sophocles, Thucydides, Cicero, Virgil, Horace and Tacitus have not written for youths, who, not penetrating them, cannot be improved by excellencies which are beyond their mental reach.

As far as composition is concerned, our modern languages, so easily learned and so useful in many regards—at least the French, Italian, German and English—are as grand and spirited, and certainly as logical and perspicuous as Latin or Greek.

The shallow cosmopolitan indifference that underates national pride and honor is the forerunner of national corruption and decay. One of the great duties of public Education is to strengthen and elevate the national feeling and love of country, and to foster the better genius of the nation.

A thorough acquaintance with the English language, its poets, historians and philosophers, would far more benefit us than the present Latin and Greek pretense.

Modern nations have poets equal to any of antiquity, and, certainly, historians and philosophers; but their scientific writers and thinkers are unquestionably more exact and solid than any Greece or Rome had produced, and these modern languages and literatures are infinitely richer in productions and are more applicable to educational purposes than the languages of antiquity.

The antique state was despotic, whatever its form was. With modern nations freedom of the individual and organic development are foundation principles of civilization, and these we best promote by the study of great modern authors.

The great Vico deprecates the influence of the ancient poets on the passions. Their heroes are not only without humanity, but even without manliness. Agamemnon pierces his unfortunate suppliant with his spear, and setting his foot upon his body pulled it out. Hector drags through the dust dead Patrocles, as Achilles does Hector; and the Greeks are represented, one after another, stabbing the dead remains of the latter hero. Sovereigns are massacred and their bodies left a prey to dogs and vultures; sucking infants are dashed against the pavement, and ladies of highest rank are made to perform the lowest acts of slavery. Blood, fraud and meanest cowardice are the features of Homer's brutal heroes. Murder is no sin with Homer,

neither fraud degrading, nor cowardly skulking before superior strength unbefitting his heroes, who,
being cruel and inhuman, are not truly heroic,
though eminent for savagery.

Hecuba, in Euripides, is chained like a dog to
Agamemnon's gate. Prometheus, in Æschylus, is
fastened by a chain, nailed one end to a rock, and
the other end to his breast bone. In the Electra
of Sophocles a woman is represented murdered by
her children. In the tragedy of Alcestis, Admetus
insists upon his beloved wife to die for him,
and scolds his father indecently to do the same
thing.

With such brutal and cowardly acts these writers
are teeming, and they are held up to us as our
models. What wonder, then, that there is so little
moral progress among us!

We do not like to lift the veil from what is most
reprehensible in the life and writings of the ancients.
Their bordering on the brute state of man may be
taken for an apology for that; but they must not
be forced upon us as patterns. We may cut out all
the passages in which that animalism appears in all
its nudity; still, should we clear the classics of all
that springs from that spirit, little would be left,
and, hence, we protest against the idolatry made
of the classics.

So coarse and indelicate were the Romans that

whipping was a punishment inflicted on even high officers in the army.

To live by plunder was held honorable among the Greeks; for it was their opinion that the rules of justice are not intended for the restriction of the powerful. The policy of the Greeks and Romans in war was to weaken a state by plundering its territory and destroying its people.

The Romans eternally warred upon other nations. Let us take Lucullus' behavior toward Cauca, a city he attacked, for it is but an illustration of other similar acts. They surrendered upon his promise to garrison them for their own protection. Instead of which he enriched himself by plundering the city, leaving 20,000 dead upon the spot. Cæsar, Pompey, Crassus and all the other Romans were men of rapacity and lust; and as their deeds are learned by our youths in an old and difficult tongue they fall deep into the soul and form their hearts and minds upon these execrable models, and, hence, our cruel disregard for the victims of our greed.

When we consider men, such as Sir Robert Peel, Lord Brougham or Ashley, and their life-long labors in the British Parliament in behalf of the working people, does it not seem as if the genius of humanity and industry presides over us to-day, and that under its inspirations the rising generation would make better men, than under the influence of rapacious Rome or cruel Greece? It may be well for the man to know what was practiced at Greece, Rome or somewhere else; but must we, therefore, make the minds of our susceptible youths the sinks of execrable wickedness?

We belie, degrade and render weak and inefficient our modern standard of moral excellency, which is a pure spiritualism, by making our models in Education the ancients, the life and soul of whom are rapacity, power, lust, deep dissimulation—as bloody Cæsar playing democrat or Cicero augur, consulting mice and chickens on mighty affairs of state—and a sensuousness bordering on pure animalism.

Let none think that the intellectual culture, generally derived from the study of the classics, outweighs the moral disadvantages; for, if we take the results of the inquiry of the Royal Commission on Education of Great Britain, a most insignificant minority of the students of the best colleges of England are at all profited by their Latin and Greek. "The number of well taught classical scholars at the university notoriously form a small proportion." "Very few coming from Christ Church, Oxford, to the university can construe accurately in Latin or Greek a piece from an author they have studied. It would be useless to try them with a new passage, a test they could not stand at all."

Dr. Fitch says before the British Association for Social Science: "Of the many who have studied Latin, how many of them ever open a Latin book? How many have caught the spirit of ancient Roman life or polity, or acquired an insight into Roman literature, or have a trace of their school-Latin left on their minds and opinions?

" The study of the classics usually ceases before the student begins to profit by it, and is, therefore, utterly useless. It is like mounting up a steep hill, and then stop outside the temple on the summit."

" The study of the classics comes in far too many cases to absolutely nothing; that it rather deadens than awakens thought ; that it stimulates no literary appetite, and that it is not even indirectly helpful in enabling the pupil to write his own language with fluency and grace." Mr. Fitch, speaking before the British Association in this manner, is recognized by this most learned body as a man of great authority and experience in Education, having been the principal of eminent training colleges and holding the position of one of Her Maj- ˙ esty's Inspectors of Schools.

Dr. Hey gives his testimony as to the many hopeless youths sacrificed in the Latin schools to the hopeful few for the sake of making a good verse maker.

The royal commission and the witnesses brought

before them, though all classical men, admit " The public Latin schools send out the ablest scholars and also the idlest and most ignorant men." " Of the time spent at the Latin schools by the generality of boys much is absolutely thrown away, etc." " With a great mass of men it takes them to twenty or twenty-one to construe a Latin and Greek book they have studied already at school, to master three books in Euclid and to solve a quadratic equation."

But, notwithstanding these unwilling confessions, the very able men of the Royal Commission on Education are statesmen, and as long as the domineering spirit and the diplomatic ability of prelates, nobles and kings are to be trained, for such work the schools of the Cæsars and of the Athenian oligarchs are by their nature most fit, and, hence, their high encomiums upon Latin and Greek for the high classes in society.

We see the impediment to progress in so many symbols as there are words in the Chinese language, which the scholar has to learn before he can give himself up to the acquisition of valuable knowledge. But is our devoting years to Greek and Latin grammar any less retarding us in our progress ?

The question has often been propounded before, why do men so rarely continue their Education and self-improvement on leaving school? Our answer is, because during their school years their brain powers or molecules have been absorbed by the impressions of useless things forced upon their attention, and on their entering the world things can make but a dull impression on minds scribbled all over. Teach children what has a bearing on their future occupation, and it will turn up in their mind with freshness; it will shed light on and deepen similar impressions and ideas, and form between them all possible interconnections of cause and effect, setting them thus to think and improve and educate them through life.

Admitting the Greeks and Romans were the first in civilization in the order of time; must we, on that account, waste our years on them? Must we ride on a log because this was the shape and nature of the original wagon before the wheel—not to speak of steam—was invented?

Much of what we advance has been said before us by Locke, Vico, Lord Kames, Korner and others, but is not less true for that, and will be repeated after us until it is profitably applied by the schools.

Has there no progress been made in civilization, or the art of thinking and writing? If the hundred generations of philosophers since the days of Greece and Rome—for every generation has its philosophers—have not sufficiently improved upon one another in that long stretch of time so as to lose out of sight in the gloom of the past Greece and Rome, pity man and his poor capacity. He better give up at once the futile attempt of ever learning or knowing anything and set about eating grass like any other ox.

Hosanna! it resounds from all over the land, great is the goddess Diana! Let pedagogues moderate their shoutings and their fears, our railings will injure neither the goddess nor their trade, for, if peradventure we have said anything sensible, the crowd will be sure not to mind it.

THE PROPER EMPLOYMENT OF TIME.

We do not trust business transactions to the un-aided memory; why, then, should the golden sands of life be allowed to run down without a daily and hourly account? Time, says our immortal Franklin, is not short, but poorly managed. The relations of life are too multifarious to be properly attended to if left at loose ends. Self-knowledge, so material to self-improvement, requires an exact account with ourselves, and the sages of all ages, down to Bacon, Montaigne and our own Franklin, have all insisted upon managing our time and keeping a systematic journal, in which we render account of our hours and very minutes.

Such an account will keep us in mind that our life is not wholly our own, but belongs to the race. Our cash account does not add to our cash—the account of our inner life is a most valuable addition to our spiritual capital. We keep strict account of our means and let the power that creates them float away unheeded. A continual watch over our thoughts, desires and actions will grow into a spontaneous self-control, until, in the course of ages, action, reflection and self-control will be one and irseparable in the race.

A strict training to a steady and regular employment of time is an excellent means for the formation of habits which, growing functionally and organic, become in the end unmistakable features of the race.

Only through the close observation of the self-recorded thoughts and feelings of ages will we attain a veritable mental science, which is alike indispensable for a correct Education, the treatment of criminals and the insane, the government of men by laws, and for a proper conduct in life.

To record honestly, therefore, our inner life, is to lay a foundation, without which every science of man, his life, actions and happiness is impossible.

The slow moral progress is a sad riddle to many. But does improvement in morals not mean improvement in self-government? And how can we

improve in this, if we do not improve in self-knowledge by keeping a steady watch over the employment of our time, life and actions.

MEN, WOMEN AND THEIR SPHERES.

The preservation of the race being the end of
Education, man, as the natural provider of the
family, must be industrially educated; and woman,
the mother of the race and the guardian of the
family, must be brought up with a view to these
her natural functions, which are to-day sacrificed in
a most pernicious manner—both in school as well
as in the factory—to the most material injury of
the race. Life is much shorter in districts with
textile industries, where women work, as a rule, in
factories; and our daughters, who are put through
the higher course of studies in our seminaries and
high schools, do not, as a rule, enjoy the good
health their mothers did.

Forgetting that language is as often the medium
of error or falsehood as of truth, we make reading,
writing and speaking the whole of Education. We
ought to remember that the art of reading and
writing is not culture, it is the mere opportunity
for it, and is often unused and forgotten by the
masses after they have acquired it. The aim of
popular Education must be something higher and
more substantial. Next to the preservation and

improvement of the race, the chiefest care of Education must be industry, which alone can lead to universal culture and the reign of eternal truth and justice, or the kingdom of God upon earth.

INDUSTRY, HEALTH, COMFORT AND HAPPINESS.

Industry must take the place of sloth and idleness—the fountain head of pauperism and all the hellish brood at its heel—and the satisfaction arising from an intelligent and well-ordered activity must banish the unhealthy craving after low pleasures with their demoralizing effects upon individuals and communities.

The preservation of the race being the true end of Education, the comfort, health and happiness of the individual must be all secured, and, hence, the science of life must take the place of the empty formalism of word teaching. Food, fabrics, houses, windows, stoves, and the bearings of the like things upon human health and happiness, are matters falling under the observation of the senses, plain to the young understanding, and are best suited to prepare for further scientific knowledge and practical work.

THE SCIENCE OF THINGS.

The science of things and common sense must be brought to bear upon the health and comfort of

the individual, and our elementary course of instruction must be made as full of things as it has
hitherto been full of words.

The effort scientific England is making to lift up
the masses to a higher level of culture and well-
being through spreading among them the rudi-
ments of a scientific knowledge of the things of
life, art and industry, industrial training, cheap
publications, art, industrial and economical museums, command our attention, and exhort us to
enter with like earnestness upon the same work.

French, piano, dancing-masters, and the semi-
barbarous, haughty and disgusting airs of ridiculous
vanity notwithstanding, as far as solid excellency
is concerned and the things leading to usefulness,
efficiency, health, comfort, goodness and happiness,
not the first step has as yet been taken in raising
man rightly; and yet this is the highest work of
the state as well as of the family.

We grow, of course, by the law of nature and by
necessity; but man ought to be his own maker,
and the state ought to be a providence shaping man
to a noble purpose. There is nothing greater nor
more divinely beautiful than a noble man or woman, and the time will come and is even near at hand,
when a child from the cradle to full maturity will
be physically, morally, intellectually and industrially the tender care of the state as well as of the
family.

If the system we propose is utilitarian, our principle of utility is of the highest order, referring, as it does, to the preservation and improvement of the race. To-day, alas! we make money, and unmake man; but we shall soon find out that even in the material order of things the making of man must precede the making of money. An efficient industry requires health and science, and a prosperous commerce is impossible without confidence and honesty, which rest upon a universal moral consciousness.

THE CULTIVATION OF ALTRUISM.

We may daily hear in the shops or read in the works of philosophers that old prejudices are dying away and new ideas are acquired, but society is not improved. Still, John Stuart Mill adds in his memoirs, this cannot be due to the unalterable disposition or nature of man. For just as well as Education, habit and public opinion make men willing to fight and die for the state, they can also be disposed to work for the good of society.

Race Education as a whole and a system replacing selfish individualism by an altruistic disposition rendered hereditary by the training of generations, will ultimately save humanity from the miseries and troubles of the present fratricidal struggle, and mitigates the want and the sufferings

15

of the masses of to-day by insisting upon a varied industrial training as one of the chief elements in the Education of the people.

LABORERS MUST MAKE THEIR OWN MARKET.

The connection between ever-recurring stagnations of trade and the uncertainties of foreign commerce has long been noticed, but the deeper and more universal cause of the restriction of the home market, and its possible removal, have hitherto escaped economists. The producing masses living in large cities have no means left for purchasing manufactured articles, rent and provisions consuming their wages. With our present powers of locomotion, this difficulty can be surmounted, and the excess of the mischief of city life in every other direction, as life, health and Education, will soon force us to seek relief from these and other troubles in suburban residence.

The reader may suspect us of forgetting that we are writing about Education, as we obviously lose sight altogether of Latin, Greek, grammar, stump-speaking and the like school accomplishments of the present day, considering, as we do, mainly the housing, clothing and feeding of the people, their health and decent living, all of which being achieved not so much by each striving for himself as for humanity, we leave refinement and culture to take care of themselves. To this we plead guilty, but hope for an honorable acquittal at the bar of the future.

The present movement of the population toward large cities gives ascendency to deteriorating tendencies, and is an important question of civilization.

For, if the people are not sound in body, neither can they be sound in mind, government, or politics. Corrupt blood necessarily produces corrupt morals and institutions. The hectic flush of a consumptive people is apt to repeat itself in the appearance of the state and government, as private madness is apt to end in public folly, and private suicides in civil war, in which a nation ends its own life.

All great statesmen, writers and economists agree that nothing is more apt to lay a firm foundation for social order and conservative interests in a society of democratic tendencies than a multitude of small property owners, in whom the state is always certain to find the element of order and the spirit of industry and peace. This system of small properties, introduced by Napoleon in France and wherever his arms proved victorious, has been long on trial; and the economy, the prudence, the industry, the order it spreads, have everywhere brought it in favor. The wildest revolutionary elements of the large cities of France have been unavailing against it; and in this republic, too, nothing but a solid wall of small industrial property owners will secure the peace of society.

Capitalists will find it as well to their advantage as to the advantage of the laborers to locate in the country. And how vastly preferable is to the young the companionship of nature with her sublimities and beauties to the dense city with its crowded lanes and squalid abodes—nurseries of meanness, vice and crime.

Capital, labor, human life, government and civilization would not only be great gainers by the industrial classes domiciling themselves on the lands surrounding our large cities, but their very existence imperatively demands it, as the moral poison engendered where great masses of population concentrate, is positively destructive to the social health of society.

The city breeds moral, social, economical and political pests and is the hearth of general disorder. Vice, crime and corruption among high and low are at home there. Close contact between the rich and opulent and the poor and the miserable, fills the latter with bitterness, which ends in strikes and agrarian disorders. Matrimonial bonds, recklessly formed by the hopeless laborer, swell the population beyond reason. Then come the pests, crowding breeds, which are more destructive, because more constant than the pests of the Middle Ages. In three generations the city laborers are swept away with nothing left behind them but plenty of graves, showing by their small size that their occupants had but few days here, and these full of misery. The country population fills the gap, to be soon swept away like those of whom they took the place. And thus the moloch of the city devours the children of the land, until all health is gone. In the moral confusion attending such social corruption the turbulent and the ambitious soon find their account, and the government proves as short-lived as the people.

The country gives the laborer a home; it gives him plenty of heaven's pure air, light, pleasure, sensibility, happiness, contentment, health, energy and peace and good-will. It gives him stability, character and efficiency, and personal consideration. In the city he dies from want of all this. His heart fills, therefore, with bitterness. He is a houseless, forlorn vagabond, full of unrest and unstable, without property, a home or anything to live for or to look forward to and hope for. He feels as an outcast, an Ishmael, with everybody's hand against him, and his hand is, therefore, against everybody.

An intelligent and industrious people, with our vast country for our home, under the sweet influences of green fields and the smiles of the wide heavens upon us, our future might be as long as God's own years; but double our tenement population and we perish. Still, how is it with London, Paris, Berlin, Vienna and the like cities? Well, they are hotbeds of revolution, burning craters watched by half a million of soldiers, whose organizations can only be kept up by an occasional war costing the trifle of a half a milliard.

But what has all this to do with Education? Simply this, that with a tenement population the Education of the heart, mind and morals is absolutely impossible.

A healthy community is impossible without the union of the schoolhouse, the home and the workshop, symbolical of the head, heart and stomach of which they have respectively to take care.

The sacredness of human life is the ethical aspect of Education, the natural function of which we have shown to be self-preservation.

The bloody strife has but been transferred from the battle-field to the exchange, but the victims are as vitally affected in the one case as in the other. If common laborers are not sure of their to-morrow's bread, capitalists are no more safe nor spared; though with them it may be a matter of months or of a few years. According to mercantile statistics but 5 merchants in 100 in Boston, 4 in 100 in New York City and 3 in 100 in Philadelphia succeed in business.

The fact is, modern life has not as yet accommodated itself to the great revolution of our grand industry working with steam and machinery.

The new system requires manufacturing on the largest scale for the largest market. Cheap manufacturing alone does not answer; for, when wages are very low, the masses cannot be consumers of articles of manufacture; business comes, therefore, to a standstill and a deadly stagnation follows.

As international commerce has taught us that the prosperity of neighboring nations is indispensable to our own national success, so does the necessity of a home market teach us the necessity of caring for the prosperity of our own people.

Nothing but a thorough industrial Education and understanding of the economical interests of society can lead to the necessary union between labor and capital, and give peace and prosperity to the present disturbed and suffering industrial world.

As machinery is expensive, rapidly wearing out and liable to be superseded by mechanical improvements, it must be used to its full power, especially as the additional cost is not at all in proportion to the increased production, and, hence, the tendency to over-production, over-trading, financial crises, business stagnations and want of employment. But even in times of prosperity the usual trades cannot afford to pay for the labor of one man wages sufficient to buy for his family bread, meat, lard, butter, milk, vegetables, clothing, to pay his house rent, incidental house expenses and insure him against sickness and death. It is evident a man must have all this; still his claim upon it is not a question of right, but of fact. Does he produce it? he certainly does not. Communism, socialism or co-operation do not solve this problem, which becomes more troublesome daily with the increase of improved machinery, the increase of population and the decrease of real wages. To our mind there is but one solution of the social question arising from the new condition of things, which is, in proportion as the increase of improved machinery supersedes human exertions, man must employ his labor more upon the soil, in which rooted, he will like a firm tree weather every storm. Every workman must have his house and his acre, he must raise his meat, his milk, his butter, his vegetables, live rent free, and with his factory labor he must provide for all other family wants. There is hope and encouragement in the acquisition of a homestead. A man should not be paralyzed by the fear of houseless misery, neither should all his wants be secured to him without the full display of his energies in his daily labor. The rendition of man to the soil removes a thousand complications.

Unscrupulous demagogues incite the masses to

claim the share due to capital. Thoughtless capitalists propose no remedy, and call upon the armed power to put down the strikers who, of course, have no right to disturb the public peace. But hunger does not stand upon right, it asks for bread. Meanwhile riot upon riot demoralizes the people, class is arrayed against class, and anarchy and despotism are growing upon us until at last we cannot sleep in peace without an army standing watch over us, and industry is ground between the upper stone or a standing army and the nether stone or the starving masses, and the expenses in which they involve the state in a thousand ways. To some there may be no problem in our present social condition; bayonets and starvation will mellow down the work-people to work at half starvation wages. But if the masses are half starved, who are to be our customers? and a system of labor which converted the people into a herd of vicious criminals and incendiaries is dear at any rate. We must improve the condition of the masses, for with them we live or sink in the end. Whatever assists the people in moving from the city to the country and aids them in acquiring homes there, contributes to the health, peace and prosperity of society, and spreads a healthy civilization.

We have been driven to the conclusion, as machinery supersedes human hands, labor must employy

15*

itself on the soil; but this is but half and perhaps the lesser half of the truth, the more important part is, as the production of our material wants needs less labor, more labor will be bestowed upon man himself and upon his Education, and as this will be better understood, the blessings of machinery will be more appreciated. The fewer hands are needed for the production of articles of comfort, the more and the longer can children be left to the school and its humanizing influences, and the more can woman devote herself in the school and the family to the work of Education, fitting humanity for peace, for order, for love and for happiness; and the more can be shortened the hours of labor and manly toil mingle with study and contemplation.

We dwell here only upon physical deterioration and its effect upon morals. But the action of every mental and moral power and faculty oscillates between extremes, and, hence, the constant tendency toward aberration from the perfect and the danger of mental and moral deterioration.

At one phase of civilization the reason and conscience of the age are all in a torpor; at another, the one is all subtlety and the other sensitive to morbidity. And even at the same age all phases of civilization are simultaneously produced in people living in different conditions.

One end of society living in want of everything inclines to brutality, while the other end living in luxury runs into effeminacy leading to corruption of another sort.

The animalism of the masses must be corrected by the application of science to the common occupations of life, and the effeminacy of the over-refined must be overcome by the association of physical labor and exercise with intellectual culture; for reason and the senses are correctives of one another, and must prevent the brutality of barbarism and the corruption of over-refinement; and, hence, we see the necessity of combining science and industrial pursuits with the customary branches of Education as the correctives of the respective vices of the classes which occupy the opposite extremes in society.

Disparaging these opposite vicious tendencies, and favoring science and genuine culture, we discard but scholastic verbalism, as out of time and place in the industrial world of to-day.

The struggle for existence is as inexorable a factor in society as it is in nature, and that Education is, therefore, the best which, increasing the bread-winning capacity of the masses, sustains them in that struggle and gives them a chance under the law of the survival of the fittest: and that, Industrial Education alone can accomplish.

PART VI.

THE PEOPLE AND THEIR HOMES.

As the homes are so are the people, is an adage Race Education cannot afford to overlook. The shell is no more part of the oyster than the home is part of the man, who is more made by his home than his home by him. What light and heat are to the plant, home is to man. As climatic influences modify organic forms, so does home, the climate of man, ever modify man and his faculties.

The plant is no more rooted in the soil than man is. Myriads of ages man has wandered in the forests and green fields under the sweet influences of the azure sky, and their presence is to him health and strength. This ocean of light and beauty streaming into the eye is the quickening power of the life and activity of the brain and the nervous system, to which it is what the vivifying air is to the blood. Death and disease, like vice and crime and every other poison, ripen in the shade, and are in very deed the work of darkness. Place man in his correct relation to nature, and every possible

(348)

discord disappears from the individual and collective life of man.

The country is man's natural home. In the city his health deteriorates and his intellect degenerates by lack or excess of mental exercise; luxury or want debases his morals; politically he is made the dupe of demagogues or is enslaved by tyrants; his life is shortened, his very type is lowered, until within a few generations the stock itself becomes extinct.

What disadvantages attach to the homes, or rather barracks, of the masses in the city, which are insalubrious in respect to light, heat, air, dampness, soil, construction and surroundings, besides the effect of fearful crowding, deadly competition, temptations to vice and crime, evil associations, causes and opportunities for envy, hate and strife, while in the country all the elements and surroundings contribute to strengthen and invigorate man for his work and his duties, everything calming his passions and supporting his reason.

We hold with the old tradition that man is not made to become Godlike in knowledge, but to work the ground; and this command to cultivate the earth of which we are taken—which nurses us and to which we return—is binding alike upon princes, poets, tailors or presidents. We are all better off by complying with it, and invariably suffer for disobeying it.

Every school should cultivate a taste for agriculture as well as for the mechanic arts. An hour or two daily devoted to the cultivation of a garden patch will add to our effectiveness in our calling by improving our health of body and soul, by enlivening us through change of labor or exercise, and by bringing us into a more living sympathy with nature, and the great masses, whose whole life is devoted to the cultivation of the ground.

It has been well observed that as development in the organic world depends, according to Darwin, on variability and permanency in the genesis of forms, so is social improvement conditioned by legality and progress or conservatism and reform—which are in the political world, what the centripetal and centrifugal forces are in the cosmos, and of which the one would end in the rigidity of death while the other would bring infinite division and atomic isolation.

The city represents change and reform. The individual is driven from position to position by a mass of events he cannot control. We are changed and carried away by a whirlwind of events. We hardly can collect ourselves or assimilate facts and experience into elements of internal growth, character and a harmonious individuality.

The country is conservative. There man can master the impressions which rush in upon him

with less impetuosity; and as they are coming less
from the heated strife of an artificial world and
more from objects of nature, their effect upon man
is invigorating and less apt to incline him to
feverish activity.

Organization, stability and law were of the
greatest necessity, when in the infancy of the race
communities were forming, and, hence, the agricultural state in which the legal and conservative
spirit predominates was then most conducive to
human civilization. After men have become order-
loving, cities best serve the cause of civilization,
by bringing life, motion and progress into human
affairs. The present system of manufacture causes
a steady rush into already populous cities, and dis-
turbs the balance between the two principles of
permanence and reform, represented by country
and city, the union of which our means of communication render feasible, as the space our dwellings spread over becomes daily a matter of less importance, as we annihilate it by the power of steam.

By associating the conditions of city and country
life, we unite the progressive tendencies of the one
with the conservative of the other, and thus keep
up a healthy social development, while the country
alone leads to death through stagnation, and the
city through revolution to anarchy and dissolution.

Freedom is the chief element of man's moral

nature. But freedom is a fiction without power which property of some sort or other bestows. There is hardly manhood or dignity without as much property as will give a man standing room in the world. Property is, therefore, a moral necessity. In the Middle Ages, when the feudal lords owned the land, the industries in the cities gave the people a moral existence by giving them an opportunity to achieve property. To-day, when the manufacturing interests in the cities are owned by our industrial lords, the people must acquire homes and property in the country or become again penniless vagabonds without moral or political existence, the slaves of a *régime* more powerful than any of the past.

Manufacturing in large cities must give way to manufacturing all over the country, or the deterioration arising from trade diseases, combined with the deterioration peculiar to crowded cities, will degenerate humanity. And this putting side by side the manufacturer and the agriculturist, or the cotton and wool raiser with the spinner and weaver, is the solution of many a troublesome problem in social philosophy. For it decreases the machinery of transporting raw material and manufactured goods and turns men and capital engaged in the carrying trade into manufacturing, which is enlarged, while commerce, speculation, bank operations, panics--

always springing up from the latter or sudden calling in of credit—business stagnations and public distress will be lessened.

Land without men and men without land are equally valueless. Combined they enhance each other's value. In proportion as men crowd into small areas, the land reaches a fabulous figure and a man's worth falls below that of the brute.

Let men spread all over the land, and the value of both will be equally enhanced. Henry C. Carey says with much truth, by this law alone we can escape the miseries and not far-off revolutions of England, the civilization of which is the last an honest republic would try to install. Not foreign commerce, but home trade and manufacture we must enlarge; the first is full of danger and uncertainties, the latter is safe and reliable. A country with resources sufficient for the support of 200 millions population can grandly prosper on the internal trade and manufacture of an industrial population of fifty millions.

England, not as large as many a one of our forty states, and with colonies all over the globe, seeks above all, foreign commerce; and its economists pretend to favor this course upon scientific principles. But a glance at the condition of England shows that foreign commerce carried on to excess is a curse to any nation.

According to a late competent observer the *élite* of skilled mechanics in England, by rigid economy, may manage to subsist in tolerable comfort, though not without the wolf growling audibly at the door.

Next rank the wages of the skilled craftsman. After supplying him with clothes and shelter, they leave him about half enough to eat. Half-starved clerks may be ranked with this class.

Farm laborers, porters and the regular employees of commerce, systematically famish upon their wages.

Next comes the job laborer, who fasts when he can get work, and starves when he is without it.

Lower yet is the shop girl, on duty fifteen hours a day, for a pittance inadequate to the supply of her necessary wants—the seamstress earning four shillings a week, slowly dying of over-work and privation—and the servant girl to whom is doled out a shilling a week and one hour recreation once a fortnight.

Lower still are millions without regular work, or home, or food, hopeless, starving, dying—literally dying upon doorsteps, where they have crowded for shelter under hedges, where they have lain down from the wind; upon heaps of ordure, where they have groveled for the warmth derived from the reeking exhalations. The cities of England are crowded with this unhappy class of beings. They meet the eye upon every street—too numerous to attract attention or sympathy.

Thus the very élite of labor in England is famine-pinched and hunger-driven. Millions pine, hopeless, joyless, slowly famishing upon wages insufficient for subsistence, and the homeless outcasts of the cities perish for want of employment.

With such a certificate from the famishing masses of England, we must be excused if, without giving here any further reasons, we prefer our American system to the commercial system of England, in which there is no more science than in the lion on the British flag.

We dwell on the economical aspects of homes and dwellings, for whatever produces wealth produces health and strength and civilization, and whatever destroys wealth destroys life and health, and spreads all the evils attending barbarism.

There is no more powerful agency than home. Schools and compulsory laws are of no effect without it, and whatever undermines it must be put down as most hostile to the cause of civilization.

Expensiveness of living in large towns makes pregnant mothers overwork themselves to the very hour of delivery, the result of which in the newly-born child is marasmus—constitutional weakness—the natural disease of the higher stages of old age. The same cause necessitates them to work in fac-

tories and to deprive their infants of their most
natural food—the mother's milk—through which
they fall tenfold a prey to disease and death.

The same expensiveness of living in large towns
forces mothers to go out to work and leave their
little ones locked up in an empty room where brutal
isolation trains them to idiocy.

This same expensiveness of living in large towns
which has forced the mothers to leave their home
for the factory, forces children to leave the school
for the same place, and thus deprives the masses
of their Education and the means of bettering their
condition. Worse than all this, a home without a
wife, without children, without any attractiveness,
in which hardly anything but misery, death and
disease are bred, make the family burdensome to
men and women who, shunning such a state, avoid
marriage and live in all sorts of vicious indulgences,
ending in crime and corruption and the dissolution
of society. All this may be of no moment to some
men, but the expensiveness of living in large towns
absorbs all the earnings of the work-people for bare
bread and shelter, and leaves them no means for
procuring articles of manufacture. This, too, may
be of no importance to some. But when the masses
do not buy, the small traders do not sell. This
looks a little more serious and assumes its full importance when we consider that, if the retailers do

not sell, neither can they buy, nor can the whole-
sale man sell or the factory manufacture, and, hence,
misery and stagnation overtake all classes.

The masses may be the lowest and least noticeable portion of the community, but it is also the
foundation of the whole structure and the pyramid
of society, which tumbles into the dust when its
broad basis is withdrawn.

There is not a consideration of health, life or
death, of Education, morals, government or economics but is in favor of workmen's homes in the
country. But facts speak louder than arguments,
and we shall turn our attention to them, as we are
convinced that we serve best the cause of Education by urging homes for the people. For, if the
people have good homes—if they have schools or
not—they have the best part of a good Education
anyhow; while, if they have no homes, the best
schools are but whited sepulchres full of dead bones.

To illustrate the condition of the people and their
dwellings in populous factory towns, we need not
cross the ocean. Writing in the midst of a city of
over half a million of tenement population we are
surrounded by misery appalling in degree and frightful in extent; but as our responsibility for what of
this sort is happening right at our door is blinding
us to the condition of the homes of our people,
we shall at first transfer our social studies to

a more remote scene, where we can afford to be more impartial witnesses of events—to France and England—countries ahead of all others in manufacturing, and which may serve us as a warning, as in proportion as we adopt their system the same results will follow, and which, perhaps, has already transpired to an extent we are unwilling to admit.

A study of the industrial classes in France shows them in the smaller towns pleasantly located in neat houses, with savings in proportion to wages. In large cities, where the houses are unpleasant and the family is anything but attractive, higher wages bring only dissipation. Of 12 to 15 children, 3 to 4 survive. In Rouen, of 3,000 children, 1,100 die before the expiration of the first year. Most of the children of the factory people are farmed out, and 83 of 100 are left to die from starvation. Expensiveness of living forces the mother to go to the factory as well as the father, where they both work long and hard; the children, neglected and suffering, die, leaving but few, and they are crippled and puny, to the dissatisfaction of the grumbling conscription officer, who feels himself cheated out of his recruits. Here, as in all great centres of industry, dwellings are poor, and, consequently, drunkenness, misery and the ravages of licentiousness eat up the people.

The alleys, houses, rooms and furniture are filthy

and miserable beyond description, left most of the
time to the neglected little savages, the mother
having neither time nor strength left to clean, wash
or sweep, cook, or feed her little ones. She can do
nothing for her family, neither can she take an
interest in it nor be a companion to her husband,
who, coming home, finds nothing but filth most
repulsive, insufficient and poor food, children he
hardly knows, and a woman work and misery have
reduced to a veritable slave. And what of the
children during all the day? There is not an hour
of affection or joyous childhood for them. The
dingy home, the factory, the hospital and the
grave are all of life, and the last is the best.

The child of six is kept home partly from weakness and partly to take care of two, three or four
little crying children. The school may keep some
of the children five to six hours, but, of course, the
parents stay away twice as long. The women can
neither sew, mend, knit or do any housework. Not
half the work-people, when their children are sick—
which is only too often the case—have money for
bedding, food, medicine, or even fire. The physicians
say in half of the cases good food is all that is
needed, but they dare not tell it to the family who
have not the means.

And yet all this misery is as nothing. This want
of bread, these rags, these dingy, dark and damp,

chilly, miserable chambers and cellars or garret-rooms, and even loathsome diseases and burning fevers, they are as nothing compared to the soul-devouring poison that grows in such foulness. Hardened by misery they are used to and know not how to escape, fathers spend their nights in drinking places, while their children die with hunger, mothers become indifferent to the vices of their daughters and act as their confidants and counsellors in prostitution, and neither father nor mother incline to save their children from the perdition which threatens them.

The mortality of Rouen—as in other industrial centres—is simply murderous. Devilliers shows that of 100 children the best situated citizens lose 10 under the age of 1 year, the work people lose 35! Of the children farmed out by the factory people, 90 in 100 die in the first year in most of the departments of France. In Eure-de-Loire 95 of 100 die. Of 27,219 children in this department 8,037 died within one year. There were 1,389 illegitimate children, of whom 1,333 died after one year (1862). In the asylum of Loire-Inférieure 90.50 per cent., and in Seine-Inférieure 87.36 per cent. of the children died under one year.

Hunger-driven mothers work to the hour of delivery, and, hence, this mortality among their feeble children, who have not the strength to overcome the additional misery that is put upon them. Poor mothers! all day at work and nursing all night with empty breasts, children starving all day, this is killing game for mother and child.

What a city home! father and mother gone; an empty room; no fire in the stove; a baby in the crib; a girl of six doing the work of a mother. Or little dirty, ragged children fighting in the filthy lane about a dirty thing, hard to say what it is and which is beneath the notice of dogs, they are locked out, and vagabondage is forced upon them. If the children live to eight or ten years, their days of factory slavery begin. The working people in the large cities of France are worse housed than prisoners. No jailer would keep prisoners with so little air, light or food. Their dwellings are simply murderous. No room for anything, for attending to anything or even for turning around. No separation of sexes or decency possible. Men, women and children sleep all in the same bed. The room is often in the cellar or under the garret, exposed to wind or rain; everything rots, and the inhabitants are constant victims of rheumatism and skin diseases. There is no accommodation for anything; everything has to be bought in smallest quantities and in the most expensive way. The chimneys are often poor and the smoke blinding. In most contagious diseases, so common in such quarters, isola-

16

tion is impossible. Coming from his labor to such a dark, damp, uncomfortable hole, the poor man is repelled and almost driven to the public house, which completes his ruin.

Villermé showed under these conditions in the industrial cities of France the average life of the factory people to be just nineteen years, while that of people in a normal condition is forty-three! The mortality among the children of the factory he showed to be a veritable extermination. The misery of the parents forces children of six to seven years into the factory. Of course, children so young are made to work by compulsory means. The parents soon lose all influence with these young factory hands, among whom a fearful demoralization prevails, and who at the age of twelve years smoke, drink, visit saloons and have their girls. So Villermé found it thirty years ago and so Jules Simon finds the condition of the factory people in the populous centres of industry to-day.

The physical and moral ruin of the people in the great manufacturing towns of France is beyond description.

The family, with all its saving influences, has given way to universal vagabondage, misery and depravity, which can hardly end otherwise for France than in the desolation of its large cities lighted up by maddened petrolleuses. Let this lesson written over the lurid sky be read and noticed all over the world.

Far from having overdrawn the picture of the working classes in the large cities of France, we dared not half tell the truth, which is too shocking for a straightforward recital.

Men, women, boys and girls being everywhere thrown together in the factory and upon the litter like brutes, decency and cleanliness of body become impossible, and this looseness ends in the complete destruction of all principle and character and in the ruin of society.

The working girls in their want and desolation abandon themselves and become mothers before they reach maturity of age, at sixteen to fourteen and earlier. Men fear the responsibility of a family ; seeing as they do the misery of their fellows in the bonds of wedlock, they will not marry. Poor women are forsaken when their greatest need has come, the poor children are farmed out, and from eighty to ninety-five of a hundred die in less than a year. The men shift from woman to woman and the women from man to man, and abominations, best left unmentioned, fill the land and destroy the nation.

The same corruption we find everywhere in proportion as the people are crowded into tenement houses of a low order. Little Bavaria has an annual crop of 35,083 illegitimate births; Wurtemberg, 12,216; Prussia, 47,961, and Saxony, 12,057.

A digression may not be out of place here in reference to Sweden, which seems to contradict every principle of social philosophy; for, while its population is almost entirely agricultural, well schooled and religiously trained, crime abounds to a degree found nowhere else. Laing found one in one hundred and thirty-four of the population in the country and one in forty-six in the towns convicted of crime, while in Ireland the proportion was in the same year one in seven hundred and twenty-three. Stockholm had annually (1851-55) 1,788 legitimate births and 1,477 illegitimate ones! The fact is, though the country inclines us to virtue and the manufacturing town with its attendants to vice, none exerts such a power as may not be overcome by other influences. The nobility of Sweden, though but one in three hundred of the entire population, possesses more than one-eighth of the land, taxation presses hard upon the poor and their industries, who beside earn scanty wages and can hardly work six months in the year on account of the severity of the climate; half the people, therefore, live worse than English paupers. Add to this that nine-tenths of the population are peasants, treated by all classes with the uttermost contempt and whose degradation is completed by a most debasing penal code, and we certainly cannot wonder that a people whose sensibilities are blunted by daily misery, and despised by all lost its self-regard, is not improved in its morals by the schoolmaster, the Church or the country. Sweden, thus, of all the countries, confirms our rule that the school is powerless where the people are kept in a pauperized condition that blunts their better feelings; and that the bringing together in our large cities the very rich and the very poor—robbing the latter of all self-regard, the safest defense against vice, immorality and crime—destroys them.

As to the condition of the working people and their dwellings in England, let Joseph Kay's pages answer. Fathers, mothers, sons and daughters crowd together in a state of filthy indecency, and are much worse off than the horses in an ordinary stable. Sometimes a man is found sleeping with one woman, sometimes with two, and sometimes with young girls; sometimes brothers and sisters of the ages of eighteen, nineteen and twenty are found in one bed together. . . . . Men and women, three and four found sleeping together, are not ashamed, but answer remonstrances by laughter or sneer. . . . .

In 1844, 20 per cent. of the working classes of Liverpool, 11¾ per cent. of those of Manchester and 8 per cent. of those of Salford lived in cellars.

And so it is all over England, and the farming
hands in the rural cottages don't fare any better.
The population is denser to-day and time has
brought no relief. Look beneath all the display
of objects of literature, science and art, and what
is there but a pauperized and suffering people. To
maintain show we have degraded the masses, until
we have created an evil so vast that we now despair of ever finding the remedy.

A committee appointed by the statistical society
to investigate the condition of dwellings and the
people, say : " Your committee has given a picture
in detail of human wretchedness, filth and brutal
degradation, the chief features of which are a dis-
grace to a civilized country and which is but the
type of the miserable condition of the masses of
the community, whether located in small, ill-ventilated rooms of manufacturing towns or in many
of the cottages of the agricultural peasantry. In
these wretched dwellings all ages and all sexes,
fathers and daughters, mothers and sons, grown-
up brothers and sisters, stranger adult males and
females and swarms of children—the sick, the dying and the dead, are herded together with a prox-
imity and mutual pressure which brutes would resist ; where it is physically impossible to preserve
the ordinary decency of life ; where all sense of
propriety and self-respect must be lost, to be re-

placed only by a recklessness of demeanor which necessarily results from vitiated minds."

Officials, clergymen and surgeons from all over England, give a description of the condition of the people in their crowded dwellings too shocking for recital. The promiscuous mingling of the sexes in the bedrooms has been increasing and producing year after year worse consequences, until it has become so common among the poor as to destroy all modesty and virtue among women, and threatens to annihilate the foundations on which are based all the national and domestic virtues, and to make want of chastity before marriage and want of delicacy and purity after marriage common characteristics of the mothers and wives of our working people.

We shall conclude these statements of Joseph Kay, which we could follow up by others of equal authority, with the significant statistical figures of 60,000 illegitimate births per annum in good Old England.

We are at a loss where to begin and where to end, or how to press into a few brief lines all the miseries of the poor arising from crowded dwellings as sketched by John E. Morgan. The poor are huddled together in a manner that health and strength for their daily work is fairly impossible. Their dwellings are forcing-beds of disease, where

the plague originates. Here lies the very canker
at the root of our social system. The day's work
of our laborers, so wearing on the nervous system
as well as on the muscles, is in their insalubrious
dwellings followed by loss of appetite and loss of
sleep.

What harvests of preventable deaths! Fifteen
or sixteen deaths in a thousand is the normal death-
rate. In sixty of the worst streets of Salford the
rate of mortality for a number of years ranged
from 36 to 91 in 1,000, the average of the whole
being 51! And Salford is no exception. Vaux-
hall district in Liverpool showed in 1864 a death-
rate of 49 in 1,000, and St. Paul's Exchange 48—
and that is not the worst.

How narrow is the life-span of our poor, and how
full of physical ailments and misery is that little!
Bad air and too little of it, kills the people. Thousands around us are annually dying, starving for
want of a breathable air.

In Salford 25,000 people suffer intensely from
air-poisoning ; in Manchester 80,000 ; in Liverpool
and Glasgow are an equal number of sufferers from
pestilential quarters, and London has fully a half a
million of inhabitants, who suffer enfeebled health
from the bad state of their crowded, stifling dwellings. Without naming the towns, upon a thorough
knowledge of which the statement is based, of the

12,000,000 of the town population of England and Scotland, fully 2,000,000 suffer from want of proper dwellings.

Dr. Hunter positively states that the dwellings are more crowded by 10 per cent. to-day than they were 25 years ago, as the population has increased $5\frac{1}{3}$ per cent., and the dwellings have at the same time decreased $4\frac{1}{2}$ per cent., as many buildings have been appropriated for other purposes. Typhus, measles, scarlet fever, smallpox and other diseases come and go; there are signs of a widespread physical deterioration; chronic ailments are the rule; dyspepsia, bronchitis, scrofula and consumption are common, and the thread of life is deplorably fine spun, and many seem to cower around the open mouth of the grave.

From these crowded poor one million of paupers gains its recruits; prisons and reformatories look to them for their largest supply; and it is among them that diseases originate that revenge themselves on society at large. So far Dr. Morgan, a public officer in 1869, than whom none is better informed upon the condition of the laboring masses and their dwellings.

THE TENEMENT HOUSES OF NEW YORK CITY.

We beg the reader to notice that we closely follow the Official Reports of the Board of Health, published for the last ten and more years, by which every one of our statements may be verified.

The majority of tenement houses in this city are old structures built for other purposes, partitioned off within so as to give each family a living room 10 by 12 feet and a bedroom 6 by 4 feet, while no regard is paid to ventilation or domestic conveniences; twenty, thirty, forty to one hundred and fifty such apartments are constructed, and into each a family of from three to five persons is crowded. The danger from crowding in these tenement houses is a hundred-fold increased by their being packed together in blocks. Rear tenement houses aggravate the evil beyond measure. They are built upon the rear of the yard, close to the rear tenement of the opposite lot, leaving a small cold and damp space between the front and rear houses, not inappropriately called the *well hole*. Not only are fresh air and sunlight thus effectually excluded from the living and sleeping apartments of most of the inmates, but the buildings become damp and cold, and in time saturated with the poisonous and filthy excretions of the inmates.

The result of this effective overcrowding in badly constructed dwellings is shown by the fact that this half of the population of New York yields 75 per cent. of the total sickness and mortality. Tenement houses of a capacity for ten families were found by the Board of Health, in which, beside other diseases, typhus prevailed, and in six months twenty persons were stricken down by this terrible malady. In other buildings a mortality of 55 in 1,000, or 1 in 18, died! which is 40 more deaths to every 1,000 population than there is absolute necessity for.

Tenements, with two houses on the same lot, suffer also from the super-added nuisance of privies located in the middle space. The air in these areas is always impure from the noxious gases arising from the privies, and even without these necessary nuisances the air is too confined for the proper supply of human beings. Tenements have been examined by the Board in which the apartments consisted of one living room of 14 by 8 feet and a dark bedroom of 7 by 8 feet, with no means for ventilation and full of filth, furnishing constant work for the undertaker, the ambulance and the hospitals. The privy vaults and everything else, of course, was in a most loathsome and killing condition.

A description of the kind of homes work-people at times find in tenement houses may interest. The roof leaky as a sieve, affecting the comfort of the inmates down to the second floor; the walls, ceilings and woodwork of the whole house shaky with age and bad usage and rotten with filth; the fireplaces destroyed and dangerous; the partition walls thin, ill-fitting planks, covered with foul and ragged paper. The alleyway dark, extremely filthy and dangerous in every respect. The basement walls crumbling; the ceiling below the level of the street; no light, except through the door, and occupied by four beds; the steps decayed and dangerous. While the wood and other materials of such structures undergo the process of dry rot, the wretched tenants waste and die from a disease expressively termed the "*tenement house rot.*"

The debasing effects of such houses have never been overdrawn. Mr. N. P. Willis gave the following vivid description of the tenement class of people immediately after the riot of 1863: "The high brick blocks and closely packed houses in this neighborhood seemed to be literally hives of sickness and vice. Curiosity to look on at the fire raging so near them brought every inhabitant to the porch or window, or assembled them in ragged and dirty groups on the sidewalks in front. Probably not a creature who could move was left indoors at that hour. And it is wonderful to see and difficult to believe that so much misery and disease and wretchedness could be huddled together and hidden by high walls unvisited and unthought of so near our own abodes. The lewd, but pale and sickly young women, scarce decent in their ragged attire, were impudent and scattered everywhere in the crowd. But what numbers of these poor classes are deformed; what numbers are made hideous by self-neglect and infirmity, and what numbers are paralytics, drunkards, imbecile or idiotic, forlorn in their poverty-stricken abandonment for the world! Alas! human faces look so hideous with hope and vanity all gone! And female form and features are made so frightful by sin, squalor and debasement."

The degree of overcrowding in the tenements of New York City exceeds that of any of the large cities of the civilized world.

The density of population was to each acre in 1870:

NEW YORK.		LONDON.	
11th Ward	328	Strand	307
13th "	311	St. Luke's	259
14th "	275	East London	266
17th "	289	Holborn	229

The highest allowable population is 80 to 100 persons to the acre. The effect of this excessive crowding in badly constructed dwellings upon the death rate is that double as many of these tenement inmates die as of the people living in the country. Sickness and death are, however, but a fraction of the sum total of damage which overcrowding and defective house accommodations do to the poor. The gross immorality, the huddling up of all sexes and ages, leads them on to a total self-abandonment and every species of vice and crime.

Gotham Court may be taken as a representative of tenement houses, their character, accommodations and influence on the population. Two barrack-buildings furnish tenements to 146 families or 584 individuals. At times it has been packed with nearly double that number. The roof is a general playground for children and a place of deposit for ashes, garbage and to a large extent used as a privy by the tenants. The plaster and woodwork of the hallways is out of repair and extremely filthy; the stairs are dangerous; the cellars are dark, horribly foul and filled with mud, rubbish and human excrements. They are not used for storage of wood or coal, as neither property nor life are safe in these cellars on account of rowdyism rampant around this court. The privies are horrible breeding tanks of disease; the horrible odors rising from this immense receptacle of filth spread between the two piles of buildings—each five stories high—which are separated only by a distance of nine feet wide. The poison thus concentrated is very directly applied to each and every apartment in the buildings. Added to the filth of the privies is the filth of the yard, into which much rubbish and garbage is thrown. For a long time this court has been the nightly resort of a crowd of loafers, bummers and roughs, who kept the tenants in a complete state of terrorism. On Sunday especially this is the playground of these rascals—boys and half-grown men —who fight among themselves and pick quarrels with the tenants. Women of the street are dragged in, under the back-stairs and into the cellars by these miserable youngsters, and vice, drunkenness and terror reign rampant. The police will not follow them into these dark cellars and recesses. The agent and housekeeper dare not interfere; and the police, I fear, are content to leave the court pretty much to itself. Ventilation is impossible, and even if it was not, the air is already poisoned before it would enter the rooms. This was the condition of Gotham in 1870. In 1865 the Health Officer found the mortality in these buildings 30 per cent. of the children born, 7 per cent. of the entire population, which is three and four times as great a mortality than there is an absolute necessity for. Of 504 inmates 146 were more or less sick, some with smallpox, some with typhus, some with scarlatina, dysentery, chronic diarrhœa, etc.

All zymotic, epidemic and contagious diseases make especial havoc in our tenement houses, as they are usually overcrowded, badly ventilated, damp and filthy; the relapsing fever, however, is peculiarly a disease resulting from overcrowding and destitution, while typhus is a disease which finds its cause in overcrowding alone. Miserable living and sleeping in damp, filthy cellars and unventilated apartments produce this epidemy, by which thousands of the inhabitants of the tenement houses have been attacked in 1870. This epidemy has been for the last few years raging all over the *civilized* (?) world among the *destitute laborers*, who are living in unwholesome and crowded apartments.

The cholera of 1866 left the inhabitants of the clean and well-to-do sections of the city of New York unvisited, even while this terrible pest has slain hundreds of victims in the overcrowded, badly ventilated, damp and filthy tenement houses. In 1867 the mortality of children of one year of age amounted from week to week one-fourth to one-half of the entire death rate. In some of the crowded tenement neighborhoods 80 per cent. of the mortality occurred among the infant population. The unhealthfulness of the dwellings is most telling upon the delicate constitution of infants; and, hence, the slaughter among them. In many cases it was observed, though death was imminent, removal to the country and its pure atmosphere terminated the disease as if by magic. The filth and foul air of tenement houses furnish the ferment for contagious and miasmatic diseases, and fresh air, pure water and plenty of sunlight are the best preventatives of zymotic as well as of other diseases.

In the report of 1874, we read that large numbers of cellars in the lower wards of the city were occupied as dwellings and lodging-places, which were totally unfit for such occupancy; many of them nests of crime, and all in a condition to become on the slightest appearance of pestilence the centres of disease. In most cellars the walls and ceilings were found damp; the floors resting on damp earth were rotting away or were resting upon stagnant water, which would be forced up below the boards at the slightest pressure of the foot upon the floor. Many of the lodging-cellars were found to be long rooms divided into small apartments by pieces of curtain, while in others the beds were arranged alongside of each other without such partition and occupied indiscriminately by lodgers of both sexes. In the second sanitary inspection district 315 persons were found living in damp, unventilated cellars. They suffered from alcoholism, and rheumatism in all its stages.

In the Fourth Ward 176 cellars were found in a deplorably filthy state, and radical measures were recommended for closing them and redeeming the wretched occupants of those cellars from early graves, lives of drunkenness and prostitution. In numerous instances damp, dark, filthy cellars were rented from $25 to $75 per month. " The system of tenement dwellings is so radically wrong that to suggest improvements would end in a suggestion that the present houses be all torn down. Cleanliness in them is impossible without light and air, and this cannot be had with front and rear buildings. Volumes of air vitiated by the disagreeable smells of cookery of the lower stories are always sent up through the halls and narrow courtyards, also the exhalations of decaying vegetable matter and the like. The walls and ceilings of the halls become soon covered with a coating of animal matter deposited upon them, and the floors become soaked with moisture, filth and dirt, which is never removed."

We might have presented more sensational pictures—we have preferred to describe the homes of the working people in the very words of our noble sanitary inspectors, and the misery of their occupants can be easily inferred upon the principle of Mr. Godwin : " As the homes, so the people."

Our sanitary inspectors are doing their best to improve the condition of the tenement houses. But as the population increases and the business houses encroach and narrow the field of the tenement houses, and the proportion of the inhabitants to the area is already three times as large as health permits it, all their measures cannot bring permanent relief. Besides, their powers are too restricted to do all the good they would like to do.

Is it in Boston, the Athens of American intelligence, any better? The State Board of Health of Massachusetts tells us that the homes of the laboring classes in Boston are overcrowded and unwholesome, abodes of misery, affecting injuriously the health, the morals and the political purity of the community; they are disgracefully unfit for human habitations, and nothing can be added to a true notion of their badness, as their character for squalidness and unwholesomeness is known to all.

The State Board is tired of telling over the story of the miserable abodes of the people, and we shall follow the description of the Rev. Edward E. Hale in his " How the People Live in Boston, and How They Die There."

The mortality of the infants in Bethlehem, which has made every Christian mother curse the name of Herod, is more than equalled in the terrible sufferings of the children in Boston. *Seventy-five deaths among the children of the poor happening just from cholera infantum alone in twenty-four hours!* And almost all under one year of age, and coming out of all proportion from the tenements of the poor. Not a child on the dead-list from Beacon, Chestnut or Pinkney Streets, nor deaths in Union Park, Worcester or Springfield Streets, or from Chester

Square ; in short, not one death from the very nice
streets.   The largest part come from two neighborhoods—the quarters of the dingy homes of the
poor.   But let us glance inside these hells, called by
a misnomer homes.   Well, here we are in the room
of Mrs. K——, who lost a boy—it was her only
child.   The air was damp, chilly and dark, because
the sun never kissed it.   The floor of the entry was
wet from the overrunning of the water-faucet, which
supplied the house, and all the region was damp, as
the cellar is apt to be, which is much below the
tide-level.   Just seven people lived in four rooms,
which put together would have made one of twenty
feet square.

One of the deaths happened in the house opposite, in which thirty-one persons lived (?) in fourteen
so-called rooms.   What had been the yard of this
house had been taken up by another tenement
building.

Another one of the deaths occurred in a four-
story tenement, in which forty families are packed,
and which looks very much like a menagerie cage.

13 E—— street is another such feeder of the
cemetery.   Two tenement houses adjoining each
other, with thirteen families in the one and ten in
the other.   The water pipes are put up in the most
shameful manner.   They must of necessity freeze
up at the very first frost.   There are but two fau-

cets for twenty-three families to draw from, and no
way to get to them without wading through dirty
water. Two of the most filthy privies, entirely open
for these twenty-three families, are so much out
of repair as to be dangerous to enter. The apartments are miserable places, out of repair, the plas-
tering of the walls and ceilings give little chance
to whitewash, as it is broken off to a large extent.

One of the poor innocents was sent to its rest
from one of the tenements in Phœnix Place. There
is a melancholy uniformity in this class of buildings. They are lightly built of wood, all on the
same plan. Think of it, sixty adults and sixty-five
children packed away in sixty rooms, each of which
was about twelve feet square. The summer atmosphere of these places is odious, but the winter atmosphere is worse. The lots are so small that all
privy arrangements and deposits of offal are horribly near the open windows. It was wretched to
hear the woman talk, as if the child died of course,
and she never ought to have expected that it would
live. The poor feel they are doomed and become
reckless.

It would be a sad and endless repetition to say
more in detail about this matter, as the dwellings
assigned for homes to the laboring poor in Boston
all are pretty much of the same description.

In 1865, a thousand children died in less than a

hundred days from an epidemy that raged among the dear little ones. The Bostonians, who live in comfortable circumstances and neat homes, are surprised to hear it. It did not touch them—it raged among the poor.

But the worst of all is that it is not only New York City, Boston, Baltimore, Cincinnati, St. Louis, Louisville, New Orleans, in short, the very large cities; it is fully as bad in the smaller manufacturing towns everywhere. Take, for instance, the tenement house called "Buffum's Block," in Linn, Mass. It is eighty feet long, thirty feet wide, containing a basement, two stories and an attic. In the basement, below the level of the street, three families live, and the house contains not less than forty-six persons. The privies are foul and beyond approach by a decent person. Additional complaint was caused by the privies of the neighboring tenements which, being on higher ground and faulty in construction, were overflowing into this yard. Here is a sample, and we take the first—there is not much choice—from Salem, in the same State, at No. 18 Congress Street. At the time of the inspection by the health officer, this house stood in the midst of a pond of stagnant water. In the same watery lot was an overflowing privy-vault, and a piggery added its contribution to the general filth. Sixteen persons occupied the house, which was in a condition to poison the atmosphere of the whole neighborhood. All the tenements of the laboring classes in this district, says the State Report, should be condemned as nuisances.

Here, as an illustration—and we take again the first at hand—from Springfield, T—— Block. The house, when inspected, was greatly out of repair—its windows broken, its stairs dangerous, its roof leaking. The vaults of the privy were brick receptacles, entirely above ground, and as one of them was broken, the abundant contents had settled away, a filthy mass of excrement overflowing. Most of the tenants declined to use these privies, and resorted to expedients which can only be hinted at.

This is not impracticable fault-finding. Quick transit opens a highway that leads out of these and a thousand other abominations equally destructive to the people, who are to-day unreasonably herded in miserable tenement houses.

Quick transit gives the working people the means to live out in the country in their own cottages, where God Almighty's untampered sweet influences will keep them sound in body and soul, sound in principle and in action, and in all the relations of the individual to himself, his family and the state.

A home in the country with a garden patch attached to it, owned by every working-man, is the only possible solution of a thousand problems which press for an answer.

Once every mechanic looked forward to the time when he would be master and have his own shop. To-day, once a factory employee, means always one; he is a hopeless vagrant; he cannot invest and does not economize, and ever remains without a home, hope or property. In unemployed spells, a general crisis, or a change or cessation of his trade through the invention of new machinery, in sickness or old age, he becomes homeless, breadless and penniless.

Must not such uncertainty be unbearable to intelligent laborers, spread discontent among them and dispose them to anything that threatens the overthrow of the present order of society? This terrible uncertainty must give way to something more reasonable, just and better. Our workmen are perishing body and soul in our city slaughter-pens, called tenement houses.

The population living in private houses in New York City number a half a million, and their mortality was in 1872, 11,097, or about 22 in 1,000; the other half a million of tenement population had in the same year 21,550 deaths! or more than 10,000 above their proper share. And as there are fourteen cases of sickness to every one case of death, the workmen of this city had 140,000 more cases of sickness in their families than they would have had in more wholesome dwellings. What loss of human life, what sufferings, what expense and what loss of labor are implied in these preventable deaths and diseases, the latter of which, again, by enfeebling the bodies and minds of the people multiply pauperism, drunkenness, premature orphanage and widowhood, prostitution, crime, retributive violence and consequent prison life and suffering.

Most unfortunate for the people they are the children of God, for were they horses they would not be left to perish for want of a little more stable room.

This social murder could be stopped by the double measure of quick transit and strict sanitary regulations in reference to tenement buildings. " Houses that produce death cease to be property. If a man sells unwholesome meat, the law interferes; if he sells the use of a room with fever in it, the public do not complain. Officers of health point out such places, but the public still refuse to destroy them, and great numbers are slain annually by this indirect and legal method, while the strictest measures are taken to prevent a few annually being killed by arsenic. The time must come, and the sooner the better, when it shall be enacted, that no land shall contain more people per acre than can live healthily thereon. The same thing must be said regarding houses, though this is more difficult to attain."

At Muhlhausen, in Elsace, a workmen-town was built, giving laborers facilities for acquiring property, and what a change it worked! what a revolution! a blessed revolution that destroyed vice and misery, and led from the improvement of material conditions to a moral regeneration.

At Lille, in France, houses have been built for the workmen with gardens attached to them, and are sold to the laborers on easy terms. At Rouen the same system is attended with the same blessed results.

To illustrate this system, we may add a word more about Muhlhausen, the first great success of a workmen-town. One hundred houses were built in 1853, an additional 428 were built in 1859, and 560 in 1863. Of these, 700 belonged to the workmen in 1866. They paid $4.60 per month, and in 14 years each house held at $600 was paid up, interest and capital, having paid but little more than a high rent. Each home has a garden of 30 by 36 feet attached to it. The government has voted $2,000,000, a loan to building societies under the following conditions: 1. The properties must be sold to the workmen at cost price. 2. No purchaser to be allowed to sell his property before ten years, so as to prevent speculation. 3. The building company not to charge the workmen more than 4 per cent. for capital until it is paid up. 4. A public building, uniting a reading-room, restaurant, bathing and washhouse and a bazar, where all articles of common consumption are sold to the workmen at wholesale prices, must be built in the centre of the town.

The Industrial Building Society at Muhlhausen has complied with these conditions, and received from the government in addition to their original capital of $25,000 a loan of $80,000. In this comparatively small manufacturing place 700 toiling families were changed from hand-to-mouth living renters into provident and independent citizens and property holders, each living in his own comfortable home undisturbed by the often unwelcome company of drunkards and other incongruous and even infamous characters thrust upon decent men in tenement houses, living in cheerful quarters, and as if it were under his own fig-tree. No more driven from cheerless and filthy rooms to the debauchery of the public house. What moments he can save he bestows upon his garden, and the boys and the mother are happy to second him with the hoe as he goes ahead of them with the spade, now and then stopping and blending his solid reflections and well-meant counsel to his family with his labor of love. They make arbors for shade and plan improvements, beautifying the homestead. When old, he need not blush to live from the earnings of his sons, for he has done his duty to them and all the family. And father and mother, after a life of toil, but which was not without its blessings, die on the homestead with the children, leaving them not only property, but a good name and a model life. Not only property is thus made, but character is built up and kept like a jewel.

What a difference between such workmen and those who are driving about like vagabonds and semi-savages. Jean Dolfus, who started this noble work at Muhlhausen, deserves well of the human race for this illustrious example given to manufacturers and workmen.

At Guebwiller, also in Elsace, a hundred cottages with gardens attached to them, were built in 1866.

Beaucourt had in 1864, 97 cottages. Colmar built in 1864, 50 houses. At Sedan, the workmen own their houses and gardens, and are as respected for their character as they are useful by their labor.

What touching stories could be told about many a workingman who, under the old system, became dissolute and was daily nearing a drunkard's grave, but who has been redeemed at the first opportunity of acquiring a piece of property, a home for his family and old age.

At the Ashton colony of workmen, in England,

none have yet applied for charity; in 35 years
hardly a breach of law has occurred, and illegitimate births are becoming scarce. The people look
healthy, and even those who work in an atmosphere of 80° Fahrenheit are strong and vigorous,
having but one-half day of sickness in a whole
year. The intercourse between employers and
employed is marked by regard and confidence.

Get railroad advantages, give us opportunities
for cheap country homes, and societies will spring
up which will enable the poorest laborer to live in
his own house.

England has over 2,000 such building societies
with 800,000 members and $80,000,000 loaned on
buildings. London alone has over 700 societies
with over $20,000,000 advanced on property to its
members. Scotland has over 88 building societies
with over $65,000,000 advanced to its members.
These building societies afford manufacturers the
best opportunity for providing their workmen with
homes, and have been used for that purpose by
the noble Arkroyd, Crossley, and others. Belgium, Germany and other countries have been
benefited by the opportunities building societies
offer to the poor for owning homes, and there is
no reas n why building societies should not prove
a success in New York and other cities in the Union
as well as in Philadelphia.

We consider that this step must be taken of all others first, if the great and momentous questions of civilization, which crowd around labor, are to find a peaceable solution.

The massing of the people in a few centres is productive of a thousand mischievous consequences, which threaten capital as well as labor and every other element of civilization—yea, the body and soul of man with utter destruction. Avoiding general argument and steering toward convincing facts, we refrain from entering upon the moral, political, social and economical tendencies of the present movement of population toward the great cities, and will strengthen our position of the importance of the workingmen acquiring homes, with an authority like that of Le Play, a most thoughtful and competent writer, who has devoted a lifetime to the study of the condition of the industrial classes, and who sees the only means of preserving society and the prevention of the dissolution and the relapse of society into barbarism through a variety of corrupting influences, undermining the family first and society next, in restoring the ancient custom—*the family owning their hearth.* Only by this means good habits and wholesome customs are preserved and revered, parental authority honored, woman's influence a blessing, economy fostered to acquire the home, character developed, reliability

and trustworthiness gained and roving and indifference overcome.

In regard to the workmen reaching their homes
in the country and their places of work in the city,
we agree with Dr. S. Smith's sanitary report of
1871, from which the following page is taken:

"The workmen must depend upon the railroad,
which has not and probably will not give him cheap
fares without compulsory legislation, and such legislation we believe should be at once obtained. As
a slight return for the privilege which railroad companies enjoy within this city, especially in the monopoly of large areas of valuable land, they should
be compelled to provide cheap transit for the poor
and laboring classes. Such legislation in England
long since compelled all new railroads entering
London to provide penny trains at suitable hours.
These cheap trains proved a marked success. The
Legislature of Massachusetts recently passed a law
compelling the railroads to provide cheap trains
morning and evening, and charging one cent a mile
for yearly tickets, and this law has been there in
force since 1862. The same kind of legislation
should be obtained in this State in regard to all
railroads entering New York City."

Homes for workmen out of the city is nothing
but what is just and proper; it is in the interest of
all parties, the capitalist as well as the laborer, and

the family as well as the state. It is approved by philosophers and statesmen, and has been put into practice with success by manufacturers on a sufficiently large scale to judge its success.

Sir Robert Peel, whom nobody will accuse of impracticable radicalism, says: "Our large cities offer the workman only opportunities for continuous labor and gross and degrading pleasures. Give them small properties in the vicinity of the manufacturing districts, this will wean them from drunkenness and improve their moral character." He further says: "*It must be confessed that the condition of our workmen is not what it ought to be, and that the mere production of wealth is not the highest aim of government, which ought to care for the happiness and well-being of the people.*"

Sir J. Coleridge, a member of the Gladstone ministry, said: "Our laborers live hardly, work very long, and have at the end of life nothing to hope for."

Neither religion, Education, nor temperance, nor courts of justice can elevate a people living huddled up like pigs, says the good and learned Dr. Blakie. The same great authority continues: Typhus, consumption, scrofula, etc., are wasting away the laboring people in the densely populated tenement houses, and the victims of typhus alone among workmen in the prime of life, number

annually doubly the fallen on the battle-field of
Waterloo. Love of home, says this same philan-
thropic divine, is associated with regard for father
and mother and their precepts. Filthy tenements
are no home, and, hence, no lesson to the heart;
all the purer feelings even of a mother and sister
are deadened by them. The cleanest can be but
untidy, dirty, wretched, discontented and disorderly
in such hovels, and the preference for the public
house to such quarters become a necessity. The
vice and filth in the crowded dwellings of the poor
counteract all the lessons of religion and humanity.
A miserable hovel destroys all home feeling and
family ties, and plants atrocity, barbarity and crime
in their place. The only remedy are small, neat
homes out of the city the laboring man can even
become proprietor of; he is stimulated by this
method to saving, and, being provident and accumulating property, becomes a useful citizen every
way. There are 8,000 to 10,000 such workingmen
who have got their own homes about Birmingham.
Happy homes are the chief cause of the prosperity
of a country. Such are the thoughts and the experience of the learned Blakie.

Purity, affection, thrift and industry are lessons
of a clean, neat and attractive home. " Lille in
France," says the thoughtful Fix, " with a most
dense population, is also the most miserable, most

17*

drunken, obscene place, with nothing but dirt, misery and vice."

The same author says : " Love of labor, of order and economy will always be found in a home that attaches the workman to his family ; there he sacrifices low desire and studies thrift for the sake of the children and a home that is attractive."

Self-respect, regard for himself and his place in society, is one of the mainsprings of keeping aloof from every degrading vice, be it drunkenness or any other moral defilement. But can any one reared in the horrid filth of the tenements of crowded cities be conscious of human dignity? Or is it not rather a mockery to speak to such men of the high dignity of their being? Provident thrift or care for the future has no room in a man who is suffering from a thousand present ills. The poor everywhere suffer partly from want of intelligence, sobriety, thrift and self-respect, and their surroundings foster these very defects. And yet, regard for ourselves is intimately connected with regard for our fellows, for human nature, and, therefore, for the rights of other men. Regard for human nature leads to trusting in it and believing in its upward tendencies, which lead to hope, exertion, improvement and elevation. Vagrancy is one of the chief causes of crime, and miserable hovels lead to it by destroying all home attachment. Let all who study

the sources of crime notice this connection between
the homes of the people and vagrancy and crime.

Clean homes certainly should be made possible
to the honest laborer, a privilege not even denied
to crime (Hill). When the prisons are in better
order than the homes of laborers, crime is encouraged.

So killing are the crowded dwellings of the poor
that the English Commissioners officially report
that the laboring population of large cities would
soon be gone, if the influx from the country would
not make up for the slaughter. Dundee, with its
once proverbially splendid Scotch population, alas!
what a spectacle it offers to-day!

What haggard looks the spinners of Lyons or
those of Spitalfields in London present! And yet,
the moral debasement of which the physical degradation is the cause as well as the index, is the worst
feature of the whole.

These squalid homes, says Buret, drive children
from 4 to 8 years into horribly dirty streets, where
they already young contract vagrant habits.

Rev. Canon Girdleston, of the English Episcopal
Church, said in a meeting of his brothers in the
ministry: The laborers live in hovels without
ventilation or the surroundings necessary for ordinary decency. Not one of those present would consent to stable their horses in these hovels; hovels

which bred a race of men who, from want of domestic comfort, spent their lives in the pothouse, and who had nothing to look forward to but to be buried in a pauper's grave; hovels which bred a race of women whose maidenly blushes were blutched in consequence of the scenes they were obliged to witness through want of proper sleeping accommodations. The clergy might keep aloof from the labor question because it might be supposed that social questions were not within their province. He was bound to acknowledge that the clergy could not consider themselves free from blame, and that a great weight of responsibility lay at their doors. They ought from the pulpit deliver themselves more frequently from this responsibility. He solemnly declared that the man he should fear most to meet at the last great day was the poor laborer, who, perhaps, if he himself had exercised his ministry more faithfully and more fearlessly in denouncing social abuses, might have been spared a life of misery and penury and a pauper's grave.

A voice as clear, powerful and bold, that once thrilled the people of Boston from the pulpit in Music Hall, said: " Look at the houses the poor live in, without comfort or convenience, without sun, air or water; damp, cold, filthy and crowded to excess. In one section of the city there are thirty-seven persons on an average in each house. Consider the rents paid by this class of our brothers. It is they who pay the highest rate for their dwellings, paying often 30 per cent. on valuation. If your bills of mortality were made out so as to show deaths in each ward of the city, I think all would be astonished at the results. Of one hundred children of poor working people in Boston only thirty-eight live five years, only eleven become fifty! The mortality among the poor is greater in Boston than in any city in Europe, and the death rate among their children is increasing." So far Theodore Parker.

Another friend of the race, the great and gifted Channing, speaking of the influence of the poor man's dwelling on his domestic affection, says : " The delicate sentiments find much to chill them in the abodes of indigence. A family crowded into a single and often narrow apartment, which must answer at once the ends of parlor, kitchen, bedroom, nursery and hospital, must, without great energy and self-respect, want neatness, order and comfort. Its members are perpetually exposed to annoying petty impertinence. The decencies of life can be with difficulty observed. Woman a drudge and in dirt loses her attractions. The young grow up without the modest reserve and delicacy of feeling in which purity finds so much of its defense. Coarseness of manner and language, too sure a consequence of a mode of life which allows no seclusion, becomes the habit almost of childhood, and hardens the mind for vicious intercourse in future years. The want of a neat, orderly home is among the chief evils of the poor. Crowded in filth, they cease to respect one another. The social affections wither amid perpetual noise, confusion and clashing interests. The poor often fare worse than the uncivilized savage in his ruder hut, which he can leave for the bright light and pure air of heaven. The poor man in the city must choose between his close room and the narrow street. He has a home without the comfort of a home."

There is hardly a faculty or virtue in man but it is fostered by a home that is deserving of the name. Franklin's motto, "Do everything in its proper time, in its proper place, use everything in its proper use," or orderliness, industry, thrift, taste or a sense of beauty, delicacy of feeling, kindliness, self-regard, culture, purity, serenity, joy and happiness, contentment, meditation upon our past conduct and forethought as to the future, family discipline and regard to the duties and relations between parents and children or wife and husband —nothing of all this is possible in an unclean den, in which all persons and functions are mixed up in one general confusion and disorder, and everything is out of time, place and joint.

Orderly homes among the working people are the best means for the spreading of a higher civilization through the moral elevation of the masses, and the preservation of the family in all its elevating influences. Facilities for the acquisition of these homes cannot fail to reconcile labor to capital and to attach the workmen to our present state of society. There is no other means by which pauperism as well as crime can be destroyed, and the individual, the state and the race can be saved but by the home and the family, the school and nursery of the civilization of the race.

Aside from moral considerations and economical reasons, sanitary facts of the gravest sort demand the formation of workmen settlements in the country.

We shall shift our studies to Prussia, that we may have the double advantage of observing the effects of crowding under other skies and through other eyes, which cannot but correct or confirm our observations made in France, England and the United States.

The efficient statistics of Prussia show that while in Westphalia the proportion of occupants to each house was, in 1855–1858, 6.91 to 1, and in the Rhenish Province, 6.04 to 1 ; the proportion in the

district of Gumbinnen was at the end of 1855, 8.97
to 1, and at the end of 1858, 9.19 to 1, and here it
was that typhus became epidemic and raged like
a pest.

Dr. L. Muller writes: "I was soon convinced
that the time, locality and origin of the disease, as
also its gradual spread, was the effect of human
or animal perspiration accumulating in close places,
and that it thence spread to other places and became epidemic."

Dr. C. Canzow, the medical inspector of the Gumbinnen district, in his account of the origin of the
typhus epidemy in the overcrowded dwellings of the
laboring people, says: "It is not saying too much
that spotted fever has become endemic among the
permanently suffering workmen of this district."

Dr. Pappenheimer, the celebrated sanitarian and
medical adviser, says in his publication on Sanitary Police: "The study of typhus in lodging-
houses, in certain town quarters, hospitals, work-
houses, ships and prisons leads always to the same
result. Every epidemic typhus, which is not the
effect of hunger and want, is the result of overcrowded and filthy localities. Filth and overcrowding produce typhus, very often becoming epidemic,
and affecting impoverished nations or such as are in
a suffering condition in consequence of a commercial
crisis, war or the failure of crops. We physicians

cannot cure such national sufferings. We have no medicine against hunger, nor can we prevent the overcrowding of houses, the home and origin of typhus." Such is the medical experience in reference to crowded dwellings in Prussia.

The greater part of 60,000 illegitimate births, and of probably 20,000 annual infanticides in England, are traced, in the Transactions of Social Science, to the disgusting conditions in which the masses are forced to live. The London *Times* says: "If we wish to prevent infanticide, we must guard a woman against the cruel conditions in which the crime is usually perpetrated. Is everything really done by us which ought to be done? Most assuredly it is not done. As long as the poor have to live in a manner, which makes the separation of the sexes impossible and renders impracticable the observance of common decency, these crimes will be perpetrated. . . . . Let us make a real, earnest exertion to improve the dwellings of the poor, and with the dwellings the morals of the inhabitants will mend."

Dr. Farr says: "The children of that idolatrous nation that passed its children through the fire, an offering to Moloch, were hardly more in danger of losing their lives than those born in our large cities."

Of a hundred children born, live to the age of five years, in

Norwegia	. . .	83	Prussia	68
Sweden	. . . .	80	Holland	67
England	. . . .	74	Austria	64
Belgium	. . . .	73	Russia	62
France	. . . .	71	Italy	61

But the very low mortality rates of the well situated lower the average mortality of the whole, and hide the real state of the case, which is ugly, indeed, as the mortality among the laborers crowded into the tenements of large cities rises to the fearful proportion of 50, 60, 70 and even more in 100!

Villermé showed that the mortality was in French arrondissements:

With	7	per cent poor dwellings	. .	1 person in 72
"	22	"	"	. . 1 " 65
"	38	"	"	. . 1 " 45

In England, sanitary investigations show a mortality in dwellings of

202 square yards to each person	. . . .	1 in 49
101 " "	. . . .	1 " 41
32 " "	. . . .	1 " 36

Of all the deaths from cholera in London, in 1849, belonged to the

Higher classes	26 in 1,000
Middle "	157 " 1,000
Laboring "	817 " 1,000

This, of course, is entirely out of proportion to the number of the various classes.

In Brussels, die

In the quarter, with the best dwellings . . 1 in 53 persons.
" " " poorest " . . 1 " 29 "

In Zurich, in Switzerland, the average life in the best quarters is 40 years, in the poorest it is 28.3.

Dr. Lankester shows the mortality in one of the best localities of London to be 11 in 1,000, in another one, among the laborers, it is 25 in 1,000. The same sanitarian shows the loss of England from insalubrious dwellings to be 100,000 lives per annum; and as, where so many die, many more are sick, a simple calculation will show that 100,000 preventable deaths imply a national annual loss of $50,000,000! And fully as much, and more, do the United States suffer, as our mortality rates are much higher, and human labor is worth more here than in England. We doubt not the interest on our whole war debt could be paid with what we lose by the annual slaughter of our working population.

In proportion to the density of population, rent, and with it pauperism, increase, the morality of the people is lowered and their death rate of mortality rises. Let the reader reflect upon the contents of the following table :

Town.	Occupants to each house.	Proportion of rent to income.	Illegitimate births.	Mortality in 1,000 population.
London . .	8	$\frac{1}{10}$–$\frac{1}{8}$ to 1	4 pr. ct.	24
Berlin . . .	32	$\frac{1}{4}$–$\frac{1}{5}$ to 1	16 "	25
Paris . . .	35	$\frac{1}{4}$ to 1	20 "	28
Petersburg .	52	. . . .	26 "	41
Vienna . . .	55	$\frac{1}{4}$–$\frac{1}{3}$ to 1	51 "	47

Minute statistical investigations show that in the same country where no other influences modify the result, crime is in proportion to the density of population and the suddenness of its increase, and, hence, so much of crime at the present movement of population from the country to the cities. Drunkenness, prostitution, scrofula, phthisis, zymotic diseases, insanity, suicide, and, at last, death, perhaps the only possible medicine against all this and other unmentionable corruption, are all in proportion to the density of population, the breeder of all that is unwholesome for the body as well as for the soul, and for the state as well as for the individual.

The rapid increase of dense city populations, says Beale, and the unchecked advance of huge masses of human misery and destitution—mental, moral and corporeal—exhibited in every country of Christian Europe must end in barbarism and despotism, if the right sort of Education does not come to the rescue.

We have already referred to the barrenness of statistics in which extremes of all sorts thrown together produce insipid averages, which hide the true condition of things. Let our sanitary authorities give us the mortality of different sections by themselves, and not throw the pestilential and the salubrious together and produce the false impression that things are just tolerable, when, in fact, this medium condition exists only on the paper where the best and the worst are thrown together, while in reality only extremes are met with. We talk of a rate of mortality of 36 in 1,000, when the fact is that in the best houses the mortality is 15 to 20 in 1,000, and in the worst it is 40 to 50 in 1,000.

Mr. Michael, the Mayor of Swansea, in England, read before the Association of Social Science a paper in which he divides his town, according to the density of its districts, into three divisions:

A	With a mortality of 11 in 1,000 population.
B	" " 20 " "
C	" " 36 " "

Or, taking the percentage of the houses in which deaths occurred, and taking groups of five houses and the deaths occurring in them during a series of five years, he found of the buildings in district

A, 21–29 pr. ct. had deaths, or	1	death in 5 houses in 5 years.
B, up to 50 " " "	2	" " "
C, 90–117 " " "	1	" " "

Out of 127 population, 29 died in 5 years in the poorest district, which gives 58 in 1,000, while the mortality of the whole district is 24 in 1,000, and that of the best portion by itself is 11.6 in 1,000.

Dr. Grunhow, an authority well known in the sanitary world, in an elaborate paper before the

Association of Social Science, shows, while the mortality of Glendale, a healthy rural district of England, for a number of years was 15.09 per 1,000, that of Liverpool was 36.35 per 1,000! And while the average annual deaths in Glendale from pulmonary diseases were 216 to 100,000 population, the average annual mortality from the same cause to the same number of population was, in Liverpool, 1,000.

The death rate of children from nervous diseases is at Glendale 40 in 100,000 population. In Manchester it is 393!

Infantile deaths from diarrhœal diseases at Glendale were for a number of years 57 in 100,000 population, at Manchester 1,945 in 100,000!

Deaths from all causes of male children under 5 years, were at Glendale, 1848–1854, 3,499 in 100,000, in Manchester there were during the same time, 13,539!

It is not the location or country that makes so striking a difference, for, as we have already had opportunity to observe, the best buildings in the cities have as low a mortality as the best rural districts have. Unwholesome employment, crowding, intemperance, want, misery and profligacy, all unite to make cities a pest. The low stature and narrow chests of the artisans in cities are proverbial.

Dr. Farr shows that the mortality of towns is in

direct numeral proportion to the density of population.

But not only does the mortality of a district increase with the density of its population, but the fecundity of a population falls with the rise in its number.

In nine of twenty towns in England, which numbered over 40,000 population, the deaths outnumbered the births, and the increase of the population in all was due to the movement of the population from the country. In Stockholm, Petersburg, Moscow, Venice, Rouen, and many other cities, the population would soon dwindle down to nothing without this emigration from the country. In no city is the proportion of births to deaths as large as in the surrounding country.

In the country districts of Scotland the annual surplus of births over deaths amounts to 1.55 per cent. of the population. In the city districts it amounts to 1.33 per cent, and in Glasgow, Edinburgh, Dundee, Aberdeen and others, the excess of births over deaths is reduced to 1.13 per cent.

It was calculated in 1857 that of the inhabitants of England and Wales 8,250,000 persons living on 2,150,000 acres, constituting the city population, the annual death rate was 25 per 1,000. The remaining 9,750,000 persons living on 350,000,000 acres, constituting the country population, show an annual death rate of 17 per 1,000, a difference of 8 deaths for every 1,000 persons, or 8,000 for every million of population. Of course, as our mortality has not as yet been reduced to that which it is in England, the annual slaughter of our working population is much larger. We are very nice about many little things, and cultivate social murder as one of the fine arts. We strain at a gnat and swallow a camel.

Low rates of life lessen the working ability of the masses eight to ten years.

The population born in large cities under the influence of noxious physical agencies is inferior in physical organization, tending to become short-lived, reckless, intemperate and little susceptible of moral improvement.

Dr. Baly showed that the mortality from cholera in England and Wales was, in 1854, in

134 districts with 915 population to the square mile, 65 to 10,000
404   "   "   235   "   "   "   "   7   "
85   "   "   122   "   "   "   "   0   "

Dr. Stockton-Hough has carefully collected the most reliable statistics bearing upon the healthfulness of city and country, and finds the old adage verified that the city is but another name for the grave. London has yearly 10,000 more deaths than births. Humanity, if living entirely in such large cities, would be obliterated in less than 200 years.

Crowding, want, misery, luxury, effeminacy, vice, corruption and crime in high and low places destroy mankind in large cities.

The mortality among children from 1 to 5 years in one hundred born is, in New York city, 50 per cent., in the country 38 per cent.

The average life in the state of Rhode Island is 31.45 per cent ; in Providence, the largest town in the state, it was but 27.9 during 15 years ending 1870.

In the country districts of England 202 out of 1,000 deaths occur over 70 years of age, in Liverpool but 90. In the country the average age is 38 years, in Liverpool it is 27 years. In the agricultural districts of England 20.7 in every 100 persons attain 45 years ; in the four great cities of the kingdom only 17.5 reach that age. The average life in the eastern district of London is 25 to 30 years ; in the agricultural regions it is 40 to 50 years. General Walker gives the average life in the United States for 1870 as 39.25 years ; in New York city and Philadelphia it is only 25 years.

18

The fertility, legitimate and illegitimate births and infant as well as adult mortality in city and country in the various States of Europe compared:

Countries.	Children to one Marriage.		Infant Mortality.		Adult Mortality.		Fertility of Marriage.		Illegitimate to Legitim'e Births.	
	City.	Cou'ry	City.	Country.	City.	Country.	City.	Cou'ry	City.	Country
			Per cent	Per cent					Per cent	Per cent
France	3.16	3.28	35.69	28.56	1:31.51	1:42.21	2.03	2.34	15.13	4.24
Netherlands	3.91	4.32	36.25	28.90	1:35.55	1:43.03	2.49	3.07	7.7	2.84
Belgium	3.80	4.17			1:34.35	1:44.31			14.59	5.88
Sweden	2.99	4.19	38.86	24.50	1:28.95	1:46.86	1.83	3.16	27.44	7.50
Denmark	3.04	3.34	29.66	22.68	1:37.41	1:49.77	2.14	2.58	16.45	10.06
Schleswig	3.50	3.69	27.42	23.42	1:35.17	1:48.49	2.54	2.83	8.38	6.37
Holstein	3.37	3.88	29.92	25.29	1:38.73	1:44.15	2.36	2.90	15.50	8.74
Saxony	4.60	4.13	39.88	36.22	1:31.10	1:34.70	2.77	2.64	15.39	14.64
Hanover	2.93	3.65	28.70	26.47	1:38.52	1:41.17	2.08	2.68	17.42	9.06
Prussia	4.0	4.44	36.02	29.47	1:27.97	1:34.46	2.56	3.13	9.80	6.60

Volumes of reflections are contained in this table, into which are crowded by the labors of great statisticians the lives, the vices, the virtues and retribution of many nations, and in which the mirror is held up to the town and country population of the civilized world.

Among 100 recruits in the country, in Prussia, 26.58 are fit for the service, in the city 19.73.

The average life in the cities of France is 35 years, in the country it is 55 years!

According to the Registrar-General of England the mortality in districts with

1 or less persons to 1 acre, is 168 to 10,000 population.
100 to 250   "   "   "   " 262   "   "

In large cities the mortality to each 10,000 is, for

London, with 50,000 persons to the square mile, 251.
Leeds   " 87,256   "   "   " 272.
Manch'ter " 100,000   "   "   " 337.
Liverpool " 138,000   "   "   " 348.

For more than half a century the rush of population has been more than what is wholesome from the country into the cities, as the following table will show at a glance as far as the United States are concerned:

	City population.	*Country population.*
1790	3.4 per cent.	94.6 per cent.
1840	8.5 "	91.5 "
1870	20.9 "	79.1 "

This same movement of population modern industry brought about in England, where the proportion was, in

	City population.	*Country population.*
1690	26 per cent.	74 per cent.
1861	56 "	44 "

To realize still more the movement of population from the country into the cities, let us consider the

growth of cities in the United States within this
century, which is for

	1790.	1820.	1850.	1870.
Boston	18,038	43,298	136,881	250,526
New York . . .	33,131	123,706	515,547	942,292
Philadelphia . .	42,520	112,772	340,045	674,022
Baltimore . . .	13,503	62,738	169,054	267,354
New Orleans . .	6,693	27,176	116,375	191,418
Cincinnati . . .	....	9,642	115,436	216,239
St. Louis . . .	....	4,528	77,860	310,864
Chicago . . .	....	....	29,963	298,977
			4,853	
			(1840)	

This movement of the population toward the
cities is not by any means peculiar to America; it
is our modern system of manufacturing, and the
people flocking to the cities to make their fortunes.
The increase of the population in England between
the census of 1850 and 1860 was for cities 17 per
cent. and for the country 3.9 per cent.

For the study of race deterioration and its prevention, this movement of population from the
country to the city is the more important, as the city
combines all the various causes of deteriora'ion,
and must the more tell upon the population.

There the air is vitiated by a lessened percentage of ozone and an increase of ammonia, carbonic
acid and other impurities and the temperature is
altered; it is there we find insalubrious buildings
and occupations, epidemics, syphilis, luxury, effem-

inacy and all sorts of extravagance, pauperism, drunkenness, insanity and crime.

The city mortality is high enough compared with the mortality in the country, and yet the worst is only realized when we consider that the rate of mortality is excessive among infants, the cities, however, receive a great influx of adult population from the country which bore the risk. So, for instance, are of the 942,292 population of the city of New York of the census of 1870, 419,091 born somewhere else, and there the greater risk of their early mortality was born. The same is the case with 111,174 out of 250,000 population of Boston. In London, of the population under 20 years of age, 26 per cent., and of those over 20 years, 53 per cent. were born outside of London. And the same is true of all growing cities, and gives them a much better sanitary aspect than they are entitled to. For many of their healthy citizens have been reared in the country, and, receiving all the time additions of adult citizens, their proportion of infant population is smaller than it is in the country, and their rate of mortality should, therefore, be much smaller, while, in fact, it is much larger than in the country.

London boasts very much upon its low rate of mortality, but 600,000 of its enterprising adult citizens are the picked men of all England, and it requires just an annual influx of 18,000 men and a

national nursery of 2,000,000 rural population, that
sends the supply and bears the heavy mortality
incidental to the bringing up of such a number of
adults, and then London and the like growing
cities boast upon *their healthy population and their
small mortality rates.*

Infants being delicate, the unhealthfulness of
city life shows itself first, but not by any means
exclusively, upon them. Though marriages are
more frequent in the city, births are less numerous than in the country; and though adults are more
numerous in the city, the proportion of men over
forty-five years is there smaller than in the country.

Just as fallacious is the comparison of mortality
rates of different cities and states, without taking
into account the proportion of immigration received
by both and their proportion of infant population.
So, for instance, have Massachusetts, Maine and
Connecticut but 10,000 infants under 5 years in
every 100,000, while some of the states, like Missouri, Nebraska and West Virginia, have over
15,000 infants under 5 years of age in every 100,000,
and, consequently, though in the latter states the
rate of mortality may be greater, their sanitary
condition may be vastly better.

Typhus fever, the disease of the prime of life, has,
as we have already repeatedly had occasion to see,
its origin in such impurity of air as is produced by

overcrowding, and is a constant cause of death, misery and pauperism. If death does not result, a low state of health becomes the rule. Bad air takes away appetite, depresses the spirits, lessens the vital power, predisposes to disease, and a relief is sought in alcoholism. The children lose all sense of decency, propriety and order, and go to recruit the dangerous classes. It would be cheaper to send children thus situated to a first-class boarding school and put them in a way to become fair, healthy and wise, than to educate them downward into thieves, prostitutes and convicts, and keep up an expensive police force, courts and jails, and lose beside $25,000,000 property per annum.

A man must not be allowed to crowd his family into less than necessary breathing space; but he is poor. Do we on that account permit him to poison or knock on the head those depending upon him? Neither should he be allowed to kill them with bad air. Instruct the people in the science of health, which has well been said, is the science of taking plenty of good air, improve what houses we have, build better ones, and protect the rising generation by positive enactments.

We protect property—that is right. But life is left unprotected—that is wrong. Herein the age is erring. Everything is allowable within legal forms that leads to wealth, however much human

life may suffer by it.   Englishmen send out armed
piratical crafts to force their poisonous wares or
opium cargoes upon unwilling nations; and England itself, a Christian nation, goes to war to force
a hundred thousand chests of opium per annum
upon hundreds of millions of men in Asia, spreading thereby misery, death and madness, and bringing ruin of body and soul upon countless people.
But then, this makes commerce.

This must cease, or we shall all perish, for a lie
cannot stand, prop it up as much as we may. *Life
must be sacred or property will soon cease to be sacred.*
The law of life and its sacredness must underlie every
other law and institution.   Hygiene must become
a religion extending its influence in every direction.   And the homes of the people must, above
all, be brought under the influence of the law of
life and hygiene.

Already three hundred years ago, under Queen
Elizabeth, the following law was passed: "No
owner or occupier of any cottage shall suffer more
than one family to cohabit therein under fine of
ten shillings."

The London *Times* and other influential papers,
agree that the legislature has a right for the protection of innocent victims to fix a suitable mini-
mum of breathing space, and to give greater power
to inspecting officers.

Sir George Strickland says: " Wherever you have an overcrowded population you will observe impaired health and morals, and, in consequence, lack of energy and self-respect. Sanitary improvement is the first step toward the elevation of their habits and tastes."

Mr. Rawlinson says: "In my large experience I have found overcrowding everywhere attended by misery, disease and crime. The people can no more help it than they can roll back the sun in his course. Healthy people may go into abominable overcrowded tenements, but nothing but disease and misery can come out of them. The formation of suburban villages for the working people, with cheap and rapid communication with the cities, would be one of the greatest blessings conferred upon the laboring population of the country."

Dr. Markham says: " It is the duty of the employer, and he should be bound by law to attend to it, that work-people—while engaged at work by him—should have proper accommodations, so that they may not have their health injured by overcrowding. People do not know that overcrowding undermines their health, and the first epidemic, be it typhus, smallpox or cholera, destroys them by thousands."

The community has a right to legislate how much of a lot must be left free by the owner for

18*

giving scope to the atmosphere and free access of light.

We cannot legislate work, but by a consistent sanitary legislation we can protect the people in their health; and when they will have this, they will find every other desirable thing.

We own we have but one idea—in Education, in science, in industry, in government, in civilization and in religion—we know no higher and no more sacred principle than even this regard for human life, which includes everything else that is of solid worth.

There is an ancient people whose religion and legislation are chiefly founded on hygiene, and what spectacle does this nation present? It has furnished the world with a code of morals and the spirit to live up in a measure to the standard placed before them. This ancient people—hardly necessary to name—is preserved to this day in spite of the ravages of time and the persecutions of men, and though its dietary code dates back thirty-five hundred years, when nature's laws were but little understood, its effects on the Jewish people are better told by the comprehensive figures of statistics than by long discussions.

The most exact statistics of Prussia show the following death rates at the various ages of a population of 100,000:

	Christians.	Jews.
Still births	143	89
0–1 year	697	453
1–5 years	477	386
5–14 "	202	151
14–25 "	155	123
25–45 "	334	231
45–70 "	614	392
70 and over	339	330
Average mortality in 100,000,	2,961	2,161

The pest in 1346 hardly touched the Jews, as the old historian Tschudi vouches. They enjoyed the same immunity in 1505, according to Fracastor. They were spared from the intermittent fever which raged at Rome in 1691, as Rammazini states. The epidemic dysentery at Nimêque, according to Degner, spared them. The Christian sufferers from the pest were, therefore, declared the victims of wells poisoned by the Jews, who, in fact, owed their immunity to their conformity to the laws of hygiene.

Human life is not altogether a physical process, it is the basis of all our social and moral relations; whatever touches it assumes a peculiar importance.

Whatever shortens the life of man degenerates his race, and by lowering his energy and powers lessens the number of great men, and strikes thereby a blow against the Bacons, Newtons and Washingtons; it makes us a scrofulous and cretin-like race, unfit to govern ourselves or the state, and renders us slaves to passions within and tyrants without.

Shorten the life of man, and knowledge and experience are not put to half their use; inventions
go prematurely to the grave; and the proportion of
the young, and, therefore, of the unproductive, of
the criminal, of the inexperienced and the foolish,
of the turbulent, of births and funerals, of widowhood and orphanage, of vagabondism, of pauperism and of vice and crime, is increased.

Shorten the life of man, and with the shortened
generations thought, action, government, institutions and systems become feverish, the constant,
silent action of time—which alone leads to healthy
maturity—is broken; everything is hurried through
as if hardly worth doing and comes into the world
with the thought of leaving it in its mind, with
paleness on its cheek, wrinkles on its brow and a
coffin on its back, for when man is short-lived his
work can be but fleeting.

Shorten the life of man, and principle, character,
moderation, good habits and wisdom—all the work
of many years—lose their power and influence, for
young people incline to change for better or
worse, just as age is conservative and preserves
the state.

Shorten the life of man, and with the fulness of
years disappears the sweetest charity, the broadest
toleration, the most imperturbable justice, the most
consummate skill in the management of great affairs,

and the steady building and developing spirit which produces in science, life and government positive and permanent results, as Socrates, Newton and Humboldt did.

Shorten the life of man, and you deprive the workshop of the strong laborer, commerce of the honest and trusted merchant, and the government of the wise patriot. Industry will, therefore, languish, commerce dwindle and the nation decay.

Shorten the life of man, and you strike infancy and ripe age; the one destroys love in the family and the other veneration in the community, and both destroy man's motive for exertion ; for, while man naturally works for his children and his own old age, an excessive mortality destroys both.

Shorten the life of man, and the strong though silent influences even upon rough men by sweet and holy childhood disappear ; the invigorating presence of men in their best estate vanishes with their health, and the earnestness of life gives way to levity when venerable age is taken from us. Every age as every sex has its own peculiar qualities and virtues, and men and institutions are only perfected by the silent mutual Education of all the integral parts of a complete humanity.

But the disastrous bearings of an excessive mortality or a puny humanity shriveled in body and mind, in thought, motive and action, are beyond numbering ; and we will only add that the wanton slaughter of our young children as well as of our prematurely dying parents, cannot but breed in us such an indifference and carelessness about life as will crop out in a thousand ways as social murder, and stamp us a fratricidal race. Love, goodness, beauty and truth are the highest functions of man, and require him to be in the healthiest condition ; an excessive mortality is of necessity accompanied by feebleness, cunning, treachery, lying and low-mindedness. A long-lived race is a healthy, free-dom-loving and defending race ; a short-lived race is a cowardly race, one that neither loves freedom nor dares defend it—it is a race of tyrants and slaves. It is a race without truth, bravery or mag-nanimity. A race hardly worth the short existence allotted to it. It is bankrupt in body and soul, and held in derision by God, man and nature ; and the best it can do is to perish and wipe out the black-est spot of creation—a race that has cast away the noblest heritage, a God-like humanity.

Do we lose sight of the great subject of our essay, Education? Surely not. But we mean to impress the all-important fact, that the miserable abodes of the people, breeding disease, vice, drunk-enness and crime, render all true Education impossible. Schools supported by dog-kennels may manufacture ciphering rascals, but to educate men and women they must have the co-operation of well-regulated homes.

We dwell upon physical comforts for the masses as the lowest round which must be passed before the highest can be reached. Destutt De Tracy, the well-known scholar and statesman, says, " Neither a legion of school teachers nor the professors of logic of all Europe can assist as much the civilization of a people, as an additional degree of well - being, which gives them *leisure*," the very thing without which the *school* is a name without a *meaning*.

We do not under-value the treasures of the mind. With Prof. Jos. Henry, Rénan and Prof. John W. Draper, we assign to perfect knowledge the highest place in the State. But we distinguish philosophical, practical and verbal knowledge or vague opinion ; the first, like the hidden forces of nature, is a life power, and all-penetrating ; the second, substantial like matter, is the very foundation of society ; and the third, like shadows vast and running before the things which cast them, spreads darkness and works confusion ; and, hence, as philosophy is attainable but by few of rare talents and leisure, we are, in the interest of truth, peace, order and prosperity, in favor of practical knowledge and industrial training for the masses.

PART VII.

THE SCOURGES OF HUMANITY.

IN a treatise on Race Education, of which the prevention of human deterioration by forestalling bad habits or hereditary evil tendencies through correct early training and teaching, forms a not unimportant part, drunkenness, often hereditary and more frequently the child than the parent of poverty, but often the parent of insanity, of suicide and of crime, claims our attention.

Morell, who has made human deterioration a specialty, mentions in his pathological studies the case of F——, who was the son of an excellent workman early given to hard drinking. He inherited the tendency to strong drink, and had seven children. The first two died in infancy of convulsions, a nervous affection. The third attained some skill in handicraft, but fell away into a state of idiocy at twenty-two years of age. The fourth attained a certain amount of intelligence, and relapsed into profound melancholy with a tendency to suicide, which terminated in harmless imbecility. The fifth is of a peculiarly irritable temper, and has broken all relations with the family. The sixth was a daughter, with the strongest hysteric tendencies, and has been repeatedly and seriously troubled in her reason.

Here is another pathological study of a gentleman of distinction and an inveterate inebriate. Four of his children perished in infancy, as the children of such men usually do ; the fifth, a son, in spite of every precaution taken by Education, was at nineteen the heir of his father's vice in an insane asylum : as a child he was extremely cruel, as many children of inebriate parents are—the terror of their playmates and of innocent little animals.

Morell cites many cases of children of inebriates cursed in later years with the hereditary bent of excessive alcoholism, leaving one insane asylum for the other, and ending in marasmus, general paralysis, in a perfect brutal condition, and the utter extinction of reason and conscience.

The same great author and physician gives the following analysis of a family under his treatment. In the first generation : immorality, depravity, excessive alcoholism and moral torpor. In the second generation : hereditary drunkenness, mania and general paralysis. In the third generation : sobriety, hypochondria, monomania of being persecuted. In the fourth generation : little intellect and homicidal tendencies ; at the age of sixteen, fits of mania, stupidity, transition to idiocy and extinction of the race.

Morell further says : " I constantly find the children of drunkards in the asylums for the insane, in prisons and houses of correction. The deviation from the normal type of humanity shows itself in these victims by the arrest of the development of their constitutional system as well as by a vicious intellectual disposition and cruel instincts."

Dr. Elam justly remarks, the children of the poor, where this evil tendency remains uncorrected by a good physical and moral Education, the surroundings are vicious, and want and misery irritate a weakened constitution, the consequences of drunkenness in the parent are aggravated, and, hence, the frightful amount of insanity among the poor.

The intellectual and moral nature of man is his very essence, and its total degradation betokens a morbidity or deviation from the normal type, which cannot be but hereditary.

A system of Education that aims at the preservation of the human race, cannot lose sight of drunkenness and its prevention, the means of which are many and decided, and form the natural elements of a practical Education, as we shall have further opportunity to show. The characteristic mental features found by Morell in the children of inebriates and which demand attention, are

an irresistible wandering from place to place, a
want of purpose, indecision, lawlessness, moral obtuseness and a taste for ardent spirits. What a
heritage! the very genius of pauperism and the
high road to crime to which vagabondage unfail-
ingly leads. The desire for stealing and the taste
for the lowest and most vicious associations, as also
a spirit refractory to all regulations, accompany the
morbid appetite for strong drink in the victim of
hereditary dipsomania.

Maudsley says, drunkenness in the parent is a
cause of idiocy, suicide or insanity in the offspring,
as also insanity in the parent may occasion dipsomania in the offspring, which conclusively proves
the deep-seated deterioration of the nervous system
arising from drunkenness, the close attendant of
pauperism.

Delirium tremens is not the worst nor is it the
end of drunkenness, which weighs down humanity
with a leaden curse, convulsing it through generations, until, at last, the spirit in man succumbs to
the demon, and every trace of divine intelligence
and power has been crushed out in the long and
painful struggle.

Alcoholism is attended by great weakness, cramps,
convulsions, partial paralysis, horrid pains, sleepless
nights, restlessness, delirium, haggardness, a complete abolition of the intellectual and moral pow-

ers, a perfect obliteration of the will and excited desires, which make the drunkard a brute, lost in indifference to all, and moving like an automaton, without motive or end, but drink, with the heart, lung and liver suffering, and ending in marasmus, dropsy, diarrhœa or delirium tremens.

Among 1,000 paralytic insane, studied by Morell, 200 were reduced to that condition by hard drinking, and of 200 inebriates, who found their way into the insane asylum, 35 were obviously hereditary cases.

Four brothers inherited the passion for drink, in which they all indulged to excess. The oldest drowned himself, the second hung himself, the third cut his throat, and the fourth threw himself out of an upper window. And there is, in fact, no end to the sad stories of whole generations of drunkards. The drinking habit of the parent is in most cases an irresistible impulse or disease in the child, uncontrolled by any motive whatsoever. Men are treated by the law as criminals, when they are in fact maniacs.

When the duty on spirits was removed in Norway in 1825, between that time and 1835 insanity increased 50 per cent., but the increase in idiocy was 150 per cent. !

Out of 300 idiots, examined by Dr. Howe in the State of Massachusetts, 145 were the children of intemperate parents.

Sweden consumes 25,000,000 gallons of spirits though it has but 3,000,000 population—of whom but half are of an age to drink—and the consequence is that insanity, suicide and crime are fearfully common among them, notwithstanding every one of them has what passes commonly for an Education.

In two hospitals at Copenhagen, of 1,000 male patients among mechanics, 34, and among day laborers, 80, suffered from delirium tremens; among the first class 61, and among the latter 104 cases of deaths were the result of liquor. Of 100 deaths among saloon keepers and bar tenders, 13.4 per cent. are caused by liquor.

Neison, the great English statistician, established from extended observations made on 6,111 drunkards, that at the ages of 21–30 the mortality among them is five times, and at 30–50 four times as high as among temperate people; and while of 6,111 common people, 100 should have died at all ages 'he drunkards lost 357.

The expectation of life is at

	With drunkards.	With common people.
20 years of age	15.5	44.2
30 " "	13.8	36.4
40 " "	11.5	28.7
50 " "	10.8	21.2
60 " "	8.9	14.2

While at 20 years of age a common man has an expectation of living 44 years, a drunkard has but an expectation of 15 years, which cuts his life short 35 years!

Drunkenness is the bridging over from pauperism to insanity, and the three together represent the complete destruction of humanity.

The statistics of England are noted for their reliability. The following table will, therefore, show the exact increase of insanity among the English poor. The population of England and Wales was in 1861, 20,061,725.

	Number of poor.	Insane poor.	Per cent.
1859	867,543	30,318	3.50
1860	854,896	31,543	3.71
1861	891,868	32,920	3.69
1862	946,166	34,271	3.62
1863	1,142,624	36,158	3.17
1864	1,011,753	37,576	3.7
1865	974,772	38,487	4.0
1866	924,813	39,827	4.3
1867	963,200	41,276	4.3
1868	1,040,103	43,158	4.3
1869	1,046,569	45,153	4.3

Whosoever can read this table intelligently and his heart does not ache for his brother, need not mistake his own quality any more. Let him set down himself for all future a heartless villain. 45,153 insane among 1,046,569 paupers, or 44 in every 1,000, in 1869; while England and Wales had 21,158 insane paupers, or 23 in every 1,000, in 1852, which gives an increase of 91 per cent. of these unfortunates in seventeen years! Think for a moment, the city of New York had 50,000 maniacs and the United States 2,000,000; well, the proportion of the insane among the very poor—we may call them paupers, they are men and our brothers still—is just the same. Is this not a degenerating humanity? And ought Education not to meet it with different weapons than grammar, spelling and geography?

A State Report of 1855, of Massachusetts, shows that the picture is as dark here as it is in England, and that insanity afflicts the poor sixty-six times as much as the independent classes.

What we have said sufficiently establishes that drunkenness most fearfully deteriorates the race, and should be met by Education, which must look to the preservation of the race. But the subject is too important to be dismissed without further remark.

George Combe maintains overwork and underfeeding to be among the chief causes which induce the craving for stimulus. The school, therefore, by spreading technical knowledge must relieve the laborer of his poorly-paying drudgery, which means much work for little pay, that leads him to the gin shop.

Prof. Fawcett traces drunkenness greatly to excessive toil and ignorance. The toiling masses are reared in such ignorance, squalor and misery, that life to them is dreary and nature without beauty, and moral beauty exists for them no more than the beauty of the physical world, for society and the laws of government oppress them, and wife and children sadden them in proportion to their love for them.

Rev. Alexander Macloid strenuously insists, that drunkenness is not a voluntary evil. The polluted atmosphere in which the poor live, the poor dwellings, the bad food, the want of temperate refreshments and of a sensible Education, which is a check on low desires, are all causes of drunkenness. The most unwholesome and exhausting trades, as the mining and iron industries, count the hardest drinkers.

To the causes of drunkenness already stated, we may add over-excitement as well as depression, chagrin of all sorts, anger, etc., need we say, hunger, cold, hopelessness, self-abandonment and shiftlessness?

In many trades an irritating animal, vegetable and mineral dust produces a continual dryness and irritation in the respiratory organs and throat, and, hence, a desire for drink.

Want of employment and a mind not finding

sufficient mental excitement in its occupation, lead also many to drunkenness.

The cultivation of higher tastes and pleasures, delight in flowers, music, song, paintings and gardening, science, literature, and whatever raises the condition and dignity of workingmen, will remove them above the low and degrading vice of drunkenness. An Education that will raise the work-people from mere routine drudges to the rank of thinking mechanics, will lift them above all temptation of drunkenness, for as skilled artisans they will cease to be poor, to want food for the body or food for the mind; as men of thought they will, as a rule, be neither over-excited nor depressed, as thinking cultivates equanimity; they will not be debarred from the higher and purer delights of the mind, and if they enter the company of the low it will not be to fall into their vices, but to raise them who are low; careful men and trained in the scientific principles of their trades, they will soon rid their work of every element that may tempt them to drink.

The *Westminster Review* says : " While men are permitted to breathe pestilential air all their life, how can we expect the love of strong drink to perish? Shorten work, or the drooping frame will infallibly have recourse to stimulants. Give the workingmen libraries, amusements, lectures and

19

leisure for attendance; good and cheap newspapers have already done much to elevate the work-people, and will do much more; park excursions, woods and fields, sky and open air, all elevate and improve man's better nature."

Taine, the philosopher and historian, says: "The depression of the workingman and his whole condition drive him to the cup and drunkenness."

The workingman, whose wages must be supplemented by those of his wife working out of the house, is driven, by the cheerless, unprovided dog-hole of a home he enters coming from his day's labor, to the more inviting public house.

The squalor of the poor separates them like a gulf from better society; it is crushing and degrading and destroys all self-regard, with which all else is lost.

The unceasing toil of men, women and children renders all culture and virtue impossible among the poor.

A practical school that uses more collections of objects of nature, art and industry than text books, will form a taste for zoological gardens, picture galleries and industrial museums.

Let us clean out our own hearts and join the company of the poor. He who had their welfare at heart did not disdain to mingle with wine bibbers. The paying out of wages at long intervals gives rise to sudden excesses and long depressions, which both favor drunkenness.

Misery leads to drunkenness and is intensified by it. Ireland drinks more than England, because it is more miserable.

Many laborers suffering ill health induced by over-exertion take refuge from exhaustion in stimulants. Many suffer from indigestion brought on by protracted in-door labor, and the appetite failing early in the morning they take a glass, and soon another one, and so on.

The London *Times*, very guarded in its statements, says : " Many workmen could not get through the work by which they gain their own and their children's bread without liquor." Of course, a man ought not to draw to-day upon his vital powers of to-morrow.

The same great journal continues in the same article : " That to many of the poor people, living in over-crowded, ill-ventilated, ill-lighted rooms, the public house is the only place in which they can enjoy a quiet evening in pleasant and perhaps instructive intercourse with their neighbors after a hard day's work, cannot be denied."

The vice of drunkenness was a hundred years ago universal ; with wealth the well-to-do classes gained in refinement ; as we spread by our humanity comfort among the masses, grace will also adorn their manners.

Careful statistics prove that in proportion that a more thorough Education and well-being spread among the working-people everywhere, in England, France, Germany and among us, in the same proportion is drunkenness lessened.

The vast capital that is wasted in poisonous liquors, the army of men engaged in this nefarious manufacture and trade, the pauperism that is made and intensified by it, the crimes that are committed under its influence, the families that are broken up by it, the brutality that is nursed by it, the idleness and loss of industry and the consequent want of which it is the cause, the army of court officers, police, jail and penitentiary officials it makes necessary, the broken-hearted widows and deserted orphans it fills the country with, the prostitutes it makes—all this, and more than all this, the low, vicious state in which we all more or less must sink living in such a community, render it difficult for us to suppress facts and thoughts calculated to throw light on a subject exercising the hearts and minds of the good men and women of this land. But our space commands us to break off—and we can only appeal to teachers to believe us or to consult perplexed boards of charities and correction and burdened tax payers, and they will find that pauperism, drunkenness, insanity and crime are not accidents, but evils of a steady and gigantic growth, defying all palliatives, and threatening the life of modern communities, which Education alone can prevent by practical training and measures all taken in view of this great purpose during the long years of the formation of men and women at school.

John Brown consents to keep John Smith at school in his early years that he may not have to keep him at a later day in jail, the poor house or insane asylum, but he positively refuses to pay a hundred dollars school tax, and deprive himself of so much comfort that John Smith may learn the name of every river in Africa, or spell at school every word between the lids of Webster's unabridged quarto dictionary.

Educators, whose horizon does not widen beyond declensions and conjugations, have long since laid aside this volume, and men interested in the race and its preservation will not shrink from the study of evils, which no amount of prudery will wink out of existence.

The virus of syphilis spreads noiselessly, and destroys the race in its very germ, poisoning the blood, disorganizing nerve and bone, and inflicting scrofula, phthisis, insanity and many other forms of disease upon the innocent, a fearful heritage of shame and woe that fills them with thoughts of self-destruction.

Neither the extent nor depth of this evil is sufficiently understood. Through hereditary transmission syphilis appears after one or two generations as scrofula, which, like the parent evil, attacks the mucous membranes, the flesh and the bones, is hereditary and amenable to the same treatment.

It is equally the opinion of weighty medical authorities that phthisis, of all deadly diseases the most common, robbing the young and the fair so often of life and hope, and the very scourge of mankind, is, to a great extent, the taint of syphilis in the blood, spread at the end of the fifteenth century, when the licentiousness of princes and prelates had reached its height, and, as Buckle says, from the Pope in the Vatican to the chambermaid, this terrible malady had afflicted all classes.

In Rome, we are informed by cotemporary writers, the disease broke out in March, 1494, and spread before the year 1495 all over France, Italy, Dalmatia, all the parts of Macedonia and Greece, Germany, Mecklenburg, Westphalia, upon the coasts of the Baltic and Roumania, and did not spend its force until the end of the sixteenth century, after every twentieth person all over Europe became a victim of this loathsome pest. This universal plague was followed by more partial ones at the

end of the eighteenth century in all parts of Norwegia, where it was brought by Russian soldiers;
in Sweden, where Norwegian soldiers introduced
it; in East Gothland, where soldiers coming from
Pomerania brought it in 1762; in Norrtige, brought
by soldiers in 1790; in Courland, introduced in 1757
by the soldiers of the Seven Years' War; in Lith-
uania, brought in 1800 by the Russian soldiers. In
1760, it raged on the banks of Lake Huron, and
made great ravages on the shores of St. Paul's Bay
among the Ottawa Indians. In 1785, 5,800 were
afflicted with this poison in the then sparsely populated Canada. It ravaged in 1791, and for many
years in Illyria, and as late as 1841 in certain localities in France. In Sweden and Norway it often
commits ravages; it is remarkably frequent and
extended in England, in large towns or where
the military are located, who make more havoc at
home by the spread of this most loathsome and
deteriorating disease, than they ever do among the
enemy with cannon or bayonet. Such is the history of the introduction of the virus of syphilis
into the blood of the living generation, and which
enforces upon us its tribute paid by scrofula, which
appears in a variety of skin and other diseases, in
the different forms of defectiveness, and, above all, as
phthisis, in which form it makes the greatest ravages; it certainly is of all the deteriorating agents

the most fearful, and demands the attention of every friend of humanity.

The virus of syphilis in the blood does not only, as Dr. Sanger says, entail upon children a mental and physical unfitness for action in the active pursuits of life, but feeds low desires, stimulates the appetite for strong drink, produces a cynical state of mind and an obliquity in the mental and moral nature of man, which renders him mendacious, hypocritical, cunning and selfish, poisoning Church and state, and answering for much that is reprehensible in both.

The insidious nature of this fearful poison calls for exact information based upon statistics which cannot be questioned.

From 1804 to 1842, 129,809 venereal patients have been treated in the hospitals of Paris, the number increasing with every year, so that while it was 2,212 in 1804, it was 5,059 in 1842, and to this day this number must have more than quadrupled. What a deterioration of the nervous system, epilepsy, insanity and suicides such an amount of syphilis must produce !

The Report of Guy's Hospital in London states 43 per cent. of all external diseases treated there are venereal. Mr. Caspar Foster states 174 cases of 285 in surgery, in 1867, were venereal cases. The Royal Free Hospital in London has daily 117 new consultations in venereal cases, or 3 in every 8 cases of a surgical nature. At the hospitals of King's and University Colleges, St. Mary's, Westminster, London, Middlesex and Metropolitan Hospitals, one-third of the surgical cases are venereal. In the hospitals for the sailors, 50 cases are daily brought in. In the Eye Hospital for Children one-fifth of the cases are syphilitic. Dr. William Remond states that in the Children's Hospital 93 boys and 105 girls, or 1 in every 5 children, were affected with syphilis. In hospitals for skin diseases one-eighth to four-fifths of the cases are syphilitic eruptions.

From 1844 to 1851 the British army, numbering 44,611 men, had annually 8,032, and the navy during the same years annually of 28,800 men, 2,830 venereal cases. From 1859 to 1860, of 1,000 soldiers in London, 422 were treated in the hospitals for venereal affections.

Recruits examined for the service in 1853 showed 250 in 1,000 the symptoms of syphilis. In 1860, the British army numbered 306 cases of syphilis in every 1,000 men, and each man averaged 8.69 days yearly loss in the hospital.

At Vienna were treated in the hospital in

	Men.	Women.	Girls.	Children.	Total.
1860 . . .	3,550	62	1,440	1	5,463
1861 . .	3,375	73	1,753	5	5,206
1862 . . .	4,000	77	2,019	5	6,901
1863 . . .	5,808	90	2,224	6	8,128

19*

Under private treatment there must have been three or four times as many.

Among 42,000 artisans in Berlin in 1856 and 31,000 sick at the hospital, were 1,800 cases of venereal, or 4.3 per cent. of the artizan population, and 6 per cent. of the hospital cases.

Syphilitic cases under hospital treatment have doubled in little Bavaria, as everywhere else. In the hospitals there were in 1859, 974 cases; 1861, 1,321 cases; 1865, 1,834 cases.

At the end of the last century the inhabitants of several districts in Denmark were obliged to submit to an official medical examination on account of the frequency of syphilis among the people.

Syphilitic children die mostly in their first infancy; still, in the hospital of Bordeaux, 1856–1861, 77 children among 2,719, or about 3 per cent., show plainly symptoms of syphilis, and 66 of this number died before their sixth year.

The following facts, gathered from the work of Dr. Sanger, show the increase of venereal poison in New York City. Blackwell's Island Hospital treated in

1854	. . . . . .	1,541 venereal cases.
1855	. . . . . .	1,549 "
1856	. . . . . .	1,639 "
1857	. . . . . .	2,090 "

The following table contains the venereal cases in the various public institutions of the metropolis in the year 1857:

Penitentiary Hospita , Blackwell's Island . .	2,090
Almshouse, Blackwell's Island	52
Work-house " "	56
Penitentiary " "	430
Bellevue Hospital	768
Nursery Hospital, Randall's Island	734
New York State Emigrants' Hospital, Ward's Island	559
New York Hospital, Broadway	405
New York Dispensary, Centre Street . . .	1,580
Northern " Waverley Place . .	327
Eastern " Ludlow Street . . .	630
Demilt " Second Avenue . .	803
Northwestern " Eighth " . .	344
Medical Colleges	207
King's County Hospital, Flatbush, L. I. . .	311
Brooklyn City Hospital, Brooklyn, L. I. . .	186
Seaman's Retreat, Staten Island	365
Total	9,847
Cases in these Institutions unrecorded . .	4,923
Total	14,770

Add to these hospi al cases the number of persons treated all over the city, privately, which must be at least three and four times as many, and we may form a somewhat correct idea of the deterioration of the race from syphilis. This estimate may appear high, but as we have for every 5 per cent. adult males one prostitute spreading the virus of syphilis, the result can surprise no one.

What a fearful amount of deterioration of the physical and moral nature of man must this poison effect! More than half of the seamen are its victims, 100 to 200 in every 1,000 soldiers suffer from it, 25 to 30 per cent. of all the sick in military hospitals are affected with it, 5 per cent. of the patients in all hospitals are sick with it, 4 per cent. of the poor and 2 per cent. of the entire population of large cities are tainted with it, 1 to 2 per cent. of innocent infants perish from it, and many more transmit it to coming generations as a fatal potency cropping out in deteriorating diseases without number.

It is the milliners, seamstresses, tailoresses, dressmakers and the like low-payed occupations, which force women into the path of vice. But one in five hundred cases was found by Dr. Sanger, in which a woman in the better remunerated trades followed this low life. "Working from early dawn till late at night, with trembling fingers, aching head and very often with an empty stomach, the poor seamstress ruins her health to obtain a spare and insufficient living."

Among 1,224 of these miserable creatures the earnings of their honest trades yielded them per week in

127 cases	. . . .	$4 00
230 "	. . . .	3 00

336 cases $2 00
534 " 1 00

Whatever fosters prostitution by interfering with woman's making an honest livelihood, or encourages concubinage by rendering the maintenance of a family by the masses of the people impossible, or undermines the family by false teachings, is the indirect means of spreading syphilis, the fell-destroyer of the race, who, unchecked, would exterminate it in the course of not many generations.

Let the school see to it, that woman on leaving it may be trained for maintaining herself honestly, and that man may be enabled to support a family with his labor, rendered effective by a practical and scientific Education.

We must banish, says a great sanitary authority, misery, educate men correctly, fill them with higher interests, make sanitary care a religion, put life under the authority of correct morals and a comprehensive hygienic legislation, restrain selfishness, and fill all with a spirit of love and mercy by a regenerated civil and penal code. Nothing so much as purity of morals and cleanliness oppose the genesis and spread of syphilis, but want and misery are hardly compatible with cleanliness and purity.

Let woman be trusted with the holy office of training and educating the race in the national nurseries of the land, and she will cease to lead the

fashion and induce extravagance; a m n will then
be able to support a family on a modest income,
and prostitution will consequently become excep-
tional. Woman in her elevation will disdain to
subserve to the pleasure of man or to live for her
own vanity sake; her labors for the race will spread
a noble spirit, and want will bring her no more to
that lowest depth of infamy which disgraces to-day
man more than her and most of all our Education,
which makes us all what we are. The school is responsible for the prostitution it does not prevent,
and the pest it does not arrest it spreads.

Our schools teach us many fine things, but leave
such matters to jails and houses of correction, which
in their turn deem it labor lost to attend to a field
overgrown with weeds.

Shall we, then, correct this race-deteriorating
evil by Race Education, which strengthens our
hands and gives them cunning and inspires our
heart to work for the race and its preservation, or
shall we make a yearly contribution of 70,000 to
100,000 illegitimate births and half as many infantile deaths, and the day of judgment may
reveal how many infanticides registered "still
births"?

According to exact statistics 700,000 illegitimate
children are annually born in Christian Europe, or
one illegitimate child to every 13.5 legitimate. In

some of the large cities every second or third man is a bastard.

In France the number of illegitimate children vere in

1844 73,950
1849 75,395
1857 76,189

Marbeau, in the Séance of the Academy of Moral Sciences, gave the following interesting social figures, expressive of the moral condition of France :

76,189 illegitimate children.
35,000 abortions.
34,000 abandoned children.
30,000 still births.
168 infanticides.

The *Medical Chirurgical Review* calculates that at the very least, a million and a half of persons are yearly infected in Great Britain with this most terrible poison. How enormous, then, must be the number of children born with secondary syphilis! how immense the mortality among them! and how vast the amount of disease and misery transmitted to coming generations! It is this that fills our hospitals, insane asylums, asylums for the blind, the deaf and dumb, our poor-houses, jails and many an early grave.

And here, then, again the question urges itself upon our mind, can Education engage in a more important work than arresting this as well as other pests which deteriorate the race and dwarf the proportions of man?

Standing armies, these ulcers of modern states, the graves of liberty, consuming the earnings of the nations and heaping up monstrous public debts, causing rates of taxation that bear heavily on all enterprise, these evils require volumes to be shown up in all their bearings, but cannot be left unmentioned where the scourges of humanity are numbered. They are sources of death and destruction in times of profoundest peace as well as in times of war, as we have shown by their rates of mortality and suicide and the propagation of the most loathsome and deteriorating disease among the nations. They are a public sanction of murder and robbery, and are a standing challenge to God and humanity.

Our prisons are another public scourge and a hotbed of human deterioration; and what else but our schools can we blame for the state the criminal is in, or for the worse laws and officials, who in the name of justice perpetrate the greatest injustice, malice and revenge, and render men's lives cheaper by their dealings than the criminal ever did in his lawlessness, creating nests breeding vice and crime of the deepest dye, which like a torrent sweep destructively over the land they were to protect, by reforming or making innocuous dangerous men.

The trades and pursuits of artisans which are

sources of pleasure, delight and comfort to all are under our present system of Education scourges to the men, women and children who actively engage in them. A description of the deterioration of the masses, arising from the numerous trade diseases, would swell our volume beyond proportion; we can but hint at the skeleton, but dare not enter the charnel house.

An observing employer remarked: "The men drop off from work unperceived and disregarded. I am quite at a loss to know what becomes of them. When they leave off working, they go, and are seen no more. Some, perhaps, become applicants for charities; but so few have I known of the ages of sixty or seventy, that leaving work, they seem to leave the world as well, a solitary one appearing at intervals to claim some trifling pension or seek admission to the almshouse." This is as melancholy as correct a representation of the end of the artisan, still let our end be like his, rather, than to be among those who can read such a summing up of a hard workingman's days without a deep pity stirring in their heart for poor humanity.

Man after man dies of decay in the prime of life and no warning is taken by the survivors. Men are generally unwilling to admit the fact of the excessive mortality of their trade. They will hardly admit that they labor under a disorder until consumption is established, and its effects apparent to every observer. To the physician's inquiry all the workers in dusty trades will say, "We are all pretty healthy," and it is only by examining each workman that the physician finds the deception.

Here is the description of an eminent physician of the operatives of a cotton factory: "The children were almost. universally ill-looking, small, sickly, etc. The men were almost as pallid and thin as the children. Among the women there was not a fresh or fine-looking individual. What a degenerate race, human beings stunted, enfeebled and depraved, men and women that were never to become aged, and children that were never to become healthy adults. It was a mournful spectacle."

The cotton dust or fibre tells on the lungs; the operative may continue at his work, but ails occasionally without being exactly ill; he has an occasional attack of sickness of his respiratory organs; he is weak and easily a prey to disease; may live on, neither well nor ill; is worn out at an early period, and sinks an old man at the age of 45 to 50. In a cotton establishment of 1,685 spinners only 22 passed the age of 50, and 8 the age of 55!

The same authority inspecting a flax mill, declares, that of a personnel of 1,079, 22 reached 40 years, and but 9 lived to the age of 50 years.

Fourteen men, taken indiscriminately from the flax mill, showed on examination great impairment of the respiratory organs. Drawn up in line, what a sight! pale, spare, emaciated, head declined, pulse feeble, subjects of disease advanced to a fatal issue, ripe for the hospital, working till they die from consumption!

Hatters, rather pale, complain of pains in the chest, are subject to asthma, and there are scarcely any old men among them.

Millers are generally pale and sickly, and often asthmatic at an early age.

Jewellers suffer in their chest, stomach, liver and head. An old jeweller is hardly to be found. In an establishment of 37 men, one had passed the age of 50.

Brass founders suffer in their respiration, cough, have often pains in the stomach and are subject to morning vomiting. Few of them live to be old men.

Masons have the bronchital membrane often in a state of inflammation from the stone dust, die frequently of consumption, and hardly ever live to old age.

We might take up trade after trade and would find each, as carried on to-day, the destruction of the artisan engaged in it. But as the subject is almost endless, we must take a larger sweep.

Arsenic, as arsenite of copperas or emerald green,

is employed in the manufacture of paper hangings, tinted paper, artificial flowers; but it enters also into the manufacture of other pigments—in printing calico, in the manufacture of glass, rat poisoning paste, not to speak of arsenic ores. Ten thousand hands in this country are engaged in these trades, and Dr. Guy, in his able report, states that out of 25 persons he examined in the artificial flower trade, 11 were considerably affected by this virulent poison, 22 were affected with a peculiar rash, sickness in the morning, weakness, feverishness, dimness of the eyes, drowsiness, trembling and convulsions. Dr. Guy gives a striking picture of the development of the miserable sickness until death steps in, and the post-mortem examination reveals fearful lesions in the mucous membrane of the stomach and in the liver. This is a sad end which is often quickly reached, but the worst is the steady deteriorating effect this virulent poison has on ten thousands engaged in these trades —but we must hurry on to still blacker trades.

Phosphorus, eating out the jawbones, makes of men engaged in manufactures using it such pitiful looking subjects, that we best turn from the sight.

More than forty thousand artisans are exposed in the United States to the deteriorating effects of lead, a metal most inimical to the system, causing the dropt hand, and other serious symptoms,

among which is the painter's colic, often stubborn
and convulsing the patient with the most excru-
ciating pains ever suffered by man. Smelters,
whitelead manufacturers, potters, painters, type
founders, plumbers and many engaged in other
trades, are deteriorated by constant contact with
this metallic poison, which especially affects the
nerves and the brain it paralyzes, and, like alcohol,
is sure to tell on future generations.

Quicksilver is used in many trades, and is most
fearful in its effects upon the system, and but few
coming in daily contact with it escape chronic poisoning. The mucous membrane, especially of the
gums, gets livid; the breath, as salivation advances,
becomes more fetid, the pulse and respiration are
retarded, and digestion becomes irregular. As the
mucous membrane is destroyed and the teeth fall
out, the patient is disfigured. Mercurial tremor
comes on, the joints pain, trembling increases,
arms, legs, the tongue, and, finally, the facial muscles, refuse service, and the man is but a grimace
and a mockery of himself, a pitiful sight, helpless
misery—he cannot chew his own food. Paralysis
takes from the man the use of one limb after another. The teeth have gone long ago, hair and
nails follow them; the man is all wounds, old ones
opening, all bleeding profusely, and the poor invalid perishes under hectic developments a picture

of the most horrid misery. And the worst feature
about all this is, that it is but the delineation of
the sufferings and unspeakable misery befalling
men and women in the prime of life in the diseases of many other trades.

According to the latest observations of Hirsch, the
average amount of phthisis was among the sick of

21 trades without dust	. . . . .	11.1	per cent.
"	with vegetable dust . . .	13.3	"
"	" animal dust	20.8	"
"	" mixed dust	22.6	"
"	" mineral dust . . .	25	"
"	" metal dust	28	"

Dr. Holland reports 12 needle-grinders began to
work at their trade between their 14th and 27th
years, and died between their 27th and 42d years—
the 12 men together had an average life of 30 years
and 8 months. Of 102 scissor-grinders 60 died under
40 years. The fork-grinders die before their 35th
year, the razor-grinders between 40 and 50. Among
100 sick file-cutters 62.2 per cent. are phthisical,
17.4 suffer from chronic bronchitis and 17.6 from
pneumonia. Of 1,000 glass-makers, Dr. Hanover
found 349 at the hospital. Such is the state of
health among them.

In Coster's factory, in Amsterdam, among the
diamond setters,

23 per cent. suffered from bleeding from the nose.				
36	"	"	"	asthma.

57 per cent. suffered from heart troubles and giddiness.

73.5 " of the men were pale and haggard.

Lead intoxication is common among the men; among 90 men subjected to medical examination, 30 showed symptoms of poisoning. These diamond workers are almost all sickly men, ailing with pulmonary complaints—9 of them were advanced consumptives.

Among the diamond grinders in the same factory,

8 per cent. suffered from heart complaints.

33.75 " " " headache.

40 " " " asthma.

52 " were thin and pale.

67 " suffered from bleeding from the nose.

The average life of the diamond-polishers was, in the same factory, 33.5 years, and of the diamond-setters 26.5 years !

The Report of Registration of the State of Massachusetts shows that the average lives of the following trades and professions have been in the last thirty years as stated :

Farmers	65.19	Comb-makers	51.38
Millers	57.43	Masons	50.48
Sawyers	56.67	Butchers	50.29
Physicians	55.08	Tanners	50.05
Hatters	54.55	Cabinet-makers	48.65
Clock & Watch-makers	54.43	Gunsmiths	48.57
Carpenters and Joiners	53.31	Carriage-makers	48.38
Blacksmiths	53.31	Harness-makers	48.36
Sail-makers	52.84	Brick-makers	47.99
Wood-turners	52.55	Wool-sorters	47.55

Leather-dressers	47.41	Chair-makers	41.59
Laborers	47.39	Engineers	41.57
Musical Instrument makers	47.32	Musicians	41.19
Tailors	47.19	Tinsmiths	40.96
Architects	47.15	Expressmen	40.94
Bakers	46.76	Nail-makers	40.80
Dress-makers (women)	46.49	Machinists	40.80
Seamen	46.33	Jewelers	40.29
Stone-cutters	46.30	Servants (women)	40.19
Coppersmiths	46.07	Teamsters	40.13
Silver and Goldsmiths	45.46	Book-binders	39.94
Dyers	45.35	Upholsterers	39.78
Mechanics	45.13	Barbers	39.77
Painters	45.05	Pail and Tub-makers	39.50
Weavers	44.65	Cutlers	39.23
Artists	44.56	Operatives	38.92
Shoe-makers	44.45	Printers	38.57
Brush-makers	43.40	Cigar-makers	38.31
Furnace Men	43.05	Engineers and Firemen	38.21
Founders	42.73	Drivers	38.16
Shoe-cutters	42.62	Milliners	37.30
Pianoforte-makers	42.50	Glass-blowers	37.81
Glass-cutters	42.39	Plumbers	35.43
Civil Engineers	42.34	Carvers	33.84
		Operatives (women)	27.98

How important these figures! What losses to the nation and to their own families these short lives of the workmen of the land indicate! While farmers average 65 years, workmen die in some trades at 35, in others at 38, 45, and hardly in any do they live to 55 years. It is time the public realize the ravages made among the most productive classes by the great scourge of preventable trade diseases, and stop the social slaughter that compromises the strength of the nation and its moral soundness for the sake of a few silverlings in hand.

Lombard has more than forty years ago directed attention to these statistics, which ought not to be taken as fixed quantities, but should lead us to the removal of their causes. They are not the results of unalterable conditions. The injurious elements of the trades can in most cases be eliminated, and in others rendered innoxious by shorter hours, a more hygienic life of the workmen, and the choice of a trade suited in every case to the peculiar organic condition and degree of health and strength of the individual. But only a close union between the school and the factory enables the workman to realize the inappreciable but constant action of these injurious elements, and gives him the power to eliminate them from the trades. A more substantial and hygienic living, which increases the power of resistance, is expensive, and is only within reach of a laborer well-schooled and scientifically trained in his trade, whose work is highly productive ; and, as for shorter hours, they, too, are only practicable with men, whose labor is highly productive and whose minds are stored with valuable practical knowledge, which will occupy them during the cessation of active employment ; else their short hours prove detrimental to them in more than one way.

The geat trouble is, the Education of to-day is not suited for the working masses. When the school gave only a clerical Education, only the clergy availed themselves of it; to-day, when it gives mostly a commercial and polished.Education, merchants and people of leisure alone care for it.

Give us an Education profitable for the masses of the people, and they will be sure to avail themselves of it.

Bring the school to bear upon the factory, and we shall increase the productive years of the great mass of the people at least 20 per cent. What gain to the nation and to themselves! A longer life means more health, more strength, more energy, more thought, more virtue, more manhood, more labor, more wealth, more comfort, more culture, and more everything desirable in the family as well as in the state. A longer life means less sickness, less loss of time, less expense, less poverty, less orphans, less vagabondage, less crime, less police and jails, and less taxation and public burdens, and, hence, more general prosperity.

The employment of children in factories is one of the great scourges of modern times; we can only mention this plague without unburdening our mind. Four out of five children who are from early infancy up working in factories, die before they reach the age of twenty.

The majority of children of factory people were found, by actual count, at schools attended by this class to be orphans, and by the show of the mortuary register of fifty-two deceased, forty-one only had attained the age of twenty-five.

These short lives mean volumes of misery to the laborer as well as to his family; they mean much sickness, loss of earnings, expense, impoverishment, pauperism and crime, and deserted orphans and sorrowing widowhood; they mean national loss and bankruptcy; yea, they mean injustice in a nation who is indifferent to such misery, and end in universal selfishness and dishonesty, and the consequent ruin of the country.

But the facts we have adduced speak for themselves, and the reader can make his own comments. To do justice to the subject of race deterioration as resulting from the innumerable diseases which haunt the laborer to-day, space fails us. That this deterioration is inevitable, we emphatically deny. Unite the factory and the school, labor and science, the worker and the thinker, and the laws of the intellectual order of the universe will impress themselves upon labor and its relations, and every dissonance will disappear between the worker and his work and between labor and capital; every force will become a willing tool of man, and all matter will become pregnant with use and beauty, and man will be healthier, stronger and wiser, every one standing back to back to his brother, and rendering one another every help their situation may require.

OUR RESOURCES AND OUR GREED.

The revolution which gave birth to the nation, having lasted full seven years, thoroughly aroused the people's energies, employed since in exploring resources which have grown with the population, the progress in science, machinery, quick transport and inter-communication by steam and electricity, and this feverish activity has been still more intensified by the opportunities for amassing colossal fortunes during the late war, until, at last, every other motive or principle has been smothered by the one of acquiring wealth; and, natural enough, greed for gain ended in universal disloyalty and distrust, and a final stand-still of trade. This pause brings us to our senses.

The activities of the nation are too fully aroused to be repressed; they must be directed into a channel as noble and generous as the former was ignoble and selfish. The nation must be made alive to the peril to which universal selfishness exposes its past greatness.

Or are we alarmists? and is the silent potency of the three R's sufficient to save the world without the concurrence of other social agencies? We hardly think so. Popular Education has been fostered everywhere the last hundred years, still the statistics of the steady increase of illegitimate births and abandoned children the world over, would fill a moderate volume. Offenses in France have increased from 110,593 in 1846, to 171,351 in 1853. The liberal professions, composing 2.2 per cent. of the entire population, form 4 per cent. of the criminals of France. Whilst the farmers, who form 53 per cent. of the entire population, commit but 30 per cent. of the crimes, showing at once the decided influence of work, home and a competency, and the doubtful bearing of Education on crime.

In England offenses rose from 75,859, or 4 in 1,000, in 1857, to 105,310, or 5 in 1,000, in 1865. Murders and attempts at murder in France numbered in 1830–1834 931, and increased gradually to 1,850 in 1855–1859.

Enough has been said on the score of this universally-spread fiction or swindle of what is in the clap-trap of the day styled Education. Our present Education, by getting up a false pride discouraging manual labor and putting cunning in the place of physical and creative effort, aids the progress of crime.

We talk about pauperism in Europe, and shut our eyes to the extent of the evil in our own midst.

Massachusetts, willing to probe the evil, gives us reliable statistics. It has with a population of 1,651,912, 4,342 inmates in its poorhouses, and supports partially 65,988 outside poor. It counted in 1876, 148,933 tramps! and making full allowances for duplications, it has, at least, 5,000 of this dangerous element. Massachusetts has six or seven large State institutions, beside 342 town and city poorhouses, and thousands of private families in which, at public expense, individuals are maintained; and the poor cause to the State and private charities an annual outlay of $4,500,-000. The convicts number 4,340. Whilst the poor in England, 1,037,360, are 1 in 23 of the general population, and the convicts, 28,756, 1 in 790, our poor are 1 in 22 of population, and our criminals 1 in 380.

There were commitments in the State of Massachusetts in

1871–2	160
1872–3	174
1873–4	246

In 1865 there were in the common prisons of the State 10,000 individuals, and 481 convicts in the State prison. In 1875, 20,000 were detained in the common prisons, and 852 were in the State prison. Hardly a State or country, says the State Report before us, in the civilized world, where atrocious and flagrant crimes are so common as in educated Massachusetts. Of 415 convicts sentenced to the Charlestown State prison in 1874 and 1875, 53 per cent. are born in Massachusetts, and 25 per cent. of all the convicts of 1873 came from its reformatories. Only 11 per cent. of the convicts of 1876 were illiterate, which, therefore, was not the cause of their criminality. One of every 364 natives of Massachusetts is a pauper, and 1 in every 546 a convict ; whilst 1 in every 348 foreign born is a pauper, and 1 in every 252 is a criminal. But here again we must direct the attention of the reader to the absurdity of all our statistics of pauperism. We are informed one of so many natives or foreigners is a pauper ; in other words, is an insane, an idiot, a deserted woman, an orphan, of infirm mind, sick, a cripple, an old man, or a widow —a most meaningless assertion indeed.

According to a more just and simple classification—we shall soon make clearer—we should say 1 in 100 of the population of Massachusetts is a defective; 1 in 20 is partially depending and poor, 1 in 10 is struggling against poverty, and 1 in 5 is managing closely.

This is rather gloomy, but is a fact worth while knowing. Massachusetts has :

Blind	2,512
Deaf	7,241

Dumb	129
Deaf-mutes	654
Idiots	1,340
Insane	3,637
Total	16,513

In 359 cases out of 420 cases of idiots, one or both parents departed from the normal condition of health.

Epileptics, paralytics, cripples, feeble-minded and the like classes, will swell this sum to 25,000; and what must be the nature of the tree that bears the like fruits in such abundance?

The following table shows the steady increase of pauperism in the State of Massachusetts. Vagrants were relieved in

1873	45,653	times.
1874	98,236	"
1875	137,308	"
1876	148,936	"

A glance at the population of the poorhouses of the State of New York will clearly prove our position, that widespread pauperism is evidence of physical deterioration, which has to be met by means both universal and efficient.

New York contained in its poorhouses in 1876

2,030 homeless children.	29 deaf-mutes.
278 " women.	4,047 insane.
2,081 old and destitute.	580 idiots.
795 permanently diseased.	268 epileptics.
463 temporarily diseased.	322 paralytics.

240 crippled.   394 feeble-minded.

17 deformed.   767 vagrant and idle.

303 blind.

    Total . . . . . 12,614.

The Report on Pauperism, by Charles S. Hoyt, Esq., throws further light on this subject, by showing that 4,273 of this number had each pauper relatives—some as far back as three generations. The number of pauper relatives of the paupers examined into amounted to 14,901 ; 4,968 of these relatives were known as insane, 844 were idiots and 8,863 inebriates.

What a widespread deterioration this condition indicates, and how vast must be the means that shall victoriously counteract it.

We often witness with indifference the development of a morbid formation, relying upon the remedial power of the means at our command, which, in truth, are almost invariably impotent.

We try to study the problem of pauperism ; but systematization is the first requisite to get at the nature of things, and we lump together under pauperism, a name that means social leprosy, a pest and every other thing that is loathsome—the poor insane, the idiot boy, the orphan, the widow, the sick and the man of a hundred years.

These classes are all free from personal guilt, and our dealing in such a bungling manner makes the solution of the social problem impossible, and is as

20*

much an insult to our own good sense as to humanity. The plain state of the case is, the wrecks in the poorhouses of Massachusetts, New York or any other State or country, are the flower and fruit; the outside helpless poor—call them tramps, vagrants or what you please—are the branch, and the struggling millions, who have not yet given up all hope, are the veritable tree sending forth those branches bearing the bitter fruit.

We must stop paying attention to the branches and attend to the roots of the tree. The hundred thousand outside the poorhouse must themselves be radically diseased, to yield the ten thousand physically and mentally ruined inmates of our poorhouses, and the millions—let us not be unjust —they mean as nearly right as they know. We are republicans; let us be just toward the masses, the people, the hope of the nation and of the future; perhaps the whole Education we give them is the wrong one, and we dare say this is fully half of the trouble.

An increased mortality rate may be the result of a food supply suddenly cut short by a failure of crops or a financial crisis. An increase in the rate of insanity is evidence of a deep degeneracy, the work of a long series of deteriorating causes. It is for this reason that insanity especially must occupy the attention of the social student.

Dr. Charles A. Lee said before the Social Science Association : " Statistics abundantly show that both in this country and in Great Britain there is a progressively increasing ratio of lunatics to the whole population, and the estimate of 45 per cent. increase here, as in England, in the last ten years is very probable. We know that there is an enormous and constantly increasing accumulation of chronic lunacy in every State in the Union, and that in the States which have erected the most and largest asylums, as New York, the number of insane in the poorhouses has not diminished, and is constantly increasing. Especially is insanity increasing in the United States among the middle and lower classes."

Of course, the increase of the 45 per cent. of insanity in so short a period is partly due to the preservation of the lives of the insane under their improved treatment ; still there is left a positively increased ratio of insanity sufficient to stagger the thoughtful student of social phenomena.

But whoever will read the reports of the Boards of Charities of the various States in the Union, and take into consideration the increasing numbers of the inmates of the poorhouses and the nature and composition of the latter, will of necessity come to the conclusion of Dr. Lee.

What wonder that the insane are in the most humane States penned up in cages like wild beasts, only kept less clean. Are they not, according to our most stupid and inhuman nomenclature, paupers? And yet Dr. Edward Jarvis, like his predecessor, the great Pinel, says: "Most of these unfortunates need no double doors, no bolts, no locks, but confidence and the encouragement of their own self-respect, the most important means of restoration."

The constantly diminishing yearly increase of population is another evidence either of physical deterioration or moral depravity. So, for instance, was the annual increase of population in Prussia:

1817–1828	1.71 per cent.
1828–1840	1.27 "
1846–1855	0.86 "

The annual increase of population in England was, in

1821–1831 .	1.46 per cent.	1841–1851 .	1.35 per cent.
1831–1841 .	1.46 "	1851–1861 .	1.19 "

In France the increase of population was, in

1821–1831 .	0.67 per cent.	1841–1851 .	0.44 per cent.
1831–1841 .	0.50 "	1851–1861 .	0.18 "

And when we study our own country, the steady decline of the natural increase indicates a lamentable deterioration. The annual increase was, in

1790–1800 .	2.89 per cent.	1820–1830 .	2.64 per cent.
1800–1810 .	2.83 "	1830–1840 .	2.52 "
1810–1820 .	2.74 "	1840–1850 .	2.39 "

According to Dr. Allen's statement before the Social Science Association, 10 per cent. of the marriages of Americans are childless; and whilst 1 birth upon 30 of population is the natural ratio, the ratio of births of Massachasetts' mothers is 1 in 60.

We cannot deteriorate without losing vitality and strength as a nation, and losing the chance of giving birth to thinkers and organizers and leaders in national greatness and goodness.

But the great misery of the masses is the plainest and most irrefutable proof of their deteriorating condition.

The following official items furnished by E. Crapsey, Esq., are well worth considering. There were in 1870 in

Bellevue Hospital and Charity Hospital	17,190	patients.
Hospital for Contagious Diseases . .	6,165	"
Bureau of Relief prescribed for outdoor poor	16,850	"
The almshouse poor	4,315	"
Relieved by private agencies	50,000	"
Dependent upon public charities . .	61,971	"
Inmates of prisons and reformatories .	71,849	"
Total	228,340	"

Reducing this number on account of duplications to 150,000 persons, what an army of dependents and what a problem for solution !

There is not a block of tenement houses where

mothers may not be found putting the morsel of bread they covet into the hungry mouths of crying children ; where strong men do not starve that the old people may be supported. Widows are chummed together, who are living illustrations of a sisterly spirit ; they have for years worked and starved together ; the strongest bank in the city may break, but their honor and honesty, so often tried, make them trusted for their rent during the winter months, when, also, their most modest furniture travels to the pawnbroker, to come back in the summer season and greet the presence of these, God's own dear children, who starve the year through with a never-faltering spirit. Does any one think that such stories, rising into the hearing of the Almighty Father, do not avenge the poor by confounding all in one great destruction, in order to assert, in the inexorable ways of Providence, the solidarity of the race, coldly denied by us in the cruel treatment of a brother ?

The steady and stubborn growth of pauperism proves all present attempts at preventing it rather efforts at mitigating it, an enterprise laudable, but thankless, like carrying water from the sea in a sieve, as the millions brought up and living as they are, grind out paupers by the hundred thousand, and swallow up all private and public means, rendering all our efforts nugatory.

We do not indulge in vagaries, and do not stand alone in what we blame or in what we advance. We insist upon work as well as study, and condemn the one-sided mental Education of the day, which ruins both the body as well as the mind, leading to want and misery.

The effects of our almost exclusive attention to study may be partly illustrated by the following facts. Blindness is a great source of loss of opportunity of self-support. The number of the blind in the United States is 25,000 and over. Congenital blindness is but as 1 in 10 compared to the whole class. Whatever weakens the eyes exposes them to succumb to the effects of disease or external injury, and the short-sightedness or weakened condition of the eyes, due to over application to study, has been fully established, and ranges from 5 per cent. in village schools, to not less than 68 per cent. in our highest institutions.

Of 731 collegiate scholars 296, or 40 per cent., suffered frequently headache. Of 3,564 scholars of public schools, 974, or 27.3 per cent., suffered more or less headache. In the highest class of a college not less than 80 per cent. were found sufferers from headache. Bleeding from the nose was found in 20 per cent. Spinal diseases were met with in 20 per cent., and of these 84–90 per cent. were females.

One hundred and forty-six physicians of Massachusetts have declared that our system of Education promotes consumption, and the writer in the Massachusetts Report adds to this testimony, "If this be not worthy of serious thought by our people I know of no question that can be."

"The state," says the School Commissioner of Ohio, "needs, for its material prosperity, a race of strong and healthy men and women. Widespread violations of hygienic laws as fostered by a vicious system of Education cannot be overlooked by the state."

"Education lays the foundation of a large part of the causes of mental disorders," says Dr. Jarvis.

"Insanity is the price of an imperfect civilization and an incomplete Education," says Rev. J. S. Goodman, School Superintendent in the State of Michigan.

"Our young men have a great indisposition to physical labor. We believe in that kind of compulsory Education that will fit a man for work and self-support. Of 220 convicts, in 1875, in Massachusetts, 177 were without a trade. A workman who labors and pays his way, though he is unable to read and write, is a better member of society than men educated who will not, or know not, how to earn their bread. We want more of the gospel of work." These words of Mr. Wright, the chief of the Bureau of Labor of Massachusetts, deserve consideration.

Richard Vaux, in an able article on crime in the State Report of Pennsylvania, says: "A far larger number of convicts have attended school than who never went to schools. Does, perhaps, the association of youths in school create an influence which leads to depreciate labor? This certainly would have to be considered."

Nothing but the joining of industrial work with study secures the proper equilibrium between mental and physical action, and endows the future citizen with the power of providing honestly and honorably for himself and for those who have a claim upon his support. We insist, therefore, upon a more material Education, but we lay equal stress upon a more spiritual one than the present, and one founded upon the physical, moral, and industrial relations and nature of man.

The neglect of the physical and moral Education in our schools, and the perversion of the passions this double neglect leads to, are a great cause of race deterioration. Fashion, appearances and sham in Education, leaving the heart and the higher reason empty, take the place of the more practical culture of the will, good sense, and human kindness. The state, expending millions out of the public treasury, has a right to insist upon an Education that instills in the individual, educated by the contributions of all, kindliness toward all.. The state and the government are no more interested in the scholarly accomplishments of the citizen than in his religious faith ; in the eye of the law actions alone have an existence, and are culpable or meritorious, and hence for action the public school must train us, that we may live a life useful for the state and for ourself.

When a German university celebrity, like Professor Ekhart, and a Professor Stuart, of Cambridge University, England, treat labor schools as a prime necessity of our present civilization, and such schools do prove a success, in France, Germany, Belgium, Holland, Denmark, Sweden, Austria, Italy and Switzerland, none is justified in saying, that however well such institutions may look on paper they are not reducible to practice. Reading questions from text-books, and seeing to it that the answers be exactly as printed, may be less troublesome in execution, still the world has got tired of words, and Education too must adval. from words to work.

If men make leadership in the highest department of human life their business, let them be trained for it in institutions of the severest mental discipline. But we do not want schools dabbling just enough in Latin and Greek to spoil a boy born for the plow or the shop, without fitting him for anything else.

Is the demand for a moral basis of Education, and the preservation of the race an insanity? Is the enlarging of the individual consciousness to a universal consciousness that identifies itself with all mankind, past and present, not the essential nature of human culture, and if we are to love Him whom we have never seen, are we mad for making the demand on Education to train man up for the love of a brother whom he has seen?

The realism of the Greeks must unite in our Education with the moral inspiration of the East; still, the latter must form the basis of the entire fabric of Education; for to confess our weakness, we give preference to the poor, the central figure in the civilization of Judea; for the element of beauty in the Greek world may exercise our admiration; the poor call forth our benevolence.

Education among the ancients was the business of slaves; in the middle ages it was left to the church; in our day it is a trade. But the Education of the race must become a religion, and the state and the citizen must give it their best thoughts and warmest support.

We especially insist upon orderly homes, which are for men and women what schools are for children. For we hold that the Education the family provides for all through life is of a higher order than that of the school, which is but partially provided during a comparatively brief period of life.

Home, labor, property, health, the family and Education are secured to the masses, with the opportunity of acquiring suburban dwellings, and with these elements of civilization the peace of society and the stability of the government are guaranteed.

The effects of crowding in large towns, says Charles Bray, are ill health, misery, drunkenness and degradation. Ups and downs natural to commerce, make the operative wreckless. Waste and lowest licentiousness, or starvation are the alternative. The disadvantages of the factory system may be avoided by uniting it with the culture of a garden patch, which a man can tend when he cannot sell his time to better advantage in the labor market.

Our industrial system, says Sir A. Alison, brings to-day to the masses weakness and debasement, national grandeur and private degradation. Wherever, as in the Jura, or the Val d'Arno, manufacturing employment is coupled with separate dwellings and rural residence, and the laborer can safely base his calculations upon something that is certain, there is industry and frugality, and beautiful little properties gratify the traveller in those delightful regions. On the other hand, there is not to be found among civilization a more dissolute or reck-

less race than the silk weavers of Lyons or Spitalfields, the cotton manufacturers of Rouen or Manchester, or the muslin operatives of Glasgow or
Paisley.

The national commerce bought at the price of
the strength, health and moral soundness of the
masses becomes the nation's curse. *The man who
could discover a mode of combining manufacturing
skill with isolated labor and country residence, would
do a greater service to humanity than the whole race
of philosophers.*

Dr. Elijah Harris stated most forcibly, before the
committee on crime, appointed by the Legislature
of New York, that crime in the different city wards
was always in proportion to crowding. Sing Sing,
the House of Refuge and the like State institutions
trace their criminal inmates and juvenile offenders
to the worst tenement houses. Nothing but healthful domiciles secured by a stringent sanitary legislation, can prevent wasting disease, pauperism and
crime. Overcrowding, in dark and filthy tenements, wipes out all moral distinctions. Mine and
thine lose their meaning, thieving becomes natural
and crime habitual, and hence the increasing demoralization of the densely packed populations
of growing cities.

END OF VOLUME I.

www.ingramcontent.com/pod-product-compliance
Lightning Source LLC
Chambersburg PA
CBHW052332110726
47901CB00005B/1214